HISTORY OF THE CATHOLIC MISSIONS IN NORTHEAST INDIA

A Case Study of the Bethany Sisters

HISTORY OF THE CATHOLIC MISSIONS IN NORTHEAST INDIA

A Case Study of the Bethany Sisters

Sr Marina Sequeira BS

2021

History of the Catholic Missions in Northeast India: A Case Study of the Bethany Sisters - Published by the Indian Society for Promoting Christian Knowledge (ISPCK), Post Box 1585, Kashmere Gate, Delhi-110006.

© Author, 2021

Online Order: http://ispck.org.in/book.php

ISBN: 978-81-949231-2-1

Laser typeset by

ISPCK, Post Box 1585, 1654, Madarsa Road, Kashmere Gate, Delhi-110006 • *Tel:* 23866323

e-mail: ashish@ispck.org.in • ella@ispck.org.in
website: www.ispck.org.in

Dedication

To my Parents, Brothers and Sisters who have encouraged and supported me in my educational efforts

To all the Sisters of the Congregation of the Little Flower of Bethany

To all my students and their parents who have been a great support to me in my mission field

And

To all my good friends who inspired and assisted me to complete this book.

Contents

Chapter 3: The Catholic Missions in Northeast India

Chapter 4: Origin, Growth and Activities of the Bethany Sisters

Chapter 5: Assessment of the Work of the Bethany Sisters

Acknowledgements

I give thanks to the Lord God Almighty for His grace and guidance that sustained me through these years of study, helped me and led me through the completion of this book.

The transformative journey presented through this book would not have seen its destination without the support and generous help that I received from some of the special persons of my life. First of all, I owe an immense debt of gratitude to the numerous individuals who have helped and provided me with timely suggestions, support and encouragement during this endeavor. Though it is not possible to mention the names of all the individuals, I must gratefully mention those who have been instrumental in the successful completion of my study.

In carrying out this study, I am enormously indebted to my Supervisor Dr K. Robin, Associate Professor, Department of History & Ethnography and Deputy Director of Academic Staff College, Mizoram University for his invaluable encouragement and academic guidance. He has not only played the key role in shaping my ideas and thinking-process as a research guide but also through his unique gestures, has been able to provide me with critical comments and constructive help which was instrumental in the smooth progress of the entire research work.

I owe a sincere debt of gratitude to Sr Rose Celine BS, my Superior General and her team, for allowing me to publish my research work. I wish to put on record my sincere appreciation to Sr. Sandhya BS for her support and good wishes. I am greatly indebted to all my Sisters in the congregation for their appreciation and inspiration. I would like to express my sincere thanks to all my friends and well-wishers for their prayerful support and encouragement. I duly acknowledge the valuable assistance provided by one and all towards the successful completion of this book.

I would like to remember my family members and relatives who had always felt great pride in all my academic achievements. Last, but not the least, I would like to thank all my critics for their 'valuable' criticism which has always provided me with enormous strength and enthusiasm to put in more sincere and concerted efforts towards my every academic endeavor.

Sr Marina Sequeira BS

Foreword

It is unequivocal that the histories of Catholic Missions across the globe are rooted with charitable, spiritual and religious fortification and its institutional structures are the edifying manifestations of this distinctiveness.

This work *'History of the Catholic Missions in Northeast India: A Case Study of the Bethany Sisters'* by Sr Marina Sequeira BS premises the religious fundamentals and philanthropic dimensions of Catholic Missions in Northeast India with special reference to the works of the Bethany Sisters in Northeast. In fact, this work is the outcome of comprehensive research and final Doctoral Thesis of Sr Marina Sequeira BS from the Department of History & Ethnography, Mizoram University under my Supervision.

This work explores the growth and development of the Catholic Church in India and the contributions of the Bethany Sisters in various sectors particularly for the welfare of the general public transcending geographical boundaries and of different cultures in the North East. It is in this context that this academic work assumes even more significance considering its entailing research objective.

Writing this outstanding work is indeed a phenomenal endeavor which requires tremendous research and at the same time involves huge resources which at times do not come by easily. The author articulates the core of the subject by means of simple and lucid phrases in an attempt to draw wider audience and for extensive reading of the theme. It is rather befitting for different stake holders to explore the fundamentals of this exceptional piece of research work and appreciate the core values of Catholic Missions and that of the Bethany Sisters and their works in Northeast.

I convey my heartfelt congratulations to the author Sr Marina Sequeira BS for bringing out this marvelous piece of research work into the public domain which, I am sure, would have a tremendous impact and also in adding new insights into our entire understanding on the Catholic Missions and the contributions of the Bethany Sisters in North East India.

K. Robin
Associate Professor
Mizoram University

Preface

I was a student of Little Flower School, Kinnigoli in the South Kanara District of Karnataka. On the 1st of October every year, the school used to keep up its patron's day, i.e., the feast of St. Therese, popularly known as the Little Flower of Jesus. As a student, I used to be fascinated by the value oriented and virtuous life of this young saint in the Catholic Church. Her little ways of perfection and missionary zeal captivated my mind. Although she had lived within the four walls of the Carmelite Order, she was declared as the patroness of missionaries by the Catholic Church. As a young girl, the question that disturbed me often was: 'Why can't I be a missionary and a saint like her?' Thus, I wished to become a missionary to reach out to many people far and wide. This inspiration in turn motivated me to opt for Northeast mission as a Bethany Sister.

Having worked as a missionary in Northeast region of India for the past 20 years, again I was disturbed with the question, 'What special am I doing in my mission? How is my work different from others? What more can I do to make meaningful contribution to the society? Thus, as an educator of the young minds and hearts, there grew in me a desire to make an academic contribution to the Catholic Church and the Bethany Sisters. And so I began my journey for the doctoral studies and after much reflection and consultation with some of the academicians, I decided to assess the impact of the work of the Catholic Missions and particularly that of the Bethany Sisters upon the people of Northeast. Very few research works had been conducted in the context of Catholic

Missions, especially in Northeast India. The past studies and the existing books did not assess the work of the various religious congregations or the activities of the Bethany Sisters in particular.

Thus the purpose of this study was to record the historical past of the Bethany Sisters in Northeast Region so that we are able to serve better in educating and catering to the well being of the people of Northeast. And it is carried on through a historical study by assessing the changes brought in by the missionary work of the Catholic Missions and the Bethany Sisters in particular. Further, the Bethany Sisters had completed fifty years of their arrival in Northeast. Hence this is the first attempt to give a recordable account related to the mission activities of the Bethany Sisters in Northeast from 1962 to 2012. This book points out the work of the Catholic Missions and the impact made by the Bethany Sisters in the social, political, cultural, and religious life of the people of Northeast.

Personally, this study has motivated me to explore in detail the past and present history of the Bethany Sisters and learn from it. I have some experience in this mission field of Northeast as a missionary since 1998 and those experiences motivated me to do this research work. The Bethany Congregation and particularly the Province of the Bethany Sisters in Northeast would definitely be educated by this research because it deals with the methods and approaches developed and employed by the Sisters in their missionary endeavours. I also believe that this study will be a source of help to the Catholic Church in Northeast India. It will contribute towards the understanding of the Church's role in her mission as far as the missionary methods are concerned.

Sr Marina Sequeira BS

Message from the Superior General

With much delight, I offer my heartfelt felicitations to Dr Sr Marina BS who is a member of the Congregation of the Sisters of the Little Flower of Bethany, Mangalore, for her doctoral research on *'History of the Catholic Missions in Northeast India: A Case Study of the Bethany Sisters'*. She has put her heart and soul into doing her research on a relevant theme for Bethany Institute.

Bethany Sisters stepped into the Northeast India in 1962, pioneering in Kolasib, Mizoram and now they serve in all seven states of the Northeast India, while Bethany Educational Society® Mangalore is running numerous Educational Institutions and is offering credible service to the society all over the country. Sr Marina's work will be a trendsetter, to motivate Bethany Sisters to augment their contribution to enhance the living parameters in the Northeast Society and to others to carry out research in other branches of the study.

Her historical study to assess the changes brought in by the Catholic Missions and the Bethany Sisters in their service for nearly 6 decades will be an eye opener. As she has stated, that the zealous and committed services of Sisters in various fields of Northeast India is practically invisible or is not sufficiently recognized. This study will bring to the fore the contribution of women religious of not just of Bethany, but also of various congregations working in the region, their role within the Catholic Church and their mission in the field of evangelization, education, social development, health care, and pastoral works in general, which has been the cause leading to holistic development of various communities in Northeast India. It is worth noting that people's response to the activities of the Bethany Sisters has been positive and their interaction with the people, staff, students and other organizations have had mutual benefits.

Another interesting fact is that the research reveals that most of the people have come to know the Catholic Church through the activities of religious Sisters and Fathers.

The assessment of the contribution of Bethany Sisters on the religious, social, cultural and political life of the people of Northeast will be a great boon to the Congregation in general and to the Bethany Sisters in the Northeast India in particular. Certainly, it will be an added joy to them to see their work codified and recognized through the study of Dr Sr Marina BS.

Now that the relevant sections of her Thesis will be available in a book form, it will be very useful to all concerned especially to the Bethany Congregation and Bethany Educational Society ® Mangalore. It is my earnest desire that Dr Sr Marina continues to share her learning and talents for the benefit of the people. May all Bethany Sisters be more earnest in their life and mission, and people in the Northeast especially be blessed through the selfless and generous service of the Sisters and Fathers towards building a happy, just and humane society.

Sr Rose Celine BS

Superior General, Bethany Generalate, Mangalore

The Major Areas of the Bethany Sisters' Missionary Activities

MAP

1. Bethany Provincial House, Guwahati (Assam)
2. Bethany Convent, Garchuk (Assam)
3. Madonna Convent, Kolasib (Mizoram)
4. Holy Family Convent, Silchar (Assam)
5. Holy Cross Convent, Dimapur (Nagaland)
6. Christ King Convent, Kohima (Nagaland)
7. Mary Mount Convent, Aizawl (Mizoram)
8. Holy Cross Convent, Agartala (Tripura)
9. St Joseph Convent, Viswema (Nagaland)
10. Avila Convent, Lumding (Assam)
11. Bethany Convent, Kolkata (West Bengal)
12. Bethany Convent, Kathalcherra (Tripura)
13. Bethany Convent, Depacherra (Tripura)
14. Bethany Convent, Canchipur (Manipur)
15. St Joseph's Convent, Chittaranjan (West Bengal)
16. Sacred Heart Convent, Behala (West Bengal)
17. Bethany Convent, Sihphir(Mizoram)
18. Bethany Cottage, Barasat (West Bengal)
19. Holy Cross Convent, Dharmanagar (Tripura)
20. Bethany Convent Study Centre, Shillong (Meghalaya)
21. Bethany Convent, Bazar Veng, Mamit (Mizoram)
22. Bethany Convent, Jongksha (Meghalaya)
23. Bethany Convent, Sulantu (West Bengal)
24. Bethany Convent, Nalbari (Assam)
25. Bethany Convent, Samoguri, Namsai(Arunachal Pradesh)
26. Bethany Convent, Attavar (Mangalore) Karnataka
27. St Theresa Convent, Ngherpet Veng, Mamit (Mizoram)
28. Bethany Convent, Khayerpur (Agartala)
29. Bethany Convent, Manmow, Namsai (Arunachal Pradesh)
30. Bethany Convent, Umsning, (Meghalaya)
31. Bethany Novitiate, Barasat, (West Bengal)
32. Bethany Convent, Biratnagar, (Nepal)

Chapter 1

Approaches to the Study of Religion

Introduction

Bethany Sisters are a body of people having a common organisation, serving in the Catholic Church as per the directives and rules laid down by the Church. All the Bethany Sisters live under the same laws and regulations of governance, dedicated to the service of humanity. They have a common mission for the poor and the marginalised sections of society especially women and girl children. Bethany is a biblical name of the house of Martha, Mary and Lazarus who were the friends of Jesus. Martha served, Mary listened and Lazarus befriended Jesus. By accepting this name, Bethany Sisters are expected to pray like Mary, serve and offer hospitality like Martha and Lazarus. The Bethany Sisters are known as the Sisters of the Little Flower of Bethany because Therese, born in France a Carmelite Sister who is our second patroness was called the Little Flower of Jesus.

Mgr RFC Mascarenhas, the Founder of the Bethany Sisters was a contemporary of St Therese and was attracted by her value oriented and virtuous life. He experienced special help and miracles worked by her in his difficult moments. His newly found institute experienced the fastest growth due to her intercession and he wished that the Bethany Sisters would imitate this Saint in her little ways of perfection and missionary zeal and thus would also become great missionaries to reach out to many people far and wide. According to his wish and desire, Bethany Sisters percolated into the Northeastern part of India in the year 1962.

Northeast India has 33.4 million people which accounts for nearly four percent of India's population. Known for its beauty this area also has poor roads, transport and communication, education, and health care facilities. Scholars assert that today's Northeast India is characterized by new aspirations, ethnic and political tensions, insurgency movements, flight from villages to urban centre's, erosion of traditional values, weakening of family bonds and educated unemployed. Added to that there is a disappearance of age old institutions, increasing dichotomy between life and belief, and lack of genuine leadership in society. At the same time there is a fresh awareness of her natural as well as possible resources, historical and cultural advantages and human potential, both men and women.

The purpose of writing this book is to trace the advent and growth of the Catholic Church, the Catholic Missions and the impact of the Bethany Sisters' work in the Northeast. It is a humble effort to record and chronicle Bethany Sisters' oral history so that the Bethany Sisters' in the future will know the challenging Mission and be challenged to fulfil the commission of Jesus through their Congregation. It also means to challenge the younger members of Bethany to carry on the humanitarian work, especially in taking the good work begun by the pioneering Sisters beyond this Region. The main objective of this book is to draw lessons from the past history, to reflect on them in the light of the present situation and to equip the Sisters for the future.

The advent of the Catholic Missions in Northeast India ushered in transformation and development. The Bethany Sisters have played a significant role in the social, political, cultural, and religious life of the people of the Region. The book is more of reconstructing the history of the past on Catholic Missions and the Bethany Sisters. It is more of narration and critical analysis. Hence hypothesis is not highlighted but thought of as a background to this book. Catholic Missions have effected a change in the lives of the people of Northeast and Bethany Sisters being a part of the Catholic Missions have contributed to these transformational changes through their varied activities.

The need for research on Catholic Missions and their activities particularly at the regional level was keenly felt in order to enrich and plan the ministry and work for better effectiveness. Besides, the necessity was realized to make available to the whole Catholic Church especially those concerned with the training of future missionaries, the results of research already done as well as information so that the training of personnel can be focused on areas that are required. The need to renew the missionary commitment and offer fresh enthusiasm and new incentive to those who are already in the mission field is essential so that their spirits are boosted up for better work. To give a fresh impulse to missionary activity by fostering the commitment of the members of the Province is another objective of the study.

This study is significant as it would create a common platform for all the Catholic Missions to understand the work done by them and how they contributed to the well being of the people of the Northeastern region in particular. Studying different activities accomplished by the various Catholic Missions will also give a boost to other missions to take up such studies. Evaluating the effectiveness in the mission will enable to plan out better strategies, interact more and in an effective way with the society and contribute a greater share to the well being of the people whom they cater to.

This research also needs to be perpetuated without confining within particular regions and spread across the boundaries of cultures and provinces around the country. Thus, the research is significant not only for academic reason but is also an inspiration for the younger generation, whoever will may be the future leaders of the Catholic Missions and of the Bethany Institute in the Northeast. It will help to give a glimpse of their historical past and provide for them a platform to participate in the humanitarian activities of Jesus, their Founder, leader and inspiration.

Definition of Religion

Religion may refer to scripture, rituals, myths, beliefs, practices, moral codes, communities, and social institutions– that is, the outward and objectified elements of a tradition. The term religion originated from the Latin noun *religio that* was nominalized from one of the three verbs: *relegere* which means to treat with care,[1] *religare* meaning to bind oneself back and *reeligare* means to choose again.[2] Strictly speaking no word in either Greek or Latin corresponds exactly to English word 'religion' as it is used for several meanings. All these meanings are interrelated and are connected with the belief in creator. There has been a plethora of books and articles that have attempted to define 'religion' which has a historical trajectory and in different contexts diverse meanings. Melford Spiro defines religion as: 'an institution consisting of culturally patterned interaction with culturally postulated superhuman beings.'[3]

Religion may help to understand social experiences, institutional practices besides serving as a powerful source for explaining a wide range of social attitudes and behaviors. It represents an important tie between the individual and the larger social group, both as a basis of association and as an expression of meaning for the individual and the larger social group. Professor A.C.Watson opines religion as 'a social attitude toward the non-human environment' and A.M. Whitehead opines it as 'the art and the theory of the eternal life of a person, so far as it depends on oneself and on what is permanent in the nature of things.' Thus, religion is individual and social, individual in that each person has a religious experience of one's own, and social because it is a function of a person in society. It helps to conserve social values.

Religion has also been associated with public institutions such as education, hospitals, family, government, and political hierarchies. A religion may include a vivid and inner feeling of personal values. Secondly, it consists of collective values and finds expression in social forms of life. There is an extensive evidence that social factors help to shape religious beliefs, experiences, practices, and organizations.

The individual and collective expressions of religion develop in a complex interrelationship with societies and cultures.[4]

In view of the enormous complexity of sociological phenomena, no definition seems to be totally satisfactory.[5] Thus it is clear that no sharp definition can possibly cover all of the varied phenomena which are generally grouped as religion. But there are certain characteristic forms of human activity and beliefs which are commonly recognized as religious: worship, separation of the sacred from the profane, belief in the soul, belief in gods, acceptance of supernatural revelation and quest for salvation.[6]

Various Approaches

As far as it is possible to know, some form of religious experience or activity has been common to all human beings. Religion seems to have continually played an important role in every known society and it serves some sort of purpose.[7] All societies have possessed beliefs that vary from culture to culture and from time to time. Human beings live in communities that have their cultures and religions which play a crucial role in forming, molding, and shaping world views of persons in that community. The world views of human groups tell the way in which they perceive God, the world and the humans.[8]

Religion is a complex phenomenon, focused by people on explaining the evolution of particular religious beliefs and behaviors.[9] However, religion does not refer merely to a range of human constructions and behavior connected to beliefs in transcendental beings, powers, and states. They do not just happen but are created by inspired individuals, spread by faithful devotees and structured so as to reach specific goals and serve the felt needs of adherents.[10] Scholars from a multiplicity of humanistic, socio-scientific and socio-biological disciplines have shown interest in this discipline and their work has contributed to achieving an overall understanding of religion. Anthropologists, psychologists, philosophers, theologians, and sociologists have attempted to look at the origin of religion. They have developed a multiplicity of theories which generally attempt to answer the origin and function of religion. Some theories complement each other and can be combined, whereas others are more or less mutually exclusive.[11]

Religion is an expression in one form or another of a sense of dependence on the power outside oneself, a power which can be spoken of as a spiritual or moral power.[12] Any religion normally involves certain ideas or beliefs on one hand and on the other certain observances. These observances can be positive and negative, i.e. actions and rites. Much of religious behavior of an individual has some particular goal when the religious ritual is performed. Those who carry out the rites and perform the spells desire to produce results, such as stopping a storm, bringing down rain or ensuring fertility for their crops.[13]

Fustel de Coulanges opines that the social, juridical, and political institutions of the ancient societies cannot be understood unless the religion is considered. But it is equally true that religion cannot be understood except by an examination of its relation to the institutions. The social function of the rites is obvious: by giving solemn and collective expression to them, the rites reaffirm, renew, and strengthen those sentiments on which the social solidarity depends.

Religion no longer designates some sacred, mysterious, transcendental, or metaphysical reality that sets it wholly apart from the mundane world. An inquiry to the study of everyday ordinary reality is that it seems necessary to explain for the existence, persistence and decline of religious beliefs and practices. The concern, therefore, is for an understanding of the purpose of religion as to why do people believe in god, spirits, supernatural beings and to provide an answer to the question, as to what religion does for the individuals and society. Philosophers, psychologists, theologians, and sociologists interested in a particular aspect of life have all defined religion in their own way and for their own purposes. The different approaches are valid in different ways and within their own limitations.[14]

Anthropological

The anthropology of religion involves the study of religious institutions in relation to other social institutions, the comparison of religious beliefs and practices across cultures. It emphasizes that religious traditions are not just conceptual belief systems but rather a way of life in which beliefs are embedded in and formed by the practices of faith- the rituals, symbols, and religious artefacts. It attempts to analyze the system of meanings that exist in religious symbols and their relationship to society. Besides, it also involves the observation of social life, its structures and patterns and an observation of religion helps to determine the nature of the society in question.[15]

Max Muller, a German scholar, and an exponent of Naturalism makes religion, 'a mental faculty or disposition that enables a person to apprehend the infinite under different names and under varying guises.' Further he defined religion as 'a longing or desire to know the unknown and the unknowable' i.e., the 'infinite.'[16] Edward Burnett Tylor views religion as essentially a belief in spiritual beings and it exists to help people explain events.[17] Tylor takes religion as being both belief and practice and thus deals with intellectual and not social or emotional aspects of religion.[18] According to Herbert Spencer the gods were derived from early savage experiences of ghosts who were thought to be the heroic ancestors of a particular tribe or group.[19]

George Frazer distinguished between magic and religion. The method used was seeking similar beliefs and practices in all societies, especially the more primitive ones, more or less regardless of time and place.[20] Bronislaw Malinowski argued that religion originated from coping with death. He developed some of Durkheim's basic ideas in relation to the specific functions of religion in small-scale societies.[21] However, in looking at the specific function of religion for the Trobriand Islanders, he argued that it served the social purpose of 'easing emotional stress, tension and anxiety.'[22] Malinowski noted that 'people in all societies are faced with anxiety and uncertainty. He saw religion as born from the universal need to find comfort in inevitable times of stress.

Social anthropologists such as Edward Evans-Pritchard did extensive ethnographic studies among the Azande and Nuer peoples who were considered 'primitive' by society and early scholars. His book *Witchcraft, Oracles and Magic among the Azande* is about the people of Central Africa, an attempt to make intelligible a number of beliefs, by showing how they form a comprehensible system of thought, and how it is related to social activities, social structure and the life of the individual. Throughout his work he presents Zande oracles, magic, and witchcraft as a logical, coherent set of beliefs and practices.

According to Clifford Geertz, religion is 'a system of symbols which acts to establish powerful, pervasive and long-lasting moods and motivations in people by formulating concepts at a general order of existence and clothing these conceptions with such a feeling of factuality that the moods and motivations seem uniquely realistic.'[23] Claude Levi-Strauss analyzed the complex and interrelated systems of society, understanding religious structures as the basis of social phenomena, such as kinship, marriage, language and maintained that seemingly dissimilar belief systems had the same underlying structures.

No matter how anthropologists may define religion, they characteristically see it as much more than a set of abstract ideas and beliefs. It is also a system of ordered social interaction, not only between a person and supernatural beings but also between people and their fellow human beings. The identity of the performers and participants in religious acts, the relationships among them, the nature of their acts, the values expressed in myths and rites and the occasions upon which myths are told and rites are performed are all regarded as information vital to the understanding of religion.[24]

Psychological

Psychologists of religion go beyond reason and recognize that there is a force, consciousness, which tries to apprehend the infinite in a limited way. They consider that religion deals primarily with those human experiences that go beyond ones understanding. This discipline is also concerned with those religious happenings which take place and forces which exist within the human soul.[25] U.S. psychologist, William James in his *Gifford lectures* and book *The Varieties of Religious Experience* 1902 defined religious experience as a gradual, unified consciousness, through which the person grasps spiritual realities.[26] He considered personal religious experience to be the heart of religion and defined it as 'the feelings, acts and experiences of individuals in their solitude, so far as they apprehend themselves to stand in relation to whatever they may consider the divine.'[27] This experience which is psychological and subjective becomes the basis for religion as a phenomenon and as a social institution.[28]

William James discusses religion as arising from a broad range of human experiences that are analogous to experiences in other realms. He distinguished between institutional and personal religion where the former refers to the religious group or organization and plays an important part in a society's culture. According to Sigmund Freud religion is a form of mass neurosis. It exists only as a response to deep emotional conflicts and weaknesses. Since it is nothing more but a by-product of psychological distress, it should be possible to eliminate the illusion of religion by alleviating that distress.

Freud adds that humans feel a need for and invent a source of security and forgiveness in God. At various points in his writings, he suggested that religion was a means of giving structure to social groups, and an attempt to control the outside world. Freud acknowledges that religion has played an important role in the development of civilization by helping persons come to terms with both the outer forces of nature and the internal forces of instinctual life. Religion seems to have performed services for human civilization. It has contributed towards the taming of the asocial instincts.

The Swiss psychoanalyst Carl Gustaf Jung saw religion as a projection outwards and upwards of inner neurotic conflicts and regarded it as a force for good. He suggested that religion is 'one of the earliest and most universal expressions of the human mind' and it helps people resolve their inner conflicts and attain maturity. The human psyche is 'natively religious.' Erik Erikson applied his theories to the biographies of two major religious thinkers, Martin Luther and Mohandas Karamchand Gandhi and considered religion to be an important influence in successful personality development. He considered that religious life can be psychologically healthy and even necessary for growth into full psychological and social maturity.

Religion can also be thought of as a value system. According to Milton Rokeach 'A value system is a learned organization of principles and rules to help one choose between alternatives, resolve conflicts, and make decisions.' Research consistently finds that frequent religious involvement is also associated with more extensive social support networks and this is consistently found to be connected with a variety of positive, physical and psychological health outcomes.[29]

Religion contributes to a sense of coherence and an experience of life as meaningful as well as to a hopeful outlook on life, all of which are associated with better physical and mental health. The same is true of the positive effects of hope and optimism that have been found to be associated with better health and intrinsic religiosity. The latter has been associated with higher self-esteem, less anxiety and depression. To the extent that religion contributes to one, it indirectly contributes to the other. To the extent it contributes independently to both, there may be a potentiating interaction effect.

Philosophical

Philosophers of religion examine and critique the epistemological, logical, aesthetic, and ethical foundations inherent in the claims of a religion. Questions studied in the philosophy of religion include what gives reason to believe that a miracle has occurred, the relationship between faith and reason, between morality and religion, the status of religious language and petitionary prayer.[30] It is a system for understanding meaning of life, the universe, and one's place in it. Religion claims to be more than a certain kind of experience, claims ultimate truth- to be in close harmony with ultimate reality. More specifically, it implies an interpretation of the meaning of reality in terms of its value to and for human beings, implies a consideration of the meaning of the universe for well being and reckoning with the possibility that something at the core of reality does respond to and satisfy human demands for life and fulfillment of destiny.

The task of the philosophy of religion, which is to examine, criticize, and assess the validity of at least the human elements in religious experience is thus twofold: it has the function of interpreting, evaluating and integrating the data of religious experience as these are manifest in human behavior.[31] Religious writings, the world over have recorded types and elements of this experience and have indicated that encounters of this type can take place under various conditions. Sacred rocks, trees, groves, animals, artifacts etc. are worshipped because such experiences have occurred in conjunction with or through them; thereby these objects are set apart from what is profane or unholy and are felt to be sacred by the individual or group.

Ivan Strenski says that in the phrase 'philosophy of religion,' both the term 'philosophy' and 'religion' need to be analyzed. The central questions concern whether one can prove that God does or does not exist, whether the belief in God's existence can or cannot be reconciled with the reality of evil in the world, the relationship between faith in God and reason. Caputo defines religion as 'the love of God.'[32] The definition focuses on love and thereby brings into the philosophy of religion all the phenomenological aspects of religious affections.

According to Emmanuel Kant, religion is 'the recognition of all our duties as divine commands.'[33] It is a collection of cultural and belief systems and worldviews that establish symbols and relate humanity to spirituality and sometimes to moral values. George Galloway in his book *Philosophy of Religion* opines that 'Religion may be taken as universal which touches the inner soul of a person and goes beyond all distinctions of class or group.'[34]

Every religion in its own way tries to satisfy the inner soul of its followers and its principles and practices are never meant for any particular group of people only.[35] 'No one can understand humankind without understanding the faith of humanity. Although social sciences are concerned with religion as a social construct, relating to issues that arise from human beings' interrelations with each other and the socially constructed environment in which they live, analysis of religion could take seriously the internal perceptions and understanding of reality. The theory must also balance the societal aspects of religion with the role it plays for individuals.[36]

Theological

Theologians often consider the existence of God as self-evident and explain religious claims by rationalization. In the later twentieth century, scholars discussed theologies of religion in terms of a three-fold typology: exclusivist, inclusivist, and pluralist. Exclusivism is the view that only one religion is true, and all others are false. Such exclusivism can take either an extremist or a moderate viewpoint. In fact, neither the pluralist nor the inclusivist could avoid being exclusivist at some point. Mundane and the transcendent aspects of religious life cannot be described by the concept 'religion' but with two separate concepts namely 'cumulative tradition' and 'faith'. If faith is a total orientation of human person to the transcendent, belief transfers that lofty relation into the mundane level of operation of the mind.

Inclusivism is the view that one religion contains the highest truth, but the elements of that truth may be found in other traditions. These elements prepare adherents of those traditions to accept the fuller revelation when they encounter it and sincere devotion to those truths may prove saving for those in other religions.[37] This position was popularized by Karl Rahner who raised an important issue about the salvation of those who have never had the opportunity to listen to the gospel of Jesus. John Hick in his book *God and the Universe of Faiths 1973,* opines that in the evolutionary scheme of things it is the same message of God that comes distinctly to a particular group but in a different form from the others. While theological approaches are significant in and of themselves as statements of particular forms of believing, they cannot serve as definitions of religion usable beyond those particular traditions.[38]

The German theologian Rudolf Otto treated the importance of religious experience, more specifically experiences that are both fascinating and terrifying. He saw religion as emerging from these experiences. Otto focused on moments that he called numinous which means 'wholly other' and saw religion as emerging from these experiences. He asserted that these experiences arise from a special, non-rational faculty of the human mind, largely unrelated to other faculties, so religion cannot be reduced to culture or society.[39]

Rational Choice Theory
The rational choice theory has been applied to religions by the sociologists Rodney Stark and William Sims Bainbridge. According to Rational Choice Theory, social actors will always seek to obtain their goals with the least amount of risk and cost involved. They will assess the situation in a rational way, attempt to obtain the best possible overview of alternative actions and choose what maximizes their rewards and minimizes their costs. The individuals turn to religion because they see that it gives them some sort of benefits or rewards. They will join the religious groups and movements that will give them the most rewards.[40]

These thinkers asserted that religion is able to function as compensators for unobtained rewards. They saw religions as systems of 'compensators' which are a body of language and practices that compensate for some frustrated goal. They can be divided into compensators for the failure to achieve specific goals, and compensators for failure to achieve any goal. They define religion as a 'system of compensator that relies on the supernatural' and assert that only a supernatural compensator can explain death or the meaning of life.

Sociological

Sociology of religion has as its subject the study of religion in its social context: beliefs, practices and organizational forms of religion using the tools and methods of sociology. It is concerned with the dialectical relationship between religion and society and the role of religion in society. Here the Sociologists have an interest in religion's effect on society and society's influence on religious life, in the content of religious ideas, as long as they contribute to an understanding of the interdependence between religious life and its social context.[41] They focus on understanding religious beliefs and explaining how they relate to worldviews, practices, and identities, the diverse forms of expression religion takes, how religious practices and meanings change over time, their implications for, and interrelations with, other domains of individual and social action.[42]

Two major strategies used by sociologists of religion are substantive and functional definitions. The former includes characteristics of the substance of religion which is usually based on the human belief in extraordinary phenomena that which one cannot experience with senses or grasp with intellect. Functional definitions describe the utility or the effect that religion is supposed to have for individuals and society, describe what religion does and focus on the social functions that religion has for a group or a person. Religion is considered to perform the manifest function, that is, the actual things that are clearly involved when people practice religion. It involves things like worshipping God, finding answers to social problems and the like.

Religion gives a feeling to the people that they have something in common with each other, may be a shared belief in a common God and integrating people into a sense of belonging to the same society. The social forms of religion include organization and ideology where the structures of social relations, power and other resources control the practice of religion. Organizational forms of religion extend well beyond Church, denomination, sect, cult and include temples, monastic orders, shrines, brotherhood, mosques, Sikh gurudwaras, churches, congregations, chaplaincies and missions.[43] Berger and Luckmann have argued that the concentration on institutional forms of religion has been inhibitive of a genuine sociological theory of religion.[44]

In their sociological writing, Karl Marx, Max Weber, and Emile Durkheim were reacting to the economic and social upheavals of those centuries, prompted by the devastating consequences that rapid industrialization had inflicted on the European populations of which they were part. The study of religion could hardly be avoided within this framework, for religion was seen as an integral part of the society that appeared to be mutating beyond recognition.[45] According to Durkheim, religion is 'an integral system of beliefs and practices relative to sacred things... that unite in a single moral community called the Church all those who adhere to it.'[46] It has a unified system of beliefs and practices relative to sacred things, things which are set apart and forbidden, and beliefs, practices which unite into one single moral community called a Church, all those who adhere to them.[47]

Durkheim made a clear distinction between the sacred and the profane which can be paralleled with the distinction between God and humans. The sacred, however, possesses a functional quality that is by its very nature it has the capacity to bind and unite societies. He suggests that religion arises in relation to the beginnings of society- God is seen as the projected embodiment of society, and thus religion functions as a means of creating and strengthening the social solidarity.[48] According to him religion is collective, as he emphasizes on a community as the basis of religion.[49] Religious beliefs are symbolic expressions of social realities as without them serving as a foundation, religion may have no meaning.

Durkheim viewed religion within the context of the entire society, acknowledged its place in influencing the thinking and behavior of the members leading for social solidarity, cohesion, and integration. He argued that religion itself was a manifestation of a person's dependency on, and subservience to, the collective social life which 'surrounded' that person. Attempting to explain social institutions as collective means to fill individual biological needs, he focused on how social institutions fill social needs, especially social stability. Society was viewed as an organic analogy of the body, wherein all the parts work together to maintain the equilibrium of the whole, and so religion was understood to be the glue that held society together.

The function of religion is group cohesion often performed by collectively attended rituals and these group meetings provided a special kind of energy, which he called *effervescence*, that which made group members lose their individuality and feel united with the gods and thus with the group.[50] He also suggested that religion arises out of the experience of living in social groups. Religious belief and practice affirm a person's place in society, enhance feelings of community and give people confidence.[51] He saw that religion encompasses regular rituals and ceremonies on the part of a group of believers, who then develop and strengthen a sense of group solidarity.

According to Durkheim, people see religion as contributing to the health and continuation of society and bind society's members by prompting them to affirm their common values and beliefs on a regular basis. There is also the need for individuals to understand their place in society in terms of collective relationships and responsibilities. He saw religion as an affirmation of common values, beliefs, ideals and a way of providing people with ideas they could hold in common.[52] His theory that religious ritual is an expression of the unity of society and that its function is to 're-create' the social order by reaffirming and strengthening the sentiments on which the social order itself depends is significant.[53]

Georg Simmel in his *Essays on Religion,* regarded religion as one of the abiding forms of social relations encapsulating interpersonal trust and faith.[54] He views religion as a fundamental aspect of human relations and therefore, it will always exist as a way of being.[55] Thus Simmel and Durkheim believe that religion emerges in social relations, and the individual transfers his/ her relation to a deity. Boyer claims that religious symbolism and representations are constrained cognitively by the universal properties of the mind-brain.

From these different considerations it may be suggested that human beings are part of a social world. They are dependent on the actions and forces of other human beings that can be controlled through their own behavior. However, they are helpless in the face of other's actions and forces and hence attempt to understand and control through a belief in the supernatural. The organization of the supernatural world that is constructed by human beings reflects the society in which they live. The sentiments and emotions generated by the supernatural are an important force in the enhancement of social solidarity.[56]

Max Weber acknowledged that religion had a strong social component.[57] The fundamental purpose of his research was to discover religion's impact on social change. He uses the German term *Verstehen* to describe his method of interpretation of the intention and context of human action. For him religion is 'the means by which human beings adjust to their natural, social, economic, political, and intellectual environments, the means by which these are transcended or changed.'[58] H. H. Pressler quoting Weber says that 'he insisted that the goals of religion lay a powerful hold on people and motivate them to organize their society in harmony with them. Society is rearranged by a person to conform to principles regarded as 'right' and 'legitimate.'[59]

Karl Marx described religion as a dependent variable as its form and nature arc dependent on social and economic relations, which form the bedrock of social analysis. He saw religion as originating from alienation and aiding the persistence of alienation. These are responses to the general sentiment of lack of control over a person's destiny. The persistence of religion is both an indicator of far reaching alienation and an 'opiate' which perpetuates imbalances and inequalities in the social structure.[60] 'As far as societies divided into classes are concerned, Marx's main answer is that much ideology is inevitable in a class society, because the economically dominant class requires the existence of false beliefs for its continued dominance and has resources for perpetuating beliefs that are in its interests.'[61] The dominant class must construct systems of belief about ultimate concerns (God, the universe, humanity, morality etc.), and communicate them persuasively to the masses to keep them subdued.

Impressed by these reifications, the working class develops a false consciousness, convinced that the present socio-economic order is sanctioned by the natural or eternal orders.[62] 'The ideas of the ruling class are in every epoch the ruling ideas: i.e. the class, which is the ruling material force of society, at the same time its ruling intellectual force. The class which has the means of material production at its disposal has control at the same time over the means of mental production, thereby, the ideas of those who lack the means of mental production are subject to it.'[63]

Marx agrees with Durkheim and Weber, that religion is a reflection of humanity and not of a god. The crux of his arguments was that humans are best guided by reason, but religion was a significant hindrance to reason, inherently masking the truth and misguiding followers. From a Marxist perspective, religion is considered to be a conservative social force. From this perspective, religion is a means of social control and that can be used to justify the economic and political status quo.[64] Berger sees religion as an ideological framework that seeks to explain 'the world as it is.'

Talcott Parsons' views on the nature of religious belief and practice start from the idea that all societies require a central value system, if they are to exist and develop as a society.[65] He argued that religion contributes to social integration.[66] However, societies need to develop social mechanisms, since without this mechanism, integration and solidarity could not develop across society as a whole. All the institutions in a society like family, work, education, religion have a particular set of functions which is to provide the individual with a set of meanings that help him/her to make sense of society.

Parson assumes that religion helps members of society to deal with uncontrollable events such as suffering and the problem of evil. In this way religion calms tensions that otherwise would disturb the social order, and helps to maintain social stability.[67] Religion involves a belief in a power that is higher than the individual and this higher authority can be used to represent and develop common moral codes. Common values can be reinforced and given meaning to people through the organization of collective practices and ceremonies. By making people meet to practice their common beliefs, social integration and solidarity is created. But people must develop common values/beliefs in order to create a sense of shared meaning and purpose. It does not matter what these values actually are since all that is functionally important is that common values and social mechanisms exist for propagating these values.

In pre-modern societies, religion represents an obvious solution to the problems of integration and solidarity that is getting people to live and work together. In modern societies, however, religious belief systems can be progressively undermined by the development of scientific belief systems. The concept of a higher power, for example, may be questioned by science, leading to a decline in the power of religious beliefs to create consensus. When and if this happens, societies are faced with a problem since the structural framework for integration and solidarity may start to crumble. The solution is the development of new social mechanisms such as cultural institutions like education and the mass media which serve a similar function. It is the promotion of common moral values and their practice through various forms of communal gatherings and events.[68]

Thus it can be assumed that there are variations on the general theme of religion but none of the scholars anticipate the total disappearance of religion or deny the possibility that religion could occasionally be revived.[69] Many have recognized the limitations of focusing too strongly on either side of the individual or societal function of religion. The examination of the creative interaction between the individual and the society is increasingly prominent in recent theories of religion.[70]

Religion is no longer present as 'bookish knowledge' in isolation from other 'knowledge.' It is present in the context of its cultural carriers and vehicles such as language, food and clothing.[71] The last fifty years have witnessed a remarkable revival of religious truth-claims. Religion entered public spheres and became strong identity marker both for individuals and communities. At the turn of the twenty-first century, however, a completely different situation arose: religion regained its importance, but it is no longer the same religion as that of the beginning of the twentieth century.

Religion is no longer the religion of the commandments and directives and being a member of a Church does not bring with it social advantages or prestige in the public sector. It has repeatedly acted as a motive and vehicle for change. The role played by religion can only be comprehended by viewing in terms of time, place, and its function within a historical context. Religion, like society and culture was in a continual motion, only the speed changed, at times increasing and at times decreasing due to the variations in the situation of a particular time and place, that is, the historical context. Yet religion in itself remains a powerful medium for the mobilization of human resources.[72] In its respective cultural context, religion changes, so that there are no longer simple and easily definable 'religions.'

All religions have the idea of the divine as the starting point, is transcendental and beyond any human descriptions. But religious search does not end in God alone- it moves to human community. Religion acts as the healer of the ills of life and also promotes social solidarity, unity, identity, a common faith, value-judgments, sentiments and common worship which are significant factors in unifying people.[73] Every religion does many things for the individual and also usually for the society. It helps to bear pain in the troubles of life, uncomplainingly, offers solution to the problem of evil, improves the quality of present life, offers hope for a better life in the future and outlines an ideal society. Thus, religion appears to be an essential ingredient of society. The functions of religion help to know what social and psychological problems are solved by the religious beliefs and practices and also to reaffirm the central values of a society in such a way as to maintain the social fabric of that society.[74]

Religion is one of the important contributing factor in societal integration. Religious symbols can represent the unity of the social group and religious rituals can enact the unity, allowing the individual to participate symbolically in the larger unity they represent. According to integration theories, societal cohesion and stability are ensured by the functioning of religion, education and family that represent the larger social reality to the individual and enable the individual to accept personally that definition of reality.[75] It appears that religiosity is socially beneficial, that high rates of belief in a creator, correlate with lowering rates of fatal violence, suicide, abortion and also improved physical health.[76]

Religion, as a cultural institution serves to originate new ideas and categories of thought and to reaffirm existing values. It also helps in social unity, solidarity and works as an integrating force. It holds power over people and societies. Because societies cannot be physically sensed - seen, touched, tasted, heard, or smelt. People have to be encouraged to feel that they belong to a society; they need to be integrated into society. At one end of the scale are those who consider belief in a deity is helpful while the most ardent advocates consider persons and people inherently unruly and ungovernable unless they are strictly obedient to the creator.[77] Thus it can be seen that religion has got to do with the society, is implicitly associated with social functions and has intricate social implications too.

Religion seems to be one of the most powerful, deeply felt, and influential forces in human society. It has shaped people's relationships with each other, influencing family, community, economic and political life. Religious beliefs and values motivate human action and religious groups organize their collective religious expressions. Religion is a significant aspect of social life and the social dimension is an important part of religion.[78] Religion exists in a social context, is shaped by it and in turn, often influences it.[79] Religion does give birth to and enrich social values which are visible in tribal and ancient religion. Whether modern religion like Christianity and particularly the works of the Catholic Church and Bethany Sisters as a part of the Catholic Church have contributed to the enrichment of the social values is a question under study.

Ambedkar believed that religion could be either liberative or oppressive, depending on various factors. It could function as a tool of oppression if it propagates infallibility and requires total surrender to its totalitarian perspective. It is liberative if it is open for the notion of revolution or change. The social ideal of that particular religion which is the divine scheme of governance of that religion, decides whether it is good or not good.[80] The universally accepted theory is that religion is multi-functional; hence the study of religion may give attention to a particular function or aspect of religion.[81] Therefore, it may not be appropriate to regard any one of the approaches as the only or the fundamental theory of religion and thus seeking for its universal application. The more tangible solution seems to be in the realisation of the fact that various factors at different times and place may have been responsible for the birth and growth of a philosophy like that of religion.[82]

According to Ambedkar, religion is essential to humankind for he understood religion as a social practice for establishing the righteous relations between humans. He believed that religion is necessary as a system of values and as a science of social reconstruction. For him religion is necessary for the development of an individual and it is a system of such socio-cultural values which would bring all the individuals on equal plane and would create a powerful political community. He looked at religion as the basis for social interaction and all the way he looked for a religion without exploitation and a religion that does not justify exploitation.[83]

Scholars of religion declare that religion is for all and any attempt to study religion is in fact an attempt to study humanity itself. In that vein, L.W.Grensted writes, 'No conception of religion satisfies the religious person unless it is significant for the whole of life in all its details.'[84] According to Professor J.G.Arapura, finding out the integral relation between humanity and religion is the main goal of the science of religion. For him, without humanity there is no religion and apart from the essence of humanity there is no essence of religion. Dr S. Radhakrishnan indirectly indicated that 'When properly studied, comparative religion increases our confidence in the universality of God and our respect for the human race.'[85] Thus the point becomes clear that, if any attempt is made to conceptualize a new method for the study of religion it needs to focus on life.[86]

Religion is regarded as intimately interwoven with social life. Even those who consider religion as a part and parcel of the individual private quest for 'spirituality,' do not deny the fact that religion is a social phenomenon. Religion continues to play significant role in social life and influences the process of socialization. With new knowledge and experiences society changes which in turn brings new approaches to religious thinking. Any attempt to grasp religion scientifically is bound to fail because science is based on objective knowledge, whereas religion is rooted in subjective experience. This study is focused on the cultural, psychological, and social phenomena of human life and the effect religion has on these aspects.

Religion has continued to play a vital role in the lives of individuals worldwide which shows that religion has a great survival value. Its universality is not based upon the forms of beliefs and practices but upon the social functions it generally fulfils. These functions are of great individual and social significance. All the theories of religion agree that whatever the beliefs or rituals, religion satisfies some social and psychological needs common to all people and it is considered to be an extremely important social variable in the work of all the theorists. Their approach treats the interaction and dynamic processes between religions and the rest of societies. Religion continues to be a significant dimension intertwining individual lives, collective identities, institutional practices, and public culture.

Cultural institutions, such as religion, education, and the media, form a functionalist perspective, develop as a way of giving people a sense of belonging to a particular society, create and maintain a sense of order and continuity in society. Their main function is to provide the individual with a set of values that help to make sense of society. By creating a system of common values, people see themselves as having things in common and this helps to develop a sense of belonging to a society. Religion is a very important source of cohesion and integration in society, since it can provide people with common values, experiences and interpretations.[87]

The power of religion lies in the resources it provides toward the creation and shaping of meaningfully connected individual and communal lives. Although the founding narratives of religious traditions may be seen as divinely inspired, their subsequent institutionalization is a social process. Religious institutions are social institutions whose practices evolve over time and adapt to the changing cultural and historical circumstances.[88] Religion not only helps to understand social experiences and institutional practices. It also serves as a powerful source for explaining a wide range of social attitudes and behaviors.[89]

Benjamin Franklin stated that 'religion is a powerful regulator of people's actions, giving peace and tranquility within the minds and beneficial to others.'[90] When the theory of biological evolution removed the need for a supernatural creator, concerns immediately arose over the societal implications of widespread abandonment of faith. In 1880 the religious moralist Dostoyevsky penned the famous warning that 'If God does not exist, then everything is intolerable.' Though this brings out the need and importance of religion in one's life, the essence of religion is to be sought in an inner religious experience, variously characterized as a communion between God and a person, the deep inner life or the sense of the 'sacred'.[91]

Religion is meant for personal and social transformation and it has to supply a sense of sacredness to human life. Here it may be appropriate to see how religion continues to influence society such as the networks and institutions, health and education systems.[92] Every human action is either good or evil and there is no neutral action. Vivekananda perceived good actions to be revealing one's divine nature: 'Every action that helps a person to manifest the divine nature is good and every action that retards is evil. The only way of getting the divine nature manifested is by helping others to do the same' thus helping them to live a dignified human life.'[93]

Since human beings are by nature communitarian, religion may get itself expressed also on the institutional level. Institutional religion is a term used to indicate the process by which religious feeling attaches itself to various forms of social organization. Gradually structures emerge and most important and immediately apparent activities of this kind are Churches, rituals, and dogmas. Churches are sociological institutions which give public expression to religious feeling and afford a vehicle for the transmission of faith. Some Churches are highly organized, having staffs of priests forming a hierarchy and teachers, while other Churches have been and still remain loosely knit groups of worshippers who meet periodically to express a common understanding of the divine.[94] Religious communities work with a sense of spiritual experience to help those who are in need, and address global issues that affect the earth.[95]

Religion and human development cannot be seen as two isolated fields of life but within the totality of human existence. There is a general inclination to limit religion only to the occupation of the spiritual care and subjectivity of the individual, while development is understood as economic activity in terms of production, marketing, commerce, etc. This division may be useful for analytical purposes but does not do justice to the understanding of the totality of life according to which religion and development are interwoven in human life. Little research has been made on how Christianity as a religion has impacted the development of the Northeastern society. The need was felt to establish the historical record of the history of Catholic Missions in Northeast India and to elucidate the effect of the diverse Catholic missionary efforts within Christianity.

Though Religion and particularly Catholic missionary works can be studied through various approaches, the anthropological and sociological approaches seemed apt in this study. This is because these approaches deal with the beliefs, practices, and organizational forms in their social context. The focus of study being what Christianity and more so Catholicism as a religion has done in the lives of people and how it has impacted the society could be effectively studied taking these two approaches as its background.

Catholic missionaries in the eighteenth and nineteenth centuries brought a form of health care, education and social work to the Northeastern States that encouraged the creation of new egalitarian societies. Society, however secular it might be, can recognize that religion plays an important societal role. The Church is viewed as an important agent in addressing the problems of poverty, hunger, environmental issues, social justice and so on. Modern religions have denounced many of the evils that have been counterproductive for the communities thus providing a sense of social dimension to the community and thereby making it socially relevant to the faith community.

The focus here is why religion developed, what needs it serves, the reasons for the survival, persistence and also an understanding of the social purpose of religion. Why people believe in supernatural beings, why they continue their religious beliefs, practices, the way religious behavior differs between and within societies, individuals, and the consequences for social interaction of religious activity and organization is highlighted here. What Christianity as a religion has done for the individuals and society was the focus of interest in this study.

Since the topic of investigation is the Catholic Missions in Northeast India, it is appropriate to investigate on what the Catholic Church with its missionary activities was able to do to the society in the Northeast and how Bethany Sisters as a part of the Catholic Missions have contributed to the socio-educational and cultural development of the region from 1962-2012. It was interesting to note how Catholicism and the humanitarian activities of the Bethany Sisters have helped to fulfill the purposes of religion.

The book analyzes the concepts and approaches to the study of religion and is drawn for understanding and formulating frameworks for the entire study of this work. It deals with the theories of religion and discusses the philosophical, theological, psychological, intellectual, sociological, and Marxian approaches to the study of religion. It also provides an overview of the importance of studying these theories which form the basis of this book.

History of Christianity in India and Northeast India in particular, Catholicism, its organization, the origin of Catholic Missions and their works in general are discussed at length here. In the historical background, I have highlighted the origin and spread of Catholicism as well as the Catholic Missions throughout the Northeast. The book analyses the work of the various Congregations in the Northeastparticularly the role of the Sisters within the Catholic Church and their activities.

An in-depth study of the origin, growth and activities of the Congregation of the Sisters of the Little Flower of Bethany and their activities in the Northeast region forms the crux of this book. Besides the methods, approaches and strategies employed by the Bethany Sisters in the Northeast and the extent to which they operated and liaised with elements of the State as well as civil society is further discussed and analyzed here. With the help of the archival sources, agreement files and content analysis, I tried to bring out the original purpose for which the Bethany Institute was founded and the variety of activities that the members of this Institute are engaged in. The book focuses on the work of the Bethany Sisters in the Northeast Province, the number of their institutions, their varied activities and how they have affected the lives of the people.

An assessment of education imparted by the Sisters, their social work and health care activities is presented graphically. It reveals how the Bethany Sisters interacted with the people, staff, students, and other organizations. It begins with the people's responses to the missionary activities of the Bethany Sisters, as well as how the Bethany Sisters related with the people whom they catered to. The book examines through quantitative and qualitative data the effect of the Sisters' work on the socio - economic, cultural, religious, and political life of the people of Northeast. The impact of the Sisters work is assessed through questionnaires and interviews of the parents, teachers past students, present students studying in Sisters' institutions, the Priests and Sisters of other institutions associated with the Bethany Sisters and the data collected is analyzed through pie charts.

Endnotes

[1] Christopher Augustus Bixel Tirkey, *Religion / Primal Religions*, ISPCK, Delhi, 2005, p. 17.

[2] Gregory D. Alles, 'Religion: Further considerations', in Lindsay Jones (ed.), *Encyclopedia of Religion*, Vol.11 (2), 2005, p.7702.

[3] Melford Spiro in M. Benton (ed), *Anthropological Approaches to the Study of Religion*, London, 1966, p.96.

[4] James Beckford, 'Religion', in Bryan S. Turner (ed.), *The Cambridge Dictionary of Sociology*, Cambridge University Press, UK, 2006, p.507.

[5] Madhavi D. Renavikar, *Women and Religion*, Rawat Publications, Jaipur, 2003, p. 27.

[6] John R. Everett, 'Religion' in *Encyclopedia Americana*, s.v., Vol.23, p.342.

[7] Chris Livesey, "Religion, Functionalist Perspectives." Accessed 14 May 2011. Available from www.sociology.org.uk, p.1.

[8] A. Alangaram, *Religions for Societal Transformation: Interreligious Dialogue from Subaltern Perspectives*, Asian Trading Corporation, Bangalore, 2005, p. xiii.

[9] L.B. Steadman and C.T. Palmer, *Beyond Belief, A Review of the Supernatural and Natural Selection: Religion and Evolutionary Success*, Boulder, CO: Paradigm, 2008, p.225.

[10] J. Gordon Melton and Martin Baumann (ed.), *Religions of the World: A Comprehensive Encyclopedia of Beliefs and Practices*, Oxford, England, 2002, p.x.

[11] Inger Furseth & Pal Repstad, *An Introduction to the Sociology of Religion: Classical and Contemporary Perspectives*, Ashgate Publishing Limited, London, 2006, p.3.

[12] A.R. Radcliffe-Brown, *Structure and Function in Primitive Society*, Routledge & Kegan Paul, London & Henrey, 1982, Rep.1976, p.157.

[13] Abraham Rosman, Paula G. Rubel, and Maxine Weisgrau, *The Tapestry of Culture: An Introduction to Cultural Anthropology*, Ninth Edition, Rowman& Littlefield Publishers, Inc., United Kingdom, 2009, p.256.

[14] R. Pierce Beaver et.al., (eds.), *A Lion Handbook: The World's Religions*, Lion Publishing, England, 1982, p.10.

[15] Santanu K. Patro (ed.), *A Guide to Religious Thought and Practices*, ISPCK, Delhi, 2011, p.12.

[16] Raghuvir Sinha, *Essays in Social Anthropology*, Concept Publishing Company, New Delhi, 1990, p. 175.

[17] Edward Burnett Tylor, *Primitive Culture*, (Vol. I), New York, 1874, p.30.

[18] *Op.cit.*, p.185.

[19] Varghese Manimala, *Toward Mutual Fecundation and Fulfillment of Religions*, Media House & ISPCK, New Delhi, 2009, p.234.

[20] Paulos M. Gregorios, *Religion and Dialogue*, ISPCK, 2000, p.16.

[21] Chris Livesey, *op. cit.*, p.8.

[22] Bronislaw Malinowski D.Sc., *Crime and Customin Savage society*, Littlefield, Adams & Co, Paterson, New Jersey, 1959, p.i.

[23] Clifford Geertz, *The Interpretation of Cultures*, Basic Books, New York, 1973, p.90.

[24] J.C.F, W.H. Normaan, *The Philosophy of Religion*, Oklahoma, 1967, p.422-423.

[25] W. Schmidt, *The Origin and Growth of Religion: Facts and Theories*, (trans.) H.J. Rose, Methuen & Co. Ltd., 1931, pp.3-4.

[26] Santanu K. Patro, *op. cit.*, p.13.

[27] James Beckford, *op. cit.*, pp.31-32.

[28] Helen K. Bond, et.al., (eds.), *A Companion to Religious Studies and Theology*, Edinburgh University Press, Edinburgh, *2003*, p.32.

[29] W. Strawbridge, et.al., *Annals of Behavioral Medicine, Journal of Religion and Health*, (Vol. 3), No.4, 2001, pp. 23, 68-74.

[30] Jones, James W., 'Religion, Health, and the Psychology of Religion: How the Research on Religion and Health Helps Us Understand Religion' *Journal of Religion and Health*, (Vol. 3), No.4, 2004, pp.317-328.

[31] *Ibid.*

[32] Kevin Schilbrack, "New Directions for Philosophy of Religion: Four Proposals", *Studies in Religion/Sciences Religieuses*, 2012. Accessed on 9 May 2012. Available from http://sir.sagepub.com.

[33] Christopher Augustus Bixel Tirkey, *op.cit.*, p.13.

[34] George Galloway, *Philosophy of Religion*, T &T Clark, Edinburgh, 1956, p.138.

[35] Kedar Nath Tiwari, *Comparative Religion*, Motilal Banarsidass Publishers Pvt. Ltd., Delhi, 1997, p.220.

[36] Helen K. Bond, *op.cit.*, p.92.

[37] K.P. Aleaz, *Theology of Religions, Bermingham Papers and other Essays*, Moumita Publishers & Distributors, Calcutta, 1998, p.13.

[38] Seth O.Kunin, Jonathan Miles-Watson (eds.),*Theories of Religion: A Reader*, Edinburg University Press, Edinburg, 2006, p.9.

[39] Paul F.Knitter, *One Earth, Many Religions: Multi-faith Dialogue and Global Responsibility*, Orbis Books, USA, 1995, pp. 42-43.

[40] Inger Furseth& Pal Repstad, *op. cit.*, p.117.

[41] http:// en.wikipedia.org /Theories_of_religion#cite_note-Kunin.2C_page_85-61 accessed 20 September 2012, p.11

[42] Michele Dillon, "The Sociology of Religion in Late Modernity" in Michele Dillon (ed.*), Handbook of the Sociology of Religion*, Cambridge University Press, United Kingdom, 2003, p.7.

[43] Inger Furseth & Pal Repstad, *op.cit.*, pp.13-16.

[44] Peter L. Berger, Thomas Luckmann, 'Sociology of Religion and Sociology of Knowledge', in *Sociology and Social Research*, (Vol.47), 1963. Thomas Luckmann, 'Religion in Modern Society', *Journal for the Scientific Study of Religion*, (Vol. II), April 1963, pp. 147-162.

[45] Grace Davie, "The Evolution of the Sociology of Religion", in Michele Dillon (ed.), *Handbook of the Sociology of Religion*, Cambridge University Press, United Kingdom, 2003, p.62.

[46] Anne Warfield Rawls,'*Epistemology and practice: Durkheim's The Elementary Forms of Religious Life*, p.115.

[47] Emile Durkheim, *The Elementary Forms of Religious Life:A Study in Religious Sociology*, (trans.) Joseph World Swain, George Allen & Unwin, Free Press, New York, 1915, p.47.

[48] Seth O. Kunin, Jonathan Miles-Watson (eds.),*Theories of Religion: A Reader*, Edinburg University Press, Edinburg, 2006, pp.18-19.

[49] Madhavi D. Renavikar, *op.cit.*, p.27.

[50] Roland Robertson, '*The Sociological Interpretation of Religion*', Basil Blackwell, Oxford, 1970, p.6-7

[51]*Ibid.*, p.19.

[52] ChrisLivesey, *op.cit.*, p.4.

[53] A.R.Radcliffe-Brown, *op. cit.*, p.165.

[54] James Beckford, *op.cit.*, p.506.

[55] Inger Furseth & Pal Repstad, *op.cit.*, p. 40.

[56] Abraham Rosman, Paula G. Rubel, and Maxine Weisgrau, *op cit*, p.232.

[57] Roland Robertson, *op.cit.*, p.12.

[58] *Op. cit.*, p.141.

[59] Christopher Augustus Bixel Tirkey, *op.cit.*, p. 23.

[60] For Marx's views on religion, see especially 'On the Jewish Question' and 'Contribution to the Critique of Hegel's Philosophy of Right', in T.B.Bottomore (ed.), *Karl Marx: Early Writings*, London, 1963, pp. 1-40 and 43-59.

[61] Richard W. Miller, 'Social and Political Theory: Class, State, Revolution', in Terrell Carver (ed.), *The Cambridge Companion to Marx*, Cambridge University Press, 1991, p.74.

[62] David K. Naugle, *Worldview: The History of a Concept*, William B. Eerdmans Publishing Company, Grand Rapids, Michigan /Cambridge, U.K., 2002, p.236.

[63] R. Pascal, (ed.), *Karl Marx and Friedrich Engels, The German Ideology, Parts I and II*, International Publishers, New York 1947, p.39.

[64] Abraham Rosman, Paula G. Rubel, and Maxine Weisgrau, *op. cit.*, p. 233.

[65] Chris Livesey, *op.cit.*, p.11.

[66] Inger Furseth, *op.cit.*, p.4.

[67] *Ibid.*, p. 46.

[68] Chris Livesey, *op.cit.*, p.12.

[69] James Beckford, *op.cit.*, p.510.

[70] Seth O. Kunin, Jonathan Miles-Watson, *op.cit.*, p.19.

[71] Kocku Von Stuckrad (ed.), 'Religion' in Introduction: The Academic Study of Religion- Historical and Contemporary Issues, *The Brill Dictionary of Religion*, (Revised edn.), Metzler Lexikonin (ed.), (trans.) Christoph Auffarth, Jutta Bernard & Hubert Mohr., Vol. III M-R, Martinus Nijhoff publishers, Boston, 2006, p.xi.

[72] Kenneth W. Jones, *The New Cambridge History of India: Socio Religious Reform Movements in British India*, Cambridge University Press, Cambridge, 1994, pp. 220-221.

[73] *Op. cit.*, p.xiii

[74] Christopher Augustus Bixel Tirkey, *op.cit.*, p. 22-24.

[75] Meredith B. McGuire, *Religion, The Social Context*, Fifth Edition, Wadsworth Thomson Learning, USA, 2002, p.196.

[76] http://moses.creighton.edu/JRS/2005/2005-11.html#figures accessed 14 May 2012.

[77] Chris Livesey, *op.cit.*, pp.2-3.

[78] Meredith B. McGuire, *Religion, op cit.* p.1.

[79] *Ibid.*,p. xiii.

[80] P. Mohan Larbeer, *Ambedkar on Religion: A Liberative Perspective*, ISPCK, Delhi, 2003, p.169.

[81] T.Swami Raju, *The Study of Religion: Methods & Perspectives*, BTESSC / SATHRI, Bangalore, 2004, p.27.

[82] Raghuvir Sinha, *op.cit.,* p.193.

[83] P. Mohan Larbeer,*op.cit.,* pp.160-161.

[84] L.W.Grensted, *The Psychology of Religion,* Oxford University Press, New York, 1952, p.15.

[85] S.Radhakrishnan, *East and West in Religion,* George Allen & Unwin Ltd., London, 1933, p.32.

[86] K.P. Aleaz, *Harmony of Religions: The Relevance of Swami Vivekananda,* PunthiPustak, Calcutta, 1993, p.52.

[87] Michele Dillon, "*The Sociology of Religion in Late Modernity*", *op.cit.,* p.14.

[88] *Ibid .,* p.6.

[89] *Ibid.,* p.8.

[90] Walter Isaacson, *Benjamin Franklin: An American Life,* Simon & Schuster, New York, 2003, p.58.

[91] Madhavi D. Renavikar, *op.cit.,* p.16.

[92] Varghese Manimala, *op.cit.,* p.261.

[93] A. Alangaram, *op.cit.,* p.24.

[94] *Op.cit.,* pp.268-269.

[95] Santanu K. Patro (ed.), *op.cit.,* p.172.

Chapter 2

Christianity
and Catholicism

This chapter deals with the history of Christianity, the birth of Catholicism, the organization and spread of the Catholic Church within India and in Northeast India and then the advent of the Catholic Missions to the Northeast Region.

Christianity in India

Although the exact origins of Christianity in India remain unclear, it is generally agreed that Christianity in India is almost as old as Christianity itself, taking hold even before it spread to many predominantly Christian nations of Europe. The history of Christianity in India figure in the opening chapters of the *Acts of St Thomas* which was almost certainly written in Syriac, perhaps in the third century after Christ.[1] There are two traditions regarding St Thomas. According to the Western tradition St Thomas, following the well established trade routes, reached India sometime in the middle of the first century of the Christian era. He preached the gospel and converted many, including the members of royal families, suffered martyrdom in India and was buried there. Later his mortal remains were transferred to the West.[2]

According to the Indian tradition, St Thomas came to India by sea. He first landed at Cranganore in about 52 A.D and converted high caste families and others in South India, particularly in Kerala.

He also worked in the Coramandal coast and went to China where he preached the Gospel and returned to India. On his return he organized the Christians of Malabar under some priests. He erected a few public places of worship, then moved to the Coramandal coast and suffered martyrdom. Christians believe that St Thomas, one of the twelve apostles of Jesus, died in South India and that his tomb in Madras is his genuine resting place.[3]

A. M. Mundadan ascribed the origin of the Indian Christians to the preaching of St Thomas.[4] His apostolic work was continued by missionaries from West Asia and Europe over the centuries. The ancient Church whose members are found in South India was for many centuries linked with the Syrian Church of the East sometimes called Thomas Christians and sometimes Syrian Christians. The presence of Christians was found in Western region by the end of sixth century. For centuries St Thomas Christians expanded due to their zeal, though inspired also by the apostolic spirit of their East Syrian brethren. Some monks from India went to the Far East. During the tenth and the eleventh centuries, St Thomas Christians tried to spread their faith in the Maldives' Islands.[5]

New continents were being opened up in the East and the West, and Christian missionaries were being sent forth to bear an invitation to 'strange races and peoples to take the place of millions who had strayed from the fold.' The restless energy and activity so characteristic of the fifteenth century manifested itself strikingly in the numerous naval expeditions planned and carried out in the face of enormous difficulties, which led to such important geographical discoveries. The importance of these discoveries in both East and West from the spiritual and temporal point of view was understood by Spain and Portugal. The rulers of these countries were aware of the important service that might be rendered by religion to their work of colonization.

The Portuguese pushed forward their discoveries along the West Coast of Africa till at last Bartholomew Diaz succeeded in reaching the Cape of Good Hope in 1487, thereby opening the way for Vasco da

Gama's voyage to the Malabar Coast in 1498. Though the middle ages of Christianity in India marked the arrival of Franciscan John Monte Corvino in the year 1291, history was created by Vasco Da Gama. The individuality and uniqueness of Christianity lasted until Christianity in India came in contact with the Portuguese missionaries who arrived in Kerala after the discovery of the sea route from Europe to India by Vasco da Gama in 1498 A.D.

The Christian presence is very vivid in the southern States of the country from the beginning of the first century. Christians in Kerala constitute one third population of the State. Though Christians were found in Kerala and Tamil Nadu in the early centuries, Karnataka and Andhra Pradesh had Christian presence later in the beginning of thirteenth century commencing with the coming of Dominican missionaries. Kerala has 19.31 per cent Christian population, Tamil Nadu has 5.69 per cent, Karnataka has 1.91 per cent and Andhra Pradesh has 1.82 per cent. These four States account for 28.73 per cent of the total Christian population in the country. Madhya Pradesh, West Bengal, and Gujarat have less than one percent of the total population. Christians form just 0.43 per cent in Gujarat, 0.09 per cent in Haryana and 0.08 per cent in Himachal Pradesh. In Goa, Christians constitute 29.85 per cent of the total population.[6] Elsewhere, Christians are much more scattered.

Christianity developed in India and in the course of time attained an indigenous character. In the pre-colonial period Christians were more predominant in the areas of agriculture, commerce, and welfare of the people. The contribution of Christianity in early ages before the arrival of Portuguese is the acculturation and spiritualization which provides social and socio-ecclesial life. Independence marked by the fast growth of the country economically, socially, and culturally, improvement in transportation and communication facilitated the missionaries to reach the unreachable areas of mission and development across the subcontinent. Today, Christianity is rooted from South - Kanyakumari to North - Jammu and Kashmir.

Christianity has emerged as the major religion in Nagaland, Mizoram, and Meghalaya. Among other States/UTs, Manipur (34.0%), and Arunachal Pradesh (18.7%) have considerable percentage of Christian population to the total population of the State/UTs. The total Christian population of Northeast India, which is roughly 4.3 million, accounts for 22.7 per cent of Indian Christians. With roughly 1.2 million- Meghalaya has the highest Christian population and Tripura with 47,000 has the least Christian population in the North East region of India. The three largest Christian groups in the Northeast are the Baptists, the Roman Catholics, and the Presbyterians.

Christianity in Northeast India

Christianity in North East India goes back to 1560s of Mughal and Afghan economic/political struggle period, when Arakan (Burma) King brought Portuguese Forces around Bondashill (present Badarpur) and its neighbouring areas. The spiritual needs of the Catholics were looked after by priests from South India and later by Holy Cross Priests of the Bengal Mission from 1860-76. Still later Benedictines, Capuchins, Salvatorians, Jesuits and the Salesians catered to the Catholics till this mission went back to the Canadian Province of Holy Cross in 1928 under Chittagong Diocese. The presence of the Catholics since 1860s with resident priest in Badarpur, made it possible to establish a Parish in 1880 with the first Church dedicated to St Joseph.

Catholic missionary work proper in the North East dates back since the creation of the Prefecture Apostolic of Assam, Bhutan and Manipur in 1889.[7] It was made the responsibility of a young German order, the Society of the Divine Saviour, popularly referred to as the Salvatorians.[8] Baptismal record indicated the far and wide activities and tour of the Salvatorian missionaries, baptizing people in places like Cherrapunjee, Guwahati, Shillong, Tejpur, Silchar, Manipur, Damalia, Duputtee, Krishnagar, Silcouri, Larshinga, Sonacherra etc.[9] Since then, this region has seen a number of Catholic Missions with different historical, socio-economic and cultural backgrounds.[10]

The presence of Christianity in the region is also found with the arrival of the two Portuguese missionaries on 26th September 1626. The first systematic Catholic effort to evangelize Assam was undertaken by a handful of Priests, Brothers and Sisters belonging to a young religious society that was just establishing itself and struggling to marshal adequate personnel and means for such a gigantic task.[11] Roman Catholic Missions began working in India in the fifteenth century, but there was only occasional contact with the North East prior to the nineteenth century.[12] The Foreign Missionaries of Paris (MEP) and the Foreign Missionaries of Milan (PIME) worked in this area during the nineteenth century.[13]

The Protestant missionaries first established mission work in this region in the mid-nineteenth century. They pioneered healthcare services, medical work for local people, nursing schools and Bible translation centers. They were the first to give the Roman script to most of the tribal languages, which until the advent of Christianity were only spoken languages without a script, grammar, and literature. They passed on Church leadership to local Christians. They were the first to introduce Christianity to the people of the Brahmaputra valley and the tribal people of the hills. Their missionary work can be traced back to the establishment of translation centers and schools by Serampore Mission in Guwahati (1829) and in Cherrapunji (1832). The Roman Catholic Church followed with the advent of Otto Hopfenmueller in Shillong on 27th February 1890.

Protestant Christianity spread rapidly in Mizoram with the arrival of the first missionaries in 1894. A major missionary thrust began in 1897 with the work of D.E. Jones. By 1930, most of the Mizos had become Christians. This has been called the 'Mizo Miracle' by mission historians. Lutheran missionaries, however, registered modest success among the Adivasis and the Bodos of the Assam plains. Despite the major role played by the missionaries in preventing attempts to replace Assamese with the Bengali language, their contribution to Assamese literature and publication of journals and books in Assamese and their educational and healthcare services are praiseworthy. Manipur, once a princely State, witnessed the spread of Christianity since the arrival of William Pettigrew, a Baptist missionary in 1894.

The Baptist missionaries worked among the Tangkhul Nagas with great success. Most of the Naga tribes of Manipur are Christian today, other than that there are also the Chin-Kuki-Mizo ethnic tribes in Manipur. The Naga tribes and Kuki-Chin tribes constitute 34 percent of the State's population and they are predominantly Christian. The ratio of the Christian population among the Meiteis, however, is still very less. So far as the Nagas of Nagaland are concerned, the work of the Protestant missionaries began among the Nagas in 1870. Large numbers began to embrace Christianity during the twentieth century and most members of the Ao tribe became Christians. They in turn became enthusiastic missionaries, joined the American Baptists and evangelized the other Naga tribes, especially the Semas, Chakhesangs, Angamis, Zeliangrongs, and Konyaks. In 2001, Nagaland was 87.5% Christian. Baptists followed by the Roman Catholics have the largest number of followers in Nagaland.[14]

Arunachal Pradesh, earlier known as the North-East Frontier Agency (NEFA), was closed to missionary work by successive governments in New Delhi until the 1980s. Christianity came to this bordering State during the Raj with missionaries establishing schools and Churches at Sadia and other areas. But students coming to Shillong and other towns for school and college education embraced Christianity and they in turn became missionaries to their own people. Thus, Christianity began to spread among the Adis, the Mishings, the Wanchoos and other tribes. From 1975 to 2005, nearly 20% of the tribals became Christians. Christianity was brought to Tripura in 1920 by the Baptist missionary society of New Zealand. The society established its first Church in 1938.

In the context of different political systems, plurality of religious beliefs and practices, unintelligible dialects and languages, alphabet-less communities and variations in social structure, the presence of the new faith has been of tremendous importance. This faith has helped the fragmented and isolated people for introducing various effective institutional means so that the people could successfully work in the ongoing transformed situation and create a common sense of cultural identity. Many Christian missionaries seem to have contributed to the building up of the tribal's and their rich cultural traditions.

Pandit Nehru confirmed this in his words: 'The missionaries did very good work in North-East India and I am full of praise for them.' The former President of India Dr Rajendra Prasad said, 'Christian missionaries from various countries of the world have worked among the tribal's and at great sacrifice have spread education and generally helped in effecting improvement in their living conditions. By helping the tribal's to develop, the Church has helped the nation to develop.'[15] The Christians established many schools in different parts of this Region.

Catholicism

Catholicism is understood as a distinct body within the larger Christian world.[16] The Catholic Church has always claimed Jesus of Nazareth as its Founder.[17] 'Early Catholicism' is sometimes used to refer to the Pauline Christian communities in the third generation as they are known in the Pastoral Epistles, the letters of St Ignatius, St Polycarp, and the Acts of the Apostles. Much of what is termed 'Catholic' about the third Pauline generation was already to some degree present or anticipated in the first. Paul's own perspective was from the start 'Catholic' in the sense of 'universal.'[18] One element that is peculiar to the Catholic Church is its insistence that the Bishop of Rome, the Pope is central to the self-identification of the Church in his role as the center of Catholic unity.[19] What makes the Church Catholic is the unity among all Catholic Bishops and their common unity with the Bishop of Rome, the Pope.

The word 'Catholic' comes from the two Greek words, *kath holou*, which means something like 'of the whole.' The word does occur, very early in Christian history. It is usually translated as 'Church in the New Testament and the term as used by St Paul comes from the Greek word *ekklesia* from which the word 'ecclesiastical' is derived meaning an 'assembly', 'community', or 'congregation.' The earliest stages of Christianity can be thought of as a loosely organized network of small communities in various parts of the Mediterranean world. They were linked to each other by travelling apostles, evangelists and other missionaries as well as by circulating letters like those of St Paul's letter to the Churches of Galatia, Corinth or Philippi.[20] It is within the context of this wide-ranging network of small Christian communities that the word 'Catholic' first appears. Today the term is applied to the Church founded by Christ, which is of its nature intended for all races and all times. The word is used for individual Christians in so far as they belong to the Catholic Church.[21]

It is common for many people to understand the word Catholicism to mean a particular denomination. Thus, for example, Catholics say the rosary, revere the Pope, go for Mass on Sunday, have a clergy that does not marry and those characteristics, among many others distinguish Catholics from other denominations. Catholicism can be considered as one Christian denomination identifiable as having its own distinct culture, character and sometimes dependent on ancestry and geographical location. It can be understood as a recognizable social grouping.[22] Within Catholicism there is more than one tradition (for example, there are Roman and Byzantine Catholics- all part of the Catholic Church).[23] Since the East-West Schism of 1054, the Churches that remained in communion with the See of Rome have been known as 'Catholic.'[24]

At the early stage of Christian history, Catholicity was thought to mean the unity of all the local Churches in union with each other and the common faith as it was professed in its worship, creeds and other articulations of the ancient tradition.[25] Catholic Church understands itself to be 'Catholic' as it wishes the Gospel to be preached universally to the whole world. In that sense, it seems to be a missionary enterprise[26] and not confined to any one place in the world, not limited to any one race or social class, but stands above all classes, races, nations and thus is intended for all peoples.[27] This has led to bewildering complexity of institutions, schools, literary texts, music, art, various media, forms of ministry, etc. Thus, the Catholic Church is both inclusive and expansive as it attempts to invite all people to be members of the Church.

The first important function of the Church was the spiritual one which involves educating the followers in the doctrine of faith. The second was the service to humanity which became necessary for fulfilling the teachings of Jesus Christ. According to the Catholic Directory of India-2013, the population of India was 1,210,193,422 out of which about 17,535,429 were Catholics comprising the Latin, Syro-Malabar and Syro-Malankara Catholic traditions that represent less than 2 percent of the total population but it is the largest Christian Church within India.

There are also 7 Indian Cardinals out of the total of 20 from Asia, which is a good representation of the Indian Church. There are 166 ecclesiastical units in India, 8 Auxiliary Bishops, 166 Bishops; 10715 Parishes and sub stations, 15,420 Diocesan Priests, and 7031 Religious Priests at the service of the Dioceses. 1221 Religious Priests, 250 Brothers and 4,112 Sisters, 101 persons belonging to secular institutes and 80 of them from the pious Associations totaling to about 5764 serve through various Religious Institutes.

Catholic Church runs 14148 educational institutions both formal and non-formal, 6603 social welfare centres and 2692 health service centres in the country. Besides these the Catholic Church owns 360 retreat and renewal centres as well as 668 Media centres.[28] All the Bishops in India, both Western and Eastern, form the Catholic Bishops' Conference of India (CBCI) which was founded in 1944. The Holy See's representative to the government of India and to the Church in India is the Apostolic Nuncio to India.[29] Within the jurisdiction of these Dioceses, thousands of educational and non educational institutions are functioning as an expression of its social commitment. Various developmental activities are taking place under the registered social service societies of each Diocese. Rural development activities and conscientization activities are initiated in recent times.

Since the Independence the number of services rendered by Catholics has multiplied in various forms like schools, rehabilitation centers, leprosy homes, orphanages, hospitals, dispensaries, colleges, vocational training centers, printing and visual media, social uplift programmes, social development initiatives etc. Catholicism has been a minority presence in India, although the Catholic presence is an ancient one. The Catholic Church has strong roots, with constant experiments in casting its presence in acculturated ways.[30]

Organization in the Catholic Church

The Church, from the first moment as revealed in the New Testament record, is organized in a multitude of 'Churches', one Church in each city. In each Church there are two groups, the clergy who preside over its affairs, offer the Mass, administer the Sacraments, explain the teaching and the laity.

The structure of the Roman Catholic Church begins with the Papacy. Pope is the symbol of Romanism and was called a 'Primate.' In Roman Catholic belief, the Pope is considered the successor of Peter, the apostle of Jesus,[31] as the head of the Apostolic College. The power of the Pope was supreme, and he has jurisdiction over the universal Church both in matters of faith, morals, and discipline. Disobedience to the Pope was punished by ex-communication. Thus, there was no area of the Roman Catholic Church and no person who was not subject to a direct command of the Pope. The Pope was assisted in his day-to-day administration by an organization called The Curia and different congregations. It had no authority except that which Pope gave. In this sense, the Curia acted as his personal assistants. This body addressed to the administrative problems of the entire Roman Catholic Church and particular Regions and Dioceses.[32]

The Pope personally appoints the heads of Curia offices called Congregations. The Congregation of the Consistory was established in its present form by Pope Sixtus V in 1588. It established new Provinces, Dioceses, and appointed Bishops. It also supervised the Dioceses, administration of the Bishops and received regular reports from them. The Episcopal appointment was the vital part of the centralization in the Roman Catholic Church.[33] The Congregation of Religious established by Pope Sixtus V supervised religious communities. The Pope approved any community which wished to serve in the Church at large as per the directives and rules laid down by the Church.[34] The Congregation of the Propagation of the Faith was established by Pope Gregory XV in 1622 for the missionary territory.

The Curia, the Congregations and the Court had a Cardinal as its presiding officer. The College of Cardinals was an electoral body and a senate of the Roman Catholic Church. It is the most powerful organ within the Roman Catholic Church. The Cardinals were consulted in all the affairs of the Church. The College had Cardinals who were residential Bishops and those who were not residential Bishops, expected to live in Rome and to take posts in the Papal administration.[35] The Cardinals who were members of important Congregations were likely to be the members of other Congregations as well.

A Roman Catholic Church territory always had a Bishop. The normal territory is called a 'Diocese' and the Bishop is in charge of the Diocese. The term Episcopacy is derived from the Greek term '*episkopos*' which means 'overseer' from which the English word Bishop is derived.[36] A residential Bishop was given designation of 'the Ordinary of the place' meaning that the Bishop had jurisdiction by virtue of his office. One important difference between the mission territory and the Diocese was that the Pope could limit the powers of the Vicar Apostolic, head of the mission territory who otherwise was in all other respects the effective Bishop of his territory.[37]

Dioceses are formed into a Province. Within a Province one Episcopal See, usually the oldest or the largest was called the Metropolitan See and all the others were called Suffragan Sees. The Ordinary of the Metropolitan See was by definition an Archbishop. He had neither jurisdiction over the suffragans nor any jurisdiction within the suffragan

Dioceses. The appointment of the Bishops was done by the Pope through the Congregation of the Consistory.[38]

The Parish is the basis of the Roman Catholic administrative structure and in the immediate context is the part of the Diocese under the control of the Bishop. The Parish is the place where the adherents of the Roman Catholic Church encounter the priesthood, the teaching office and the Sacramental system.[39] It is also the place where the Catholics most frequently meet the other members of the Roman Catholic community. The Parish is administered by a Parish Priest and as a rule, the Parish is defined territorially. All Roman Catholics within certain boundaries are attached to the Parish Church. The Parish is normally the centre of a certain social organization. These organizations were intended to keep the people together and offer pastoral care for the children, adolescents, young unmarried people, married people, husbands and wives.[40]

Religious Orders were founded within the Catholic Church to serve specific needs and possible challenges in the Church. All the Orders show specific peculiarities and characteristic methods organically bound up with their very essence and their special aims, most of them founded for missionary work. In India, Sisters Congregations developed for educational and charitable works. Religious Orders constituted a significant addition to the existing structure of the Church administration. They arose as a result of the individual efforts of some unique, devoted, and faithful Roman Catholic personalities. They were dedicated to the service of humanity at large and thereby they decided to demonstrate the principles of faith in action.

The Religious Orders were encouraged by the Popes because they were the effective instruments of Church administration. In short, they were important instruments in bringing about the reform of the Church. There arose also new Congregations dedicated to the education of youth, the healing of the sick and to help in the various needs of the Church.

Every Catholic believes that in Jesus Christ God has revealed himself to humanity through the humanitarian deeds that Jesus carried on during his life of 33 years on earth. This conviction has been the basis for all missionary endeavors in the history of the Church. In Canon Law the term 'mission' signifies all Districts which are subject to the Congregation of *Propaganda Fide.*

The Mission is no more just one of the activities of the Church carried out by the so-called missionaries only but it is applied to all Church related missionary work connected with the sending. In the subjective sense, it is applied to the activities which serve to establish and spread the Christian faith, to revive and preserve it. In the objective sense mission is applied to the sum of all the institutions and arrangements which have for their aim the extension of the faith. In its widest sense, it means a series of secondary activities which support and complete the main work.[41] Among these subordinate tasks include the establishment of schools and charitable activities.

The term mission, in the sense of foreign Missions began in 1622. In that year, in the Decree establishing the Congregation of the Propagation of the Faith, it appears four times and it assumed the definition that long remained: 'a body of persons sent into foreign lands for the conversion of the heathens.' The *Oxford English Dictionary* gives 1769 as the year when the term Mission first appeared in English as: 'a permanent establishment of missionaries in a country, a particular field of missionary activity.'[42] This became then a common interpretation of the word even up to recent times. People spoke about 'the Missions' by which all understood certain countries, as in Asia and Africa, where missionaries were preaching the Gospel and establishing the Church.[43] At present Mission in general has come to be a dignified, even a high sounding term for task, duty and obligation.[44]

The Catholic reformation marks the beginning of a great period of missionary expansion of the Catholic Church to all the nations. There had been a few missionary outreaches in the Middle Ages, such as Franciscan John of Montecorvino's planting the Catholic

Church in Beijing, China, in 1307. Whenever explorers were sent out from Catholic countries, so were Catholic missionaries. Despite the cruelty of some of the Spanish conquerors of the Western Hemisphere, the missionaries often fought for the rights of the native people of Central and South America. They taught and cared for the native people of the New World, as well as converted them.[45]

The Society of Jesus or the Jesuit Order, which had been the vanguard of the Catholic Reformation and a leader of the Catholic missionary effort throughout the world,[46] was suppressed in 1773 by Pope Clement XIV. It was Pope Pius VII who reestablished this order in 1814, which attracted young men by thousands. Other new Religious Orders such as the Marianists, Marists, Christian Brothers, Sisters of Charity, Sisters of Loretto, Paulists, Salesians, Society of the Divine Word etc. were begun. These Orders were engaged in a wide variety of pastoral, social and educational work. The Society of Foreign Missions was re-established in 1815. With the help of the Jesuits, the missionary activity of the Catholic Church was revitalized. The Jesuits doubled their membership during the Papacy of Pius IX and the seminaries and monasteries of all Orders were filled with new recruits.

It is still heartening to note that the present Pope Francis represents the Third World. This suggests a greater acceptability and spread of the Catholic Church in this part of the world. The Catholic Church in Asia is established in almost every country. Despite the small numbers, the Asian local Churches are normally active in many varied fields such as in education there are universities, colleges, high schools, grade schools and kindergartens. In caring for the sick they have clinics, hospitals, leprosaria, nursing schools, medical schools etc. For the poor and oppressed there are social institutes, credit unions, cooperatives, labor and management schools, grass root activities for organizing and conscientizing. In the Mass Media there are periodicals, newspapers, audio-visual centers, radio, television and film projects. Finally, there are retreat houses, ashrams, guidance centers, centers for contemplation and other such spiritual bases, to offer inspiration for human suffering and searching.

There are a number of Asian priests, religious and lay persons in apostolic work in other countries and cultures, in Africa, Latin America, and the Pacific. More than 3,000 Priests and Sisters are working overseas. Most of these dedicate themselves to a cross-cultural world, learning the language, symbols, and customs of their new home. The Church in the modern world is thought to have with all its works brought about changes in diverse fields. It has a long history of interventions in dehumanizing situations of the society and it responds to the signs of the times through its missionaries. Missionary activities of necessity demand a shift in worldviews, which means that the missionary activity requires some sense of everything from cultural anthropology to linguistics.

Missionary efforts are not the sole domain of the Ordained Priests or the vowed Catholic Sisters. Many traditional Religious Orders and some independent organizations educate and support missionaries for both domestic and foreign missionary work.[47] Every institution exists on certain religious objectives as defined in Catholicism. The function of institutions is to ensure the permanence of the pursuit of these objectives and to inculcate behavior adapted to this purpose. Every religion seems to imply the institutionalization of objectives, although the modalities involved may vary widely. Some religions are characterized essentially by their beliefs or their established rituals and these do not depend on any rigid organization of specialized roles. Others, on the contrary, like Christianity possess very strongly institutionalized structure.

A person or a small group of persons in the Catholic Church discover a certain way of living Jesus' way of life. That 'certain way' may constitute over time a series of models in the persons who have lived the way, a body of instructional literature in the form of rules, treatises and other texts, as well as a tradition about how the life is to be lived. Finally, this way of living is attractive enough to constitute a gift which the Church accepts as part of its heritage and receives the gift as a grace or charism for others to accept if they find it equally attractive.

Every school of spirituality tends to privilege certain texts from sacred scripture as central to their way of understanding the Christian life, from which they draw inspiration.[48] Those texts become particularly 'performative' in the sense that they draw from those texts a manner of living and acting. The missionary schools of spirituality take their indication from the mandate of Jesus found in the Bible of Matthew 28, to evangelize all peoples. The deeply contemplative Orders draw much from the mystical reading of the Song of Songs in the Old Testament of the Bible. Each school of spirituality has a preferred way of praying and a 'theory' about how best to attain a more perfect life of prayer.[49] These schools of spirituality almost always derive from the inspiration of individuals or small groups who conceived of them in tandem with what can be called the founding of 'Religious Orders.'

It is common to speak of the monastic school as well as the Franciscan, Salesian, Ignatian etc. It was the religious community itself that guarded and passed on the teachings of its school, but the distinctive spirituality associated with the school was available to all. If the teaching of a potential school does not adapt itself to the circumstances of history, it becomes stagnant and passes from the picture. The beauty of diverse schools of spirituality within the larger Catholic tradition is that these schools provide a way of being Catholic amenable to the personality of the individual. If a person desires to spend whole life in prayer, there are practices to encourage that. If another is more an activist there are schools that encourage such desires. Historically, these various schools of spirituality have been identified with Religious Orders.[50] Religious communities of men and women were founded to serve specific needs and possible challenges hitherto unmet in the Church.[51]

The Jesuits became the principal agents of the Catholic Reformation throughout Europe, adept at missionary work and famous for the schools they planted throughout Europe and later in various mission lands both in Asia and in the Americas. There was also the emergence of active

Orders of religious women who, freed from the restrictions of the cloister, were able to involve themselves in the active works of education, care of the sick and other forms of charity.[52] Mary Ward (1585-1645) founded a religious institute modeled on the Jesuits. The Daughters of Charity were a community of like-minded women who met together informally, eventually becoming a Religious Order with vows of Poverty, Chastity and Obedience. Those Congregations not only provided elementary forms of charity, but in time, a path for technical training, academic administration and higher learning.[53] In the nineteenth century, new Religious Orders and Societies of Priests and Sisters were formed by the Church especially to work in the missions.

Catholic Missions in India

During the British rule in India, although their religious neutrality was not conducive to missionary work, the Catholic missionaries took to establishing schools, hospitals, and charitable institutions such as nursing homes, orphanages and dispensaries. One notable result of independence was a spectacular increase in the number of institutions devoted to education and health. In accordance with the nation-building spirit, the Church threw itself into the development of educational, health and social institutions and later of community building projects.[54] Numerous Sisters, Brothers and Priests began working for the poor and the marginalized in India. They believed that even today Jesus invites his disciples to get involved in the social arena, in the struggle of the marginalized, the plight of underpaid workers, the discrimination against women, pollution of natural resources, ethical problems in politics, medicine, economy, religion and other contemporary problems.[55]

According to the statistics provided by the Catholic Sisters' Congregations in 1977, there were at that time in India 42,846 professed sisters and 3,611 novices. They belonged to 130 Congregations, 55 Indian and 75 of foreign origin. Besides the 7 purely Contemplative Congregations, there were 123 Apostolic Congregations engaged in many different activities. Five of them have founded no institutions, their members being concerned with work in animation or Catechesis, generally associated with pastoral work.[56] There is an increased record of Sisters during the year 2002-2007. In Asia, India recorded an increase of 9,398. According to an analysis, Sisters have increased in 99 nations since 2000. Altogether there are 7, 50,000 Sisters serving around the world, approximate ratio is one sister for every 9000 persons. The number of Sister's Congregations increased steadily over the century with a noticeable expansion.

In India, the foundation of local Congregations preceded the arrival of European Sisters and 28 of the 55 Indian Congregations were founded before the First World War. The foundation of these Congregations and their regional origin followed very closely the expansion of missionary activity. From the beginning of the missionary renewal, the participation of Indian religious agents was ensured by the presence of Indian Sisters, who formed a bridge between the Christians and the foreign missionaries. The development of Sisters' Congregations in India was not linked with the missions but was the result of the need to develop institutions in the educational and charitable domains.

Endnotes

[1] Stephen Neill F.B.A., *A History of Christianity in India: The Beginnings to AD 1707,* Press Syndicate of the University of Cambridge, United Kingdom, 1984, p.48.

[2] A.M.Mundadhan, *Sixteenth Century Traditions of St Thomas Christians,* Bangalore, 1970, pp.60-67.

[3] Francis X. Clark S.J, *An Introduction to the Catholic Church of Asia,* Cardinal Bea Publications, Manila, 1987, p. 15.

[4] *Op.cit.,* pp.60-67.

[5] H. Hosten, *The Mackensie Manusripts,* Madras, 1926, pp. 2-4.

[6] States: Literacy & Population by Religion, 1991 from *indiaonlinepages.com accessed on 3 May 2014.*

[7] Frederick S. Downs, *History of Christianity in India,* Vol.V, Part 5, The Church Association of India, Bangalore, 1992, p. 92.

[8] For a history of the Salvatorian work in Assam see Becker, *Catholic Missions.* Mgr. Becker published the book of which this is the second part in 1923 under the name *Im Stromtal des Brahmaputra,* and a re-edited and revised edition came out in 1927. The first part was published in 1989, Becker, *Early History.*

[9] *Souvenir,* Diamond Jubilee of the Prefecture Apostolic of Haflong, 2013, p.18.

[10] Dr Sebastian Karotemprel " The Impact of Christianity on the Tribes of North East India" in J. Puthenpurakal SDB (ed.), *Impact of Christianity on North East India*, Vendrame Institute Publications, Shillong, 1996, p. 3.

[11] C. Becker SDS, *History of the Catholic Missions in Northeast India, (1890- 1915)*, (trans. & ed.), G. Stadler SDB & S. Karotemprel SDB, Firma KLM Private Limited, Calcutta, 1980, p. vi.

[12] Dr O.L. Snaitang, *Christianity and Social Change in Northeast India*, Vendrame Institute, Shillong, 1993, p. 78.

[13] Fr Jacob Aluckal, *The Catholic Church in Northeast India*, Archbishop's House, Shillong, July 2006, p.i.

[14] F. Hrangkhuma & Thomas Joy (eds.), *Christ Among the Tribals*, SAIACS Press, Bangalore, 2007, pp.122-123.

[15] S. Devasagayam Ponraj, *Tribal Challenges and Church's Responses*, Mission Educational Books, Madhupur, 1996, pp. 17-18.

[16] Lawrence S. Cunningham, *Introduction to Catholicism*, Cambridge University Press, New York, 2009, p.12.

[17] Thomas Bokenkotter, *A Concise History of the Catholic Church*, Image Books, U.S.A, 1977. p.15.

[18] Margaret M. Mitchell & Frances M. Young (eds.), *The Cambridge History of Christianity,Volume 1, Origins to Constantine*, Cambridge Histories online, Cambridge University Press, 2006, p.123.

[19] Lawrence S. Cunningham, *op.cit.*,p.49.

[20] *Ibid.* p.3.

[21] *New Catholic Encyclopaedia*, Second edn. (Vol.3), The Catholic University of America, 2009, p. 275.

[22] *Op cit.* p.1

[23] *Ibid.,* p.2

[24] *The Oxford Dictionary of the Christian Church*, Oxford University Press, 2005. Available from http://cn.wikipedia.org/wiki/See_of_Rome.Accessed 19 July 2012.

[25] *Op.cit.,* pp.7-8.

[26] *Ibid.,* p.10.

[27] Rev. Newton Thompson S.T.D. (ed.) *A Course of Sermons by most Rev.Tihamer Toth B. Herder,* Book Company, 1947, p.72.

[28] *The Catholic Directory of India 2013:* The Catholic Bishops Conference of India, Claretian Publications, Bangalore, India, p.83.

[29] http://en.wikipedia.org/w/index.php?title=Apostolic_Nuncio_to_India & action=edit&redlink=1 accessed on 24 September 2011.

[30] Lawrence S. Cunningham, *op.cit.,* pp.257-258.

[31] John L. Mckenzie, *The Roman Catholic Church*, Image Books, New York, 1971, p.25.

[32] *Ibid.,* pp. 40-41.

[33] *Ibid.,* pp. 43-44.

[34] *Ibid.,*p. 45.

[35] *Ibid.,* pp. 57-58.

[36] Karl Rahner, Herbert Vorgrimler, (eds.), *Concise Theological Dictionary,* London, 1968, p.56.

[37] Pius Fidelis Pinto, *History of Christians in Coastal Karnataka (1500- 1763 a.d.),* Samanvaya, Mangalore, Karnataka, 1999, p. 200.

[38] John L. Mckenzie, *op.cit.,* p.69.

[39] *Ibid.,* p. 313.

[40] *Ibid.,* p. 315.

[41] W.L.A. Don Peter, *50 Questions about Catholicism,* St Paul Press, Mumbai, 1998, p.134.

[42] *Oxford English Dictionary,* under mission.

[43] Francis X. Clark, *op cit,* p.122.

[44] *Ibid.,* p.124.

[45] *Ibid.,* p.75.

[46] *Ibid.,* p.89.

[47] *Ibid.,* pp. 97-98.

[48] Lawrence S. Cunningham, *op.cit.,* p.151.

[49] *Ibid.,* p.15.

[50] *Ibid.,* p.153.

[51] *Ibid,,* p.205.

[52] *Ibid.,* p.206.

[53] *Ibid.,* p.207.

[54] *Ibid.,* p.10.

[55] National Monthly Magazine for Christian Leadership, *Smart Companion*: India, July 2012/ Vol.3 / No.6, p.3

[56] *Op. cit.,* p.149.

[57] *Ibid., p.142.*

Chapter 3

The Catholic Missions in Northeast India

Northeast India is an expansive region consisting of eight states and covering over 163,000 square miles. With 31.4 million people, it accounts for nearly 4 percent of India's population. Known for its beauty, this area also has poor road, transport, communication, education, and health care facilities. Scholars assert that today's Northeast India is characterized by new aspirations, ethnic and political tensions, insurgency movements, flight from villages to urban centres, erosion of traditional values, weakening of family bonds, educated unemployed, disappearance of age-old institutions, an increasing dichotomy between life and belief and lack of genuine leadership in society. At the same time, there is a fresh awareness of her natural as well as possible resources, historical and cultural advantages and human potential of both men and women.

The Region with its galaxy of tribes and colorful cultures has witnessed changes during the last 120 years. During this period, the Catholic Church seems to have grown and the missionaries have worked for the growth and development of the Region. Many, marveling at what has been realized in the Northeast India, opine that what has been achieved by the missionaries and their helpers in this corner is little short of a miracle. In the age of democracy the missionaries thought it useful to give importance to the training of leaders especially through the work of education, so that they could exert a salutary influence on societies.[1] The first missionary society that is the Foreign Missionaries of Milan, came to this Region in 1872, but because of a jurisdiction dispute no tangible work was done.[2]

There were many activities on the part of the missionaries during the colonial period. Their missionary work created Christian communities which seem to reflect today on the nature and goal of missionary work in North East India. Christian message seems to have had an impact on some of the intellectual and open-minded seekers of other religions. The missionary works in its institutionalized form seem to have had a positive impact on the social life of the people. The gospel values lived by the Christian communities are admired and at times accepted by people of other religions as worthy of imitation.[3]

Pioneer Missionaries

The contribution of Catholicism to the development of the people in the Northeast India is unparallel, writes Fr Jose Anchupankil, Delegate Superior of the Claretians in the Northeast India. Today there are 15 Catholic Dioceses with nearly 1.5 million Catholics in the Northeast India. Congregations like the Apostolic Carmel, Sisters of St Joseph of Cluny, Carmelites, Clarists, Sacred Heart Sisters, Sisters of the Little Flower of Bethany, Adoration Sisters, Ursulines and others were invited to this Region by different Bishops. Their work in mission centers was and is an important factor in the growth of the Church.[4] More numerous and better qualified teachers and Catechists came out from the Catholic Schools to help Priests running of the village primary schools.

In 1890, the Assam Mission, as the mission of the Northeast India then known, was entrusted to the Society of the Divine Saviour popularly known as Salvatorians who began Catholic missionary work proper in the Region. Pope Leo XIII decreed the establishment of the Prefecture Apostolic of Assam on 13th December 1889 and destined the newly arrived Salvatorians to pioneer the new mission field. The Prefecture Apostolic of Assam was carved out of the two Dioceses of Dacca and

Krishnagar, but no missionary had been sent to this area nor had any missionary activity been undertaken in Dacca. By a Decree of 15th December 1889, the *Propaganda Fide* created the Prefect Apostolic of Assam in North East India and the Bhutan territory, consigning it to the Salvatorians' care.

After the establishment of the Prefecture Apostolic of Assam as desired by ecclesiastical authorities, the first missionaries settled down among the Khasi people though at that time there was not a single Catholic among them. The Salvatorian missionaries under the leadership of Fr Otto Hopfenmueller arrived in Shillong in February 1890 when there were only Gauhati and Bondashill mission stations in the Assam territory. There was a permanent resident missionary in Gauhati. At that time, there were about 6500 Christians in the entire region of the Northeast India, but only about 350 were Catholics.

From its very inception, the missionaries devoted most of their time to the humanitarian work by learning Khasi and Bengali languages.[5] But excessive physical and mental work together with the tropical climate claimed the lives of two missionaries including that of Fr Otto within six months of their arrival. However in spite of a very severe shortage of staff in the first period since 1890 until 1897, they succeeded in establishing a number of mission stations: Shillong in 1890, Raliang in 1892, Shella in 1893, Cherrapunji in 1897 and in taking over Gauhati and Bondashill which were already in existence. The number of minor stations rose to 30, six Churches and one Chapel was built.[6]

From the very beginning the missionaries were trying to preach the Gospel, both in speech and in writing and therefore Catechism books, hymn books, prayer-books and Bibles were printed in large numbers and distributed free of cost. A major part of the year was spent by the missionaries wandering along the mountainous villages and tea plantations in valleys seeking the Catholics. In 1892, the Salvatorian Sisters joined the missionary work, whose co-operation made it possible to create many schools, orphanages, dispensaries, and homes for the aged. In early 1897, the number of Catholics had increased to

1,300. The earthquake during the same year was a great blow to the missions, destroying all the Churches and mission stations. In spite of these difficulties, two more mission stations were opened in Smit in 1898 and in Jowai in 1902. During this period, the missionaries were striving for the education of Catechists and the expansion of the system of primary schools.

Several of the missionaries who came after 1906 were better prepared with an educational qualification from England. In 1907, they started a Catechists Training Centre at St Antony's School, Shillong, to enable the Church to launch into direct evangelization, for better education and learning to read and write. Vast resources in personnel and money were spent on creating a good network of educational institutions. On the medical and developmental fronts, the missionaries made remarkable efforts to serve the people. Consequently, by 1915 the number of Catholics of the Prefecture registered to 5,176 and Catechumens totaled about 1,700. The outbreak of the First World War shattered the Salvatorian dreams of greater expansion and missionaries were interned in July 1915 by the British and expelled from India eight months later.

In 1906, Fr Christopher Becker was made the first Prefect Apostolic of Assam. On his arrival in Shillong, he studied the condition of the mission, made plans for its expansion, succeeded in getting more missionaries and saw to their proper preparation in preaching the Gospel to the natives. He succeeded in getting new missionaries for Assam. Six years after his arrival, there were already fifteen Priests and three Brothers in the mission. Loreto and St Edmund's schools were started under his patronage. By 1912 the number of missionaries increased to 18 Priests and Brothers. This enabled the opening of two major stations in Dibrugarh in 1908 and in Nougbah in 1911, while the number of minor stations rose from 32 in 1906 to 68 in 1914.

The missionary work among the Khasis gradually began to show positive results. After an intensive course of instruction, the first Khasis were received into the Catholic Church on 8th December 1891. The missionary activity among the Khasis was not limited to Shillong only but from this centre it spread out into far off areas. Sub-stations were established, several schools were opened, and the missionaries visited them frequently. Mission work was started also in areas far from Shillong and new horizons were opening for the faith. The Gospel was carried from Shillong into the Northern region of the Khasi hills. The first contact with the people were made in 1907. One of the first undertakings of the missionaries was to start a good school in Shella. Seventy boys and forty girls were admitted to the School in the first year. In course of time, schools were opened in the neighbouring villages as well.

Technical education and methods of modern agriculture were imparted to pupils in schools through the help of Salvatorian Brothers and Sisters who taught the girls home science and nursing. The Salvatorians who pioneered and laid the foundation for the growth of the Catholic Church in the Northeast India had to leave Assam in 1915 and return to Europe on account of World War I. From then onwards the Jesuits ministered to the Church of the Northeast India from 1915 to 1922. Fr Paul Lefebvre succeeded in getting the Sisters of Our Lady of the Missions to continue the work started by the Salvatorian Sisters. Soon Archbishop Stephen Ferrando founded the Congregation of the Missionary Sisters of Mary Help of Christians for service in the missions.

The people of the Northeast India have been responsive to the Gospel message. Hence, right from the beginning, much of the missionary effort was concentrated in these areas. The missionaries assert that the young and vibrant Catholic Church has been a source of strength and encouragement for them. The presence of many missionaries from other countries and other parts of India, along with a dynamic and committed laity were contributing to the growth and vitality of the Catholic Church in this Region.[7] It is an accepted fact that the Church growth also owes to the work of laity as it was they who showed the way and made the communities sprout in different villages.

Among the laity the lay associations, as well as their lay leaders and especially the Catechists, have played a role to keep the faith alive and active. A good number of laity qualified with higher education in different walks of life were becoming the voice of the rest. Frequent visits to villages, contact with people and staying with them for some time to instruct them were the secrets of Church growth in the past. But with the growth of institutions and with diminishing missionary spirit of a pioneering nature, village visits seem to have suffered in recent years. The question of learning the local language, trying to understand the feelings of the people, learning to do what is best for them in terms of the gospel, promotion of local vocations, supply of needed literature, appreciation of tribal love for music, adapting oneself to tribal ways of expression were part of inculturation by the missionaries.

From the year 1890 till 1915, the sixty-one pioneers including 31 Priests, 10 Brothers and 20 Sisters labored to make the Church grow in Northeast India.[8] Fr Otto Hopfenmueller emphasized, that it was the young society's task to prepare missionaries for the people. Accordingly, their lifestyle was set up in simplicity, modesty and the apostolic spirit was constantly held up to inspire the members. He wrote: 'I have felt the urge to contribute to foreign mission work among Christian people as well as to the nations who are still in darkness'. I chose the newly founded Catholic Teaching Society in Rome because they needed manpower and I saw that their good spirit would be fruitful in God's kingdom. My expectations were not disappointed and the constitution of my Congregation has strengthened my initiative.'[9]

At the request of Fr Becker, Mueleman, Archbishop of Calcutta sent his secretary, Paul Lefebvre to Shillong. He later became the Vice-Administrator of the Prefecture of Assam and together with five other Jesuits ministered to the Catholic communities spread over the Khasi Hills and the plains of Assam. Though some works had to be abandoned due to the shortage of personnel, they continued to cater to the Catholic community till 1922. In that same year eleven Salesians of Don Bosco under the leadership of Fr Louis Mathias arrived in Shillong to take over the Assam Prefecture. On 14th January 1906 the first group of Salesian missionaries arrived on the subcontinent whose mission field was Tanjavur in South India. Sixteen years later another group of Salesians from Europe reached the Northeast India to take over the Assam Mission.[10] From 1945 onwards, Indian Salesian missionaries joined the ranks of foreign missionaries.

When the Salvatorian Sisters had to leave India in 1915, their work was taken over by five sisters of *Notre Dame des Missions* who continued their work in Shillong. The Salesians who hailed from various European countries kept up the rhythm of mission growth and expansion. Their strategy of bringing from Europe, in large numbers, novices and clerics and forming them in Shillong seems to have paid rich dividends.

World War II however, arrested the speedy growth of the Church in Assam. Many of the missionaries from Italy and Germany were interned. After independence, the Government of India discouraged new missionary personnel coming to this Region. The Salesians started recruiting in a big way Indians into their ranks from Assam and other parts of the country. From the late 1950s, groups of Priests belonging to a Diocese were also inducted into this Diocese. St Paul's Minor Seminary was established to encourage local vocations.

World War II brought with it the added burden of the internment of the missionaries. Thus, on 10th February 1942, Mr. H.G. Dennehy, the Chief Secretary to the Government of Assam informed Bishop Ferrando of Shillong that the Government had decided to intern the citizens of Axis powers. The Assam mission suffered a great blow at this since the majority of missionaries were from Italy. Thus the missionaries were interned first at Mawlai in Shillong, then they were shifted to Deoli near Bombay and finally to the Dehradun Central Internment Camp.[11] The war brought lot of suffering to people everywhere and the Northeast India, being a border area, was subject to even greater hardships. Poverty and disease accompanied by fear of aggression reigned supreme and economic deprivations coupled with the shortage of food, essential commodities claimed many lives, especially from the vulnerable segments of society, viz, women and children.[12]

The years of World War II (1939-45) impeded the progress of the mission as the Region was affected due to the Japanese forces making inroads into Manipur and Nagaland. Towards the close of the War, Bishop Ferrando wrote: 'In these years of war we have seen 56 missionaries, Priests, clerics, and coadjutors, leaving the mission. Only 30 Priests, 20 clerics and coadjutors were allowed to stay back to continue the work. With personnel reduced, restrictions inevitable in a war zone and other grave difficulties those who remained in the field, with sacrifice and generosity were able to maintain the works.'

After the War, with the return of the missionaries, every possible effort was made to re-launch the mission activities. But in 1950 a devastating earthquake hit the Region causing huge damage. In presenting the state of Assam mission (1950-51) Bishop Ferrando wrote to Renato Ziggiotti, the Rector Major 'The past year was an exceptional year of illness for our missionaries. The great load of work, the unfavorable climatic conditions, the insufficiency of food during the long and exhausting missionary journeys etc. affect even the more robust of them. The missionaries are too few for a mission so vast. The numerous languages spoken make the transfer of personnel difficult because one cannot learn a new language in one or two years. A missionary in Assam, other than the mother tongue must speak at least three more languages.'[13]

In 1954, the first Indian Diocesan Priests from Kerala came forward to do missionary work in the Northeast India. Local Diocesan Priests and several Religious Congregations of women and men from other parts of India got engaged in missionary work in the Region. In the post-war decades, over 20 European missionaries from Italy, Spain, Belgium, and France entered Assam and an equal number of young people were recruited from Assam, Bengal, Burma and Chota Nagpur. The Naga and Mizo insurgency which began in mid 1950s and 1960's demanding sovereign States affected the mission work. The local Christian leadership was challenged to take over from foreign missionaries. The period witnessed growth of mission activities outside their home territories.[14] The contribution by missionaries to Northeast India is a chain of services for the spread of the Good News. The growth of the Church in the Region seems to bear witness to their zeal, dedication and hard work.[15]

Until the independence of India in 1947, the British government did not permit Catholic missionaries to work in Mizoram, Nagaland, and Manipur. Later, the Catholic missionaries established mission centers in those States and in Tripura especially in the field of education and healthcare services. With just over 125 years since the beginning of the Catholic Church in the Northeast India, there are about 3000 Diocesan and Religious Priests, Sisters and Brothers working in this Region. Among these an increasing number of Sisters and Priests are from the region itself.[16] People feel that there has been a qualitative change in the approach in recent times which is oriented to a more people-oriented sustainable development. Numerically, demographically and in terms of institutional presence and influence, variety of services rendered and their effectiveness is important.[17]

The creation of several small States and their interest in education and health of their people, opening of new lines of communication and increased number of apostolic workers all seemed to favor rapid expansion.[18] Assam was among the most unwanted apostolic fields. Mrs. Ladislaus Zalecki, Apostolic Delegate of India, wrote on 10th April 1892: 'The Assam Mission is the most difficult one in India, not only regarding the mission work itself, but also the conditions of life for the missionaries which require from them no small spirit of sacrifice and self- denial.' The difficulties arose from the geography of the country- trackless jungles, rugged hills, steep precipices, months of incessant, torrential rain, blistering and enervating heat, wild animals, poisonous snakes and swarming insects which brought fatal diseases, destroyed buildings, caused earthquakes and tropical storms which in a few moments demolished the work of years.[19]

A mountainous terrain, harsh weather conditions, paucity of roads, dense forests, long journeys on foot, perhaps made severe demands on the physical resources, the moral strength and the spiritual resilience of the missionaries.[20] The courage and zeal, love for the people of the land of adoption, the natural goodness and openness of the people to whom the missionaries had come were some of the strengths of the missionaries. They braved distances, isolation, lack of funds and personnel, illness, discouragement and death while the people of the Region welcomed the missionaries with open minds and hearts.[21] The number of Sisters' Congregations increased steadily over the century, responding to some of the problems of poverty, illiteracy, alcoholism and drugs.

Frederick S. Downs, an eminent historian of Christianity in the Northeast India, opines, 'Without question, the most important post War development has been the rapid expansion of the Roman Catholic Church.' He points out that the secret of success lay in the availability of personnel, means and opening up of the whole Region to Catholic apostolate.'[22] Missionaries invested in a vast network of educational institutions from elementary schools to colleges. A similar network of healthcare services contributed to the expansion of the mission. There were hundreds of Priests, Sisters and Brothers since the 1960s from South India for the expansion of the missionary work. Congregations of Sisters have also contributed substantially to the development of the society.

Since the Northeast is a vast Region, with several tribes, languages and cultures, the tribes of the Region seem to be open for development through education, health care and social work. There is social consciousness, eagerness to share the faith and a keen interest in the progress of the society. Many of the youngsters consider it their duty to share their faith with those who have not heard about it yet. The close similarities between some of the aspects of Christianity, the tribal cults and cultures might have made it easier for the Gospel values to penetrate their lives. Another factor that put the Church at an advantageous position was the dynamic nature of the people and their inclination to work as a community.

The life of the tribal's is full of festivals, dances, songs, and they find that Christianity encourages them in all these. They are also taken up by Christian love, care, sense of equality and they spend hours in prayer services, singing hymns and sharing prayer. The educational institutions, medical services and developmental works carried out by the Catholic Church attract them to Christianity.

The Church is considered vibrant and missionary in nature and in this Region is known as one of the most responsive areas of evangelization in India. There has been consistent numerical growth, establishment of various Churches and institutions in all the States of the Region. During the past 125 years steady streams of Sisters have found their way into the Northeast India. Their way of life has contributed to the growth of the Catholic Church in the Region.

Christianity and education went hand in hand and is responsible for the upliftment of the society. The modern educational institutions, health care facilities and the introduction of developmental as well as humanitarian works owe their origin to the early missionaries who were the pioneers of development in the Northeast India. As a result of its interaction with Christianity the society has undergone changes in its psychology, worldview, languages, cultures, social habits and economic activity.

Christianity seems to have brought a change in the socio-cultural environment, in the behavior, thoughts and the way of life of the tribal communities because of their acceptance of a new religious perspective. The Catholic Missions worked for the development of the poorer sections and Christianity was regarded as offering them dignity, recognition, and hope. Hokishe Sema in his book *Emergence of Nagaland* writes, 'the Christian message of freedom from fear, superstitions and above all from wild spirits did appeal strongly to the Naga minds. Every Naga believes today that the Christian religion for him is a religion from uncertainty to certainty, from darkness to light, from death to eternal life, from damnation to salvation.'

The major educational centre's in the Northeast Region pioneered by the Catholic Missions are St Agnes School started by the RNDM Sisters at Haflong in 1911, St Antony's School, Jowai, St Antony's College,

Shillong, St Edmund's College in 1927, Don Bosco Technical school, Shillong in1915, St Mary's College, Shillong by the RNDM Sisters, Loreto School in Shillong, St Xavier's school in Tura in 1948, St Joseph's College, Jakhama, Holy Cross Higher Secondary Schools in Silchar, Dimapur, Agartala and Kattalcherra, Christ King and Don Bosco Higher Secondary Schools in Kohima, Don Bosco English medium school in Karbi Anglong, Little Flower school in Kohima, Mary Mount School at Aizawl, St Maria Goretti School at Kolasib, St Paul's Higher Secondary School, Aizawl, St John's Higher Secondary School, Kolasib, St Peter's Higher Secondary School at Chhingchhip etc.

In Shillong, almost every educational institute is run by the Christian missionaries. In Arunachal Pradesh, Christianity has got the status of a private and personal affair. The State Assembly passed the Indigenous Faith Protection Bill in 1979. The Arunachalis were also attracted by the perceptive benefits of embracing Christianity and they came to the missionary schools established on the Assam-Arunachal border. The missionary organizations served as places where new generations could master the skills needed to cope with the demands of post independent India. The Christian perspective of reality is suffused with hope and it looks at the human condition positively. This sense of personal dignity appears to be reflected in the transformation that can be noticed in the villages which have embraced the Christian faith. It is believed that the families are transformed, the children are better looked after, and they are given better education due to the efforts of the missionaries.

Catholic missionaries in general are thought to cater to the poor and the needy specially the marginalized sections of the society whose quality of life changed through the intervention of the missionaries. Missionaries worked to preserve tribal cultures and identities by building the structural foundations of their spoken languages such as a script, dictionaries, grammar, and translation of the Bible, newspapers, and reviews. In times of droughts, famine, floods, and epidemics the missionaries came to the rescue of the people. People thought Catholicism brought them liberation from various shackles and helped to facilitate the transition of tribal societies into modernity. It contributed to the formation of social, political, cultural, and professional leadership of the Region and to peace-building processes in Nagaland, Mizoram, and Assam. It would seem that Christians have emerged as vibrant and distinctive communities in this Region and these States have already sent out hundreds of missionaries to other parts of India and abroad. Christianity seems to have made a unique impact on this Region.

Through modern education and healthcare, the tribal worldview is enriched and enlarged. Primitive faith has to a great extent been replaced by Christian faith, with some attempts made to assimilate its positive values and cultures by way of inculturation. On the positive side the holiness, heroic spirit of self-sacrifice of missionaries, seem to have had an impact upon the progress of the Region. The courage and determination of the missionaries in the face of constant failures and immense difficulties need admiration. Their single-minded devotion to understand the importance of the tribe has been of great help. The missionaries have contributed to the socio-cultural development as they seem to have enabled them to come out of their isolated existence. The quality of their life improved greatly through education, health care and exposure to the outside world.

On the other hand, the Churches are often thought to have destroyed the traditional cultural elements of different tribes. Talom Rukho, as quoted in a study by Atul Chandra Talukdar of Arunachal University, opines that 'the younger generation had forgotten traditional music, songs and dances following the rapid changes effected by Christianity.' Various ethnic clashes in the Region have been linked to the Church. The Churches are often alleged to have been practicing forcible conversion. People who are catered to by the missionaries are of financially poorer groups. Fr George Plathottam, Director of Don Bosco Publications, Guwahati, while denying such allegations, said: 'a widespread conception is that the Churches and the missionaries are engaged in forceful conversion. But it is a misconception fuelled by a section of people with destructive attitudes. The missionary schools are open to all irrespective of caste and creed. Most of the students in these schools for instance, are non-Christians.'

Some insurgency movements too have been linked to the Church. But the Christian leaders are of the view that by providing quality education, missionaries are making the people aware of their rights, social values, and identity. Better education enables the people to question the established system. The missionaries have liberated their thoughts and made them question the inequality and injustice in the society.[23] It is believed that Christianity acted as a stimulus, an inner urge, providing the people with a new dynamism from within, setting them on a path to transformation and change. It led to self awareness and made the people conscious of their own collective identity which provided vision that went beyond one's village, clan or tribe and gave a world view based on the Christian message of love, equality, pardon, peace and justice.

The Church in this region is believed to serve the role of educating persons who are to be the leaders of their people. Lines of communication bring medical facilities nearer home. Education introduced more hygienic living conditions. These people took to such changes much faster than those in other parts of the country. Bible centered Christian life and tradition has been built up in the villages and this makes Christian life more appealing to the people. The active participation of the laity in planting and nurturing the Church has created a greater sense of belonging.[24] Christianity seems to have given a sense of human dignity to the people and Catholicism seems to have provided a better opportunity of freeing themselves.

As Sachchidananda puts it, 'The Catholic missions with its beneficent educational and various other institutions and elaborately organized mission work among the tribal's of Chotanagpur became most popular...' The high level of literacy, the low level of infant mortality, improved status of women, the increased desire for ongoing education, health care, efforts to expose oneself to change etc. are signs of integral growth experienced when the people came in contact with Christianity. Perhaps nowhere else in India has the encounter between society and Christianity so profoundly affected and transformed as in the tribal society of the North east.[25]

It may be evident that the secret of missionary success in this region was personal contact. Those missionaries who were capable of greater warmth or great intensity of human relationships worked the bigger miracles. This refers to a deeper level of human ties based on dedication, service and sacrifice, virtues that plunge the missionary into all kinds of activities and undertakings on behalf of the people.[26] The many developments that have taken place are a means to foster such warm, personal contacts. Most of the people are happy to see that the Catholic Church in general cared to preserve their culture. The Catholic missionaries were more sympathetic to tribal customs, traditions, music, dance, architecture and to their cultural values like respect and veneration of the dead and their ancestors.

The numerous educational institutions that the Catholic Church runs are teeming with thousands of youngsters looking for missionaries. Despite many limitations the Catholic Church in the Northeast India has witnessed considerable growth during the last hundred and twenty years. It is claimed that the Catholic Church in the Northeast has done much for the poor and the deprived sections of the society. The missionaries do realize that their efforts have been too sporadic and at times too superficial.[27]

Some Sisters along with the lay people are totally dedicating themselves to working with and in the midst of the poor.[28] Through primary schools, dispensaries, house and village visits the Sisters have opened the way for the Church in many areas. Besides humanitarian and social works, some of the missionaries seemed to have failed to take keen interest in studying the land and the people, their history and culture, language and literature, religions, customs, and traditions.

An understanding of the impact of Catholic Missions in the Northeast can be gained by reviewing the development of Church institutions, which may indicate the humanitarian work done in the area. Whether Catholics are the majority or minority group in these States, the fact is that the Church is in the forefront in the field of quality education, holistic health care and people oriented developmental projects. The life and activities of various Congregations of the Priests, Brothers and Sisters in the region are prominent.

The work of the missionaries seems to have met with success especially in the States of Mizoram, Nagaland, Meghalaya, and Manipur. Historians assign several reasons for the ready acceptance of Christianity by the people. They are the natural affinity of primal religious beliefs and practices with some aspects of Christianity, the image and perception of Christian Churches as agents of social, cultural, and economic upward mobility and the fact that by and large missionaries identified themselves with the tribal people. The different aspects and facets of service and the mission of thousands of Catholic organizations across the country manifest that various Dioceses and Religious organizations follow diverse ways to meet the challenges of the time and they are rarely the same.

Diversity of Sisters' Institutes within the Catholic Church

There are more Religious women than Deacons, Diocesan Priests and Religious men combined. Taken together, Sisters represent nearly two-thirds of the total. There are more than three Sisters for every Diocesan Priest and more than four Sisters for every Religious Priest or a Brother. Nearly half of all Sisters are in Europe[29] and about a third are in the Americas. Asia claims a fifth of Sisters, well over half of whom are in India. According to the Catholic Directory of North East India, in 1997 there were 339 Diocesan Priests, 457 Religious Priests, 83 Religious Brothers and over 2000 Sisters.[30]

The Congregations of Sisters have originated as a response to the call of God to radiate His compassionate love in joyful service to the sick, needy, poor such as lepers, deaf and dumb, blind, handicapped etc.

The Founders of these Institutes seem to have realized during their pastoral ministry, the need for reaching out to the people especially the poor, the women, and children in the villages. They have visualized the fulfillment of this mission through dedicated Sisters, knowing the language and culture of the people and promoting local vocations. In the history of the growth of the Region, the contribution of the religious Sisters has been significant and vital. Usually, Religious Sisters go to mission lands due to an explicit request from the Priests or the Bishops. This was also the case in the Northeast India.[31] Education, socio-medical ministry, pastoral care, hostel and youth ministry, geriatrics and service of charity as per the needs of the society and signs of the times are the ministries of Sisters in the Northeast.[32]

Missionaries of Christ Jesus Congregation founded by Camino Sanzorio in 1944 accepted the invitation of Bishop Ferrando and opened centres at Kohima and Tura in 1948 and at Raliang in 1950. During World War II, Bishop Ferrando founded a Congregation of Sisters known as the Missionary Sisters of Mary Help of Christians. They grew fast and have been recruiting into their institute girls from the Northeast India belonging to the different tribes. Numerous other Congregations like the Apostolic Carmel, Bethany Sisters, Sisters of St Joseph of Cluny, Carmelites, Clarists, Sacred Heart Sisters, Adoration Sisters, Ursulines and other Congregations of Sisters were invited to the Northeast India by different Bishops.[33] Institutes were also started by those who were members of other Orders like Mary Kutty who was a Salesian missionary for 25 years working in the missions of the Northeast, founded The Fervent Daughters of the Sacred Heart of Jesus Congregation.

The Catholic Church has a history of the increase of new Religious Orders founded and approved by the Church at different times for different needs. Sisters have access to the strata of population which remain outside the reach of Priests and Brothers. They seem to have shown a deeper understanding of family problems and proved their unique ability to awaken the sense of personal dignity, to raise standards of human existence, to make peace, share their faith and love with people, especially the poor. In particular, the role of Religious Sisters is growing in many regions.[34] The Church depended on the Sisters for education, health care and developmental work. Most of these Congregations have a large number of local vocations, a sign of the growth of the Church.

The Sisters are responsible for the greater part of ecclesiastical activity such as teaching, health care, relief for the poor and the Mass Media. This involvement in action and the forms which this action may take, depend as a rule of the Congregation to which the Sister belongs. Some Congregations are of ancient and others of very recent origin. Some were founded in the West and so are bound up, in spite of their international character, with particular cultural forms. Others are Indian, but differ in their rite: Latin, Syro- Malabar or Syro-Malankara. Finally, each of them have developed their own special type of spirituality, associated with the charism, the life and character of their Founder or Foundress.

There are indigenous institutes founded within India but extending their services outside the nation. They are Franciscan Sisters of Our Lady of Graces, Daughters of St Thomas, Handmaids of Mary, Sisters of Adoration of the Blessed Sacrament, Prabhudasi Sisters of Ajmer, Sisters of Franciscan Clarist Congregation, Sisters of Our Lady of Fatima, Sisters of the Little Flower of Bethany, Sisters of the Sacred Heart, The Congregation of Holy Family, The Fervent Daughters of the Sacred Heart of Jesus, The Missionary Sisters of the Immaculate Heart of Mary, The Sisters of the Destitute, Ursuline Franciscan Sisters and so on.

The international Congregations that have sent their Sisters to the Northeast for mission are Servants of Holy Spirit, Daughters of Divine Providence, Medical Mission Sisters, Missionary Sisters of the Immaculate, Sisters of the Cross of Chavanod, The Congregation of Sisters of St Elizabeth, The Sisters of Charity of Sts Bartholomea Capitanio and Vincenza Gerosa, the Daughters of Mary Help of Christians who work in 89 countries and many others. There are also local Congregations founded in the Region such as Missionary Sisters of Mary Help of Christians which is the first Indigenous Institute of the Northeast India. The Visitation Sisters of Don Bosco was founded in Shillong and working in the Region with its members hailing from the Northeast itself.

Prabhudasi Sisters of Ajmer is the first indigenous Congregation of Sisters founded in Ajmer, in 1906. Congregation of the Daughters of Charity of St Vincent de Paul perhaps is the largest international Congregation spread in 91 countries, having 20,000 members in 77 Provinces. There are Indian Sisters serving in Europe, Africa, America, and the other Continents as well. There are Congregations like that of the Daughters of the Presentation of Mary in the Temple, Sisters of Mary Immaculate who devote themselves to village apostolate by means of spiritual, moral, social, and material assistance to women and children of all classes. These institutes originated solely for the upliftment of women and children, education, and instruction of young girls, to form them into good human beings and good mothers of families.

There are institutes which are Diocesan while others are Pontifical. There are institutes that cater only to health services without involving in education like that of the Medical Mission Sisters. Some Congregations have recruited into their ranks girls from the Northeast India belonging to different tribes who educate the poor children, care for the sick, visit the villages and do village apostolates. Congregations like the Missionary Sisters of Mary Help of Christians have members belonging to 41 ethnic groups of India. Most of the Congregations like that of Prabhudasi Sisters of Ajmer, Bethany sisters, Ursuline sisters etc. collaborate with the Priests and Brothers in the fields of education, care to children in the hostel especially of the girls and in the field of health care through dispensaries and health camps in the villages and work for the empowerment of women.

There are also institutes collaborating with the government in health care such as the Sisters of Charity of Sts Bartholomea Capitanio and Vincenza Gerosa. In the Northeast, these Sisters first came to work in Dibrugarh Government Hospital in 1933 in response to the invitation of the Assam Government. Just as there are institutes concentrating purely on health care, there are also Orders like the Loreto Sisters who were invited to open a school of higher learning precisely with the purpose of making Shillong, an educational centre of Assam.[35] They were restricted to education as well as the care of the girls in the boarding. They already had seven large schools in India and had a high reputation for conducting good schools for the education of girls.[36]

There are institutes bearing similar names as Sisters of Providence, the Congregation of the Sisters of the Imitation of Christ, known as the Bethany Sisters and the Sisters of the Little Flower of Bethany also known as the Bethany Sisters. But the primary objective of the former is the spiritual renewal of the Malankara Church, living liturgical life, a life of prayer and contemplation whereas the latter one was founded for the education of girls in a special way. The former plays a major role in the building up of the Malankara Catholic Church and participates in its missionary expansions. Both the institutes are indigenous, but the former was founded in Kerala whereas the latter was founded in Mangalore, Karnataka.

The members of the former Order visit the houses of the parishioners who live in faraway places as frequently as possible. Their charism is to live a life in accordance with the provisions of the Congregation, in a manner consonant with the traditions of the Malankara Church, a respectful heritage of India, the needs and aspirations of the time. Their apostolate consists of welfare of women, education, caring for the sick, protection of the orphans and the Destitute, Apostolate of the Press and social welfare activities. The activities of the latter are discussed elaborately in the next chapter. There are also the Bethany Fathers.

Institutes like Sisters of St Joseph of Cluny started during the time of the French Revolution, when Churches were closed, and Priests were hunted down, and their services were requested in the French colonies. Their Foundress worked for the formation of the African Clergy, emancipation of slaves, for mental patients and those afflicted with leprosy. The foundation of the Sisters of St Ann of Providence was connected with the humanitarian and spiritual works. The members are engaged in instruction and education of children and young girls in schools, orphanages, boarding homes, and colleges. They cater to the education and formation of children and young girls belonging to the needy without neglecting the children and young girls belonging to other social strata. Though most of the Congregations were started to cater to the poorest and the most neglected of the society, there were also Orders that did not neglect the care for the rich, reaching out to them in different ways according to their need.

Work of the Sisters

There are about 80 Congregations of Sisters working in the Northeast. The Salvatorian Sisters were the first to come in 1891 and begin educational service in Shillong, Meghalaya.[37] They were followed by the Loreto Sisters who arrived in 1908, then came the Catechist Missionary Sisters or the Salesian Missionaries of Mary Immaculate in 1913. The Sisters of Our Lady of the Missions began their rest house at Haflong in 1914 for the sick Sisters from the hot plains of East Bengal followed by the Daughters of Mary Help of Christians who came in 1923. Among the international institutes, the Daughters of Mary Help of Christians were the first Sisters to begin their work in 1958 in Manipur.[38] Among the indigenous Orders, the Congregations of the Sisters of the Little Flower of Bethany were the first to set their foot in Mizoram in 1962 and Tripura in 1968.

There are large Institutes such as the Congregation of Jesus existing worldwide with about 3000 members in 44 countries across the five Continents. The Sisters of St Joseph of Chambery number about 1500 with Provinces in France, Italy, Norway, Denmark, USA, Brazil, some regions in Ireland, Wales, Czech Republic, Pakistan, Mozambique, and Tanzania. There are also Congregations founded in India such as the Congregation of the Sisters of St Martha whose aim is to share with the working class, the poor and the needy the merciful love of Jesus, compassion and mercy through their loving service. The special end of the Institute of Ursulines of Mary Immaculate is the education of girls and instructing them in all branches of knowledge and work suitable to their condition.

Visitation Sisters of Don Bosco is a Congregation of Sisters who work with the poor, sick and ignorant of the tribal areas. Their Congregation was founded for the poor and abandoned in the villages and neglected urban areas. The Sisters dedicate themselves particularly to the upliftment of the materially and spiritually needy people especially the young, with preference given to the poorest.[39]

The Congregation of the Sisters of the Catholic Apostolate is a part of the Union of the Catholic Apostolate which consists of Priests, Sisters, and the lay people. Their members strive for the liberation of human beings from the bondage of evil, poverty and misery through the exercise of charity. An apostolate with the collaboration of the lay people is the special characteristic feature of this Union. The members promote the spiritual growth of their neighbors' by animating all to love and by forming missionaries for the work of the Church. They are completely available for works of charity and zeal through education and instruction, Parish apostolate, hospital, and social work as well as formation according to the needs of the Church, time and place.

The arrival of the Sisters of Holy Cross to India was due to the intervention of the Maharaja of Tripura whose son was studying in the Holy Cross Brothers' school namely St Gregory's High School in Dhaka, Bengal. In that same year, Fr Joseph Voorde was engaged in teaching French to the Tripura King. The Congregation of the Sisters of St Joseph of Annecy was founded as early as in 1650 in answer to the needs of the 17th century. But the Founder had put no limit to the apostolates, which the Sisters could engage in, except that they were to go in preference to the poorest and the most neglected. Their special mission is that they run leprosarium, homes for the aged and crèches. Sisters of the Cross of Chavanod have the education of the young as their mission for which they run professional and technical schools and are involved in House Management and women's upliftment.

Sisters of the Holy Spirit manage short Stay Homes and rehabilitation of women in distress, homes for the street children, vocational training centres, care centres for HIV/AIDS patients, orienting their work towards the grass root level and peoples movements based on the social realities of the Indian situation. The Daughters of St Paul, Missionary Sisters and the Sisters of Notre Dame are committed to Media Communication. They aim to make effective use of the media of social communications such as the press, radio, cinema, television, internet and audio-visual products to defend the truth and foster values in human society. They transform the message of love, compassion, and mercy into colour, sound and image to make it relevant to today's media-oriented world. Through their books and media centre's, participation in and organizing national and local book fairs, an exhibition of their products in schools and churches, organizing different animation programmes form an important facet of their mission.

Sisters' mission is to spread the Word of God through literature, films, radio, television, cassettes, slides, etc. Sisters are engaged in visiting families and schools and provide good literature for individuals and families, audio-visual programmes on variety of themes in schools and villages.[40] Their institutes are devoted to the education of women in moral, intellectual, social, spiritual and psychological aspects undertaking various activities such as teaching, social work, care of leprosy patients, schools for the blind, health programs in villages, youth animation, prison ministry, women's empowerment programs and vocational training for women.

There are orders founded by the royalty such as Laura Leroux, the Duchess of Bauffremont in France founded the Institute of the Franciscan Missionary Sisters of Sacred Heart. The vision of this institute was educating poor girls and giving spiritual support to the missions. Congregations were also founded to look after the unfortunate children during the Franco-Prussian war, which claimed many victims, leaving behind innumerable orphans. This led to the foundation of Franciscan Sisters of St Mary of the Angels.

Congregation of the Charity of Sts Bartholomea Capitanio and Vincenza Gerosa was one of the numerous foundations typical of the century. Especially in France, Belgium, and Italy this institute contributed towards the spread of new religious life pattern. It was better suited both in structure and in aims, to the actual conditions and needs of the European society, which had just emerged from the French Revolution and Napoleonic wars.[41] The suffering caused by World War II led to the founding of the Congregation of the Sisters of St Elizabeth. Franciscan Sisters of the Sacred Heart came into existence to care for the women, suffering from syphilis.

The institute like Missionaries of Charity founded by St Mother Teresa is solely dedicated to the service of the destitute. This Order does not involve in educational activities but concentrates on socio-developmental works. In the Northeast India they have 21 Social Welfare Centre's such as Nirmal Hriday, Shishu Bhavan, Homes for Children, Adults, dying destitute, unwed mothers, the aged, slum schools, leprosy rehabilitation centre's etc.

Shanti Nilayam Benedictine Abbey, Order of St Benedict is the first of its kind in India and the only one of its kind in the Northeast India. Their characteristic feature of spirituality is prayer and liturgical worship, the singing of God's praises by the daily celebration of the Mass and the Divine Office. Time outside prayer is spent in manual work by which the Monastery earns its living. They exercise hospitality by offering opportunities for retreats for small groups in the retreat houses. Sister Disciples of the Divine Master are working in 31 countries assisting in ecclesiastical offices, retreat houses, Holistic centre's, establishing houses for sick, old and the needy.[42]

The Daughters of Mary Help of Christians commonly known as the Salesian Sisters of Don Bosco are committed to the cause of education in the style of the preventive System- a system of loving kindness. They provide integral formation and education for girls. Their Congregation came into existence particularly with a view to catering to the all-round development of growing girls. From the earliest years of its existence the Congregation began to reach out to faraway lands, to the youth in need without neglecting others. They are involved in pastoral care through personal contacts, family and village apostolate and healing ministry.[43]

The members work with committed young people, parents, lay collaborators, past pupils, members of the Salesian family and other social and educative agencies for the good of the people. They aim at working for peace, justice and create family atmosphere. Every Salesian Sister is called to be particularly attentive to the needs of the young women. Their Institute plans and executes a pastoral project that aims at promoting the integral education of young people, manage Oratories and Youth centre's, give vocational training and conduct different programmes for young girls of rural settings. They work to improve the condition and position of women, undertake various works of social upliftment and network with other agencies.[44] They are engaged in knitting and sewing Schools, rendering service in the municipal hospital and surrounding villages. They have extended their field of activity to vocational guidance, marriage preparation course, Grihini schools and association of the laity.[45]

There are institutes such as the Daughters of the Heart of Mary whose immediate objective is the preservation of religious life. At that time, the very existence of religious life was threatened by the suppression of the Religious Orders in France. They offer the benefits of religious life under a new form, adapted to the changing needs of the Church. The members of the Society wear no outward distinguishing dress in order to permit greater penetration into every milieu.

The Sisters of all the Congregations profess three vows of chastity, poverty and obedience but the Hospitaller Sisters of Mercy profess a fourth vow of 'hospitality', by which they dedicate themselves to serve the sick and the needy, directly or indirectly. They are running a hospital with a department for Naturopathy since 1985 and a home for the aged. A Special feature of the Missionaries of Christ Jesus is that they make themselves available in situations of urgent need with a preference for the poor and the marginalized. They show a readiness to withdraw and hand over works when they are sufficiently established in order to open new ways.

Missionary Sisters of the Immaculate, Prabhudasi Sisters of Ajmer, Sisters of Notre Dame and Missionary Sisters of Mary Help of Christians have as their main charism, regular house visits in the villages, caring for the destitute and Differently Abled, Hostels for working women and girls, and Homes for the aged. Missionary Sisters, Servants of the Holy Spirit is a Congregation founded for the cause of propagation of the Faith. Their members are in schools, hospitals, dispensaries, catechetical and social work especially with battered women, orphans, and street children, mentally retarded and physically handicapped, aged and AIDS patients.

The Prabhudasi Sisters of Ajmer came into existence because when the French Capuchin Priests came to Rajputana Mission around 1890 and started working among the poor and illiterate village people of the area, they found that owing to the purdah system and other social restrictions prevailing among the women, it was impossible for men missionaries to approach the women. Therefore, they felt it was the need of the time to have an indigenous Congregation of women who knew the local language, customs, culture and lifestyle of the people, who could easily meet the village women to educate them.

Institutes were also founded for the sole mission of serving the families like that of the Congregation of Holy Family whose members work for an integral family life through family visits, counseling centres, etc. They have institutions like Family Apostolate Training and Research Institute, Family Renewal Centre for couples and Integral Family Development Forum. This Congregation owns a press, homes for the aged and dying. The Congregation of the Sisters of St Elizabeth serve the families, care for the mother and child, serve the sick and the aged. The Sisters try to build people through enrichment of families, empowerment of women and integral development of children with a special focus on the underprivileged. Their apostolate involves girls home, prison ministry, family counseling, village development programme, pastoral work, care and counseling for the people living with HIV/AIDS and programme for the physically handicapped.

The Congregation of the Sisters of Holy Cross (Menzingen) was founded to fill up the gap between the Gospel values and the changing world of the time. Their Founder perceived in the then existing social conditions spiritual and moral decline, which he thought of dealing with in a Christian spirit. Education of girls, who would become future mothers, was the means he adopted and the Congregation was introduced in India in 1906 to care for the sick in the Government hospitals at the request of the then ruling Maharaja of Travancore. Beside all the activities the members are specially engaged in prison ministry. They run hospitals, dispensaries, community health centre's, training schools for Nurses and Para-Medicals, TB sanatoriums, leprosy survey and treatment centre's, hospices for terminally ill cancer patients and work in hospitals of the Government and the Church related organizations.

The Institute of Sisters of Nazareth was started for the family apostolate. The members devote themselves to the service of the integral development of families. They give special emphasis on spiritual development through family visits, Home Science Institutes, Family counseling centre's, De-addiction activities, Publications for Mothers (Amma magazine), Refuge Homes to cater to the various needs of women and children, Psycho-medical centre's and vocational training centre's. Sisters of Notre Dame are engaged in communication media as well as retreat work.

Sisters of Adoration of the Blessed Sacrament have direct contact with the people through agricultural and rural development. The Institute of the Sisters of Charity of St Vincent de Paul was started as early as in 1734 for alcoholics and drug addicts. Sisters of St Charles Boromeo extend their work to Africa, Argentina, Italy, Poland, and Mexico through day-care centre's, crèches, homes for the aged, leprosaria, community development and hospice for AIDS victims.

Institutes were also founded to render service in the government institutions such as the Society of Christ Jesus rendering service in the Kohima hospital and the government leprosarium at Tura. There are Congregations that were started with the intention of sending missionaries to other countries like the Sisters of St Ann of Luzern, India. Their Founder realized that it is only a group of women with religious commitment, who would give themselves wholeheartedly to do maternity welfare. At first, they focused on health care through mobile camps and working in Government run hospitals. Their mission consists of professional training courses, vocational training, HIV/AIDS care centre's for affected and infected persons, hostels for women, training and care of the handicapped and mentally challenged, women's empowerment, prison ministry and care of the rag pickers children.

The speciality of the Sisters of Our Lady of the Missions is that they opened St Agnes, an English elementary school in 1916 for the children of the railway employees and Anglo- Indians.[46] St Mary's Convent at Laitumkhrah (1915), Shillong is the longest established and it has a Teachers' Training College–University Level, Orphanage, Higher Secondary School [English medium], Primary School [Khasi medium], Montessori Nursery School opening its doors to orphan girls and destitute children of the area. The hostel caters for the poor tribal girls, giving them the opportunity to continue their basic education.

Women for Integrated Sustainable Empowerment (WISE) as an NGO established in July 2000 in Shillong is a new social service centre. It was established by the Sisters to promote the role of women and their education for self-sufficiency, working at developing Self Help Groups among the unemployed. It targets destitute women, girl dropouts, domestic workers, and women in crisis. They come to the Centre for vocational training in fast food preparation and food processing. Girls from the orphanage get training in handicrafts, basket- dry flowers making and tailoring. Those who have completed the training from the Centre are encouraged to make use of the skills they have acquired and to take up income generating activities such as a small shop, fast food sales or livestock projects. They are encouraged to join Self Help Groups(SHG) through which they learn to mobilize their own small savings and have access to micro credit.

Apart from the Congregation of the Sisters of the Little Flower of Bethany, Ursuline Franciscan Sisters was the second Congregation that was founded in Mangalore. The charism of the Institute is to launch deeper into the life of the people.[47] Just like many other international and indigenous Congregations, the Ursuline Sisters of Tildonk also serve the local Church in whatever way they can mainly through the mission of education, health care, social and pastoral activities.[48] The Sisters of the Destitute is a unique order in the Catholic Church. Their Founder gave training to Sisters to make house visits in the locality and provide shelter and care to the abandoned and destitute with compassion as pioneers in Kerala. They choose the suited fields of service according to the needs of the times.

Thus, it is evident that the Sisters in general are engaged in a variety of activities, education-both formal and non-formal, health care services and community health, pastoral and social work with marginalized groups responding to the needs of the people. They live and work with a preference for the poor gaining a deeper understanding of their culture, tradition, and language with a desire to learn from them. There are those Sisters who are engaged in the care and education of children of all age groups. They run schools, foundling homes, Homes for the aged, welfare centre's for the orphaned/ destitute children, hostels for working girls, dispensaries, and health centre's in the rural/ tribal regions, social uplift programmes etc.

The Sisters are entrusted with the apostolic activities of teaching in the school and care of the young girls through boarding houses.[49] Among the many apostolates, the family visit on regular basis is one of the most effective means of reaching out to people which the Sisters do, realizing the significance of this mission. They maintain a good rapport with the neighborhood. Through their various activities they serve the humanity with a missionary outlook. Sisters are engaged in multiple works such as family visits, instruction of adults, childrens' hygiene and child care for the womenfolk, health care and marriage preparation courses etc.[50]

Sisters take an active part in the programmes like Youth Awareness, Youth Build and Youth Leadership Programmes. The hostels provide values and sound education to the girls which seem to have been proved by the good results over the years by those who have written their Board Exams. This becomes a source of encouragement for the students to continue to seek admission to the hostels. The hostels maintain good farms in order to educate the children in the art of working and preparing themselves for the future. The hostellers are trained to do any type of work dutifully and also to benefit out of their own land and property.

The Sisters of the different Congregations in the Northeast India set in motion and influenced a whole train of events with their charismatic personalities. Through schools, dispensaries, house, and village visiting the Sisters have opened the way for the education of young boys and girls. Sisters work for the poor, the imprisoned, the ill and the marginalized. They focus on the homeless, the destitute, prisoners and the undocumented. Marian Rona testifies, 'Because of the Sisters' hard, able and financially uncompensated work, women today are educated, competent and professional than women of any previous generations.'[51] Most of the work that excites admiration for the Church throughout the world is done by the Sisters.[52] They are multi-focus women whose power comes from their presence among the powerless.[53]

As per the data available in the *Catholic Directory of India, 2013* out of the 80 Congregations working in the Northeast India, 33 of them manage their own educational institutions, health, and social welfare centre's. Some of them work in collaboration with the institutions managed by the Dioceses or the other Religious Orders of Priests and Brothers. Though many of the Sisters run English medium schools, there are also those who manage vernacular medium schools like that of the Catechist Missionary Sisters who began an Assamese medium school in 1914 at Guwahati. They also run special schools for the deaf and the dumb, the blind, and the mentally handicapped.

Health care through its curative, preventive, promotive dimensions, through institutions as well as counseling, pastoral care, social development, and ecological awareness continue to be the Sisters' expressions of living in the mission. Justice, peace, and integrity of creation are integral part of their healing mission. Through collaboration and partnership, they continue to network with like-minded groups, participate in people's movements, capacity building for the empowerment of communities and seek to respond to the ecological crisis in a healing way. They strive to develop life-giving ways of their healing mission in response to the signs of the time.

Sisters work for the empowerment of women through Self-Help Groups and try to address the people's concerns, attend to questions of peace and justice. They help them to improve their situation and become the promoters of their own culture and society. They live and work with the indigenous people of the Region, learn to speak and pray with them in their local language, study their history and familiarise themselves with their customs.

One of the secrets for the development of the mission centres of the Roman Catholic Church in the Northeast India is the degree of autonomy and freedom for personal initiatives that each centre enjoyed. It was up to each missionary to get funds for the projects and build up the centres. Hence, family members of missionaries, their home Parishes and Dioceses supported their undertakings. The local Catholics too made their contribution in cash/ kind or by voluntary labour towards the construction of their village schools.

By and large, the Hindus and the Muslims of the plains tolerated the missionaries and even positively welcomed them into their midst for the sake of the educational, medical, and developmental benefits that they brought with them. The tribal's of other faiths, particularly of the hills, welcomed missionaries in whom they tended to depend for the education of their children, for medical and developmental projects. To this end often they offered land for schools and even helped in the building of mission centres. The Catholic missionaries were sympathetic to tribal customs and traditions, music, dance, architecture, cultural values like respect and veneration of the dead and their ancestors.

The pioneering missionaries had their individual and collective human limitations. But they also brought with them their rich individual talents, rational gifts and fortitude, specific religious spirit, charism, methods, acquired characteristics and traditional riches as well as strengths. Some were truly outstanding and exceptional in knowledge, scholarship, holiness, and abilities. Their love, dedication and untiring zeal for the human promotion and advancement of the people of the Region as well as their accomplishments cannot be denied.

An important contribution of the Religious Sisters to the Church here is the fostering of vocations to the priestly and the religious life. Earlier there was an overwhelming dependence on vocations from abroad and other parts of India. Now the trend has changed towards greater emphasis on the training of local vocations in the Region itself. The establishment of the local Religious Congregations has favoured inculturation and adaptation to some extent. Here an attempt is made to identify the specific work done by the Sisters of various Congregations to the growth and development of Northeast.

Educational Work

The most important contribution made by the Catholic Church for the growth of society may be in the field of education. The Church with a vast number of Elementary schools, Middle Schools, High schools, Higher Secondary Schools, Hostels, Colleges and Adult Education Centre's is contributing to the moulding of the society. In the minds of many especially outside the Church today, the Catholic Church seems to be synonymous with quality education. This identification may not be wrong as it reveals facets of missionary work which has marked every Catholic Mission station.[54]

The people of the Region feel that before the advent of the missionaries in the Northeast India, there was hardly any type of educational infrastructure that was accessible to commoners. Tribal areas were neglected and hence there was poverty, ignorance, illiteracy and under development. Therefore, the assertion is that the missionary contribution to education is no mean achievement.

After Indian independence and ever since the Religious Priests, Brothers and Sisters arrived in the Region, followed by the Diocesan Priests, there has been significant growth in terms of quality of life for the people because of the education imparted by them.[55] The Church has invested in personnel and money in the field of education. The All India Education Policy of the Catholic Church focuses on providing quality and relevant education, to give serious attention to deepen the authentic formation of all the students and nurture their culture. It appears that the need is to focus on the fuller development that meets the challenge of modern culture and society, and its demand for higher levels of competence. This may make it necessary to bring about significant changes in the planning and organization of the institutions, so that education promotes genuine personal development and excellence.[56]

Catholic Educational Institutions in the Northeast India

TABLE NO. 1

1.	Colleges	359
2.	Higher Secondary Schools	1,465
3.	High Schools	3,372
4.	Upper Primary schools	3,198
5.	Lower Primary schools	5,872
6.	Nursery Schools	4,428
7.	Training schools	513
8.	Technical schools	900
9.	Professional Institutions	263

Source: *The Catholic Directory of India* 2005-06, p. 110.

There is a total of 20,370 institutions with over 10 million students catered to in these institutions. According to Rt Rev.T. Menamparampil, Archbishop Emeritus of Guwahati, 54 percent of these students are girls, 28 percent are Christian and only 23 percent are Catholic.[57] The establishment of these institutions has given to the Catholic Missions a prestige and influence among the general public. The commitment of the Catholic Church to the apostolate of the schools in the Region is a commitment in personnel now numbered by the thousands, a commitment in material resources almost impossible to estimate.

The Bishops in the various Dioceses sought the co-operation of Sisters of the various Congregations or set up their own Congregations to meet the needs of education to the poorest and the most backward masses. From the beginning, a Catholic school was almost always attached to each of the mission stations. For several years, the Sisters concentrated their efforts on education. It is to be noted that a major contribution in the field of education of the young has been given by the Sisters in various rural centres. They have made it possible for children in very remote areas to reach at least Primary and High school level of education.

Various Religious Congregations of Sisters have made a significant contribution to the education of women in the Northeast India, by running scores of Elementary, Secondary and High schools, colleges in rural and urban areas of the Region. Several political, educational, and governmental leaders of the region are the products of their schools and colleges.

The Sisters found it difficult at first to get the children to school but with the spread of Christianity, the demand for schools too grew. But the establishment of Catholic schools was difficult as the government grants were not easy to get. In 1907 when the Catholics reorganized their school system to fall in line with the government syllabus, recognition was given so that by 1910 the Catholic mission could count 12 Primary schools recognized by the government. Endeavors for proper buildings, right qualifications of the teaching staff and the erection of Boarding schools enabled the Church personnel to gain the colonial governments' allocation and granting of national rights to 9 schools.

Fr Christopher Becker, records that the missionaries directed their attention from the very beginning to youth in order to instruct them in schools.'[58] By 1st September 1914, the Salvatorian Missionaries had established two English medium High Schools with Boarding houses in Shillong. They had a Higher Elementary school with Boarding house in Haflong and a Middle English medium School for local boys in Shillong. They also conducted a Girls' School for Khasi children in Shillong and two Home Science schools in Shillong and Raliang. In the same year, the Sisters opened a school for domestic science with a government grant for the building. Special rooms and furniture were provided to train girls in cooking, washing, and ironing. The Sisters had already introduced other practical subjects in the schools of Raliang, such as stitching, knitting and embroidery. They succeeded in setting up a weaving school in that locality as well.

The first Primary school for girls established according to the government regulations was opened in June 1913, by the mission centre of Shillong. Besides caring for the sick and the needy, providing a home for the aged and orphanages in every mission station, the Salvatorians laid the foundation for the education of women in the Northeast India. Only in Shillong did the Sisters conduct a girl's school for the Khasi children. The girls entrusted to them were taught various household skills and for training boys, they built an Agricultural school, a Handicrafts school with various trades, including making of silk thread and gardening.[59]

There had been a great demand for the opening of a school in Shillong for European and Anglo-Indian girls and in 1908, the Loreto Sisters from Calcutta, came to Shillong opening their school in May of the following year. The Sisters under the direction of Machtilda Costelloe set out to begin an English medium High School and a Boarding for girls which was inaugurated on 8th May 1909. The Sisters had 23 day scholars and three Boarders. The institution soon won warm praises from various civil authorities.[60]

There was great appreciation among Catholics and Protestants for the school. *Times of Assam* reported that at that time the Boarding school of the Loreto sisters was one of the best places of a summer resort. It was a place well suited to provide calm and peace to the spirit, so desirable and necessary in the education of the youth.[61] The girls were prepared for the senior Cambridge examination, for which the convent became a centre. The founding of the Loreto Convent under the auspices of the Catholic mission was an event that contributed to the name and fame of the Catholic Church.

In 1914, the Catechist Missionary Sisters took a bold step to start an Assamese medium school and a small Boarding house in Guwahati.[62] An educational institution for the girls was a much felt need since the society of that time did not easily favor the education of girls. On 15th November 1915, the Sisters of the Lady-Queen of the Missions began to work in Shillong and shortly afterwards in Haflong. But seven years were to elapse before they were able to start once more the work in Raliang. Initially they had a Primary school which later became a recognized High School. They began the school with 90 children and 42 orphans and developed into a premier educational institution in Shillong. Similarly, they made a great impact with the school started in Haflong in 1914.

In 1937, St Mary's College was officially inaugurated and affiliated to Calcutta University.[63] It also had a Teacher Training Centre which provided training for girls who had finished High school. Today it continues its valuable service in the field of education for the women of the Region.

The Congregations of Sisters had great numerical strength with qualification to impart not only academic knowledge but also a wide variety of skills and trades. They very soon made an enormous impact on the educational front. The Salvatorian missionaries had expended most of their energies among the Khasi and Jaintia people. The Salesian Sisters began the work of educational expansion which was to reach out to every corner of the Northeast except those regions to which entry was barred by the government. Primary, Middle and High Schools, both for boys and girls, Colleges and Hostels throughout the vast Region were established by this Congregation. The image of the Catholic Church as an institution which could provide educational facilities was thus firmly established from the earliest days. That image was maintained and further enhanced through the unflagging efforts of the new missionaries.

The initial choice of Shillong by the Salvatorian missionaries had been the expressed desire of the *Propaganda Fide* that the centre of the Prefecture of Assam should be there. It meant that the Khasi Hills should be the location for the apostolate of Catholic education as an essential part of that activity. That is why the Shillong area, as the mission centre, was earlier developed as an educational 'metropolis' than any other place in the whole of the Northeast India and it still maintains its pre-eminence as an educational centre in the Region. Only Arunachal Pradesh was forbidden territory for Catholic educational effort.[64]

With the setting up of the Prefecture of Haflong and its being entrusted to the missionaries of the Holy Cross, the Brothers of that Congregation opened three High Schools in the Lushai Hills. With the erection there of a separate Diocese, the schools passed under the care of the Brothers of St Gabriel. Nagaland, for so long a closed territory for Catholic missionaries, can boast of a number of Catholic schools- in Wokha manned by the Brothers of St Gabriel while the school run by the Sisters in Kohima was probably the first Catholic school in the Naga Hills. The Jesuit Fathers of the Karnataka province were in charge of a college at Jakhama which is now handed over to the Diocese. Recent years have witnessed the coming of the Fransciscan Brothers to the North East India who have a number of foundations in different parts of the region. They seem to concentrate their efforts in remote villages' where they work for the educationally less favored ones.

The pattern set by the pioneer missionaries is consistently followed in the Northeastern missions as mission and school go hand in hand and wherever possible, High schools have been established. With the gradual political transformation in Northeast India, Assam of the early missionaries became the land of the Seven Sisters. In the new situation, it proved easier to develop Primary and High schools among the hill people of Meghalaya, Manipur, and Nagaland, obtaining for this work generous help from the government. According to the 1988 statistics of the Catholic Church in the Northeast India, there are 5 colleges, 87 High Schools, 161 Middle English medium Schools, 1192 Primary and Kindergarten Schools and 56 centres for Vocational and Non-formal Training in the Dioceses of Shillong, Diphu, Kohima, Silchar and Tura. These institutions run by the various Religious Congregations provide a foundation for building up of modern the Northeast Indian society.[65]

The primary concern of the Sisters in the schools was to offer its students a milieu conducive to their integral development. Great stress was laid on forming an academic community of parents and teachers whose concern was the promotion of sound education. Though generally the first beneficiary of any school or college could be the neighborhood community, however, after so many years of service there still exists much illiteracy and social backwardness. Often the Catholic schools and colleges are accused of being ivory towers in a world of poverty, ignorance and somewhat result oriented. People have appreciated what the Sisters have contributed to the education of women in the past. They feel that educational efforts could become a vocation and a mission, and therefore, transcend the immediate goals such as excellence in academics, cultural and sports performance.[66] However, a critical survey would reveal how far the educational efforts of the Sisters have succeeded in imparting moral and social values.

Social Work

People in general are concerned with three essential choices of leading a long and healthy life, acquiring knowledge and having access to the resources needed for a decent standard of living.[67] Today the credibility of the Church's mission hinges on her interest in the matters of social justice. It is felt that people need to be taught to fight for their rights and justice in a spirit of non-violence, peace and love.[68] In certain quarters it appears that there is a growing appreciation of the Church's pro-life approach, defense of the human person, dignity and liberty, opposition to abortion and the control of the population through artificial means.[69]

In this region the missionaries come across a rich variety of peoples and cultures probably not encountered elsewhere in the world. The mission comprised the hill tribes as well as various ethnic groups which inhabit the plains of Assam. It embraced the tea garden labourers in the Assam plains and the farmers of the hills. Economically, the people whom the missionaries worked for were of the poorer group. But the new mission land offered much scope for bringing about a radical transformation of society.[70] The social work ministry of the Catholic Church communicates in action solidarity with the poor and commitment to justice.

Social justice is thought to be a part of the integral mission of the Church.[71] Down the centuries the Catholic Church has championed the teachings of social justice. The same thing is spoken in terms of Human Rights. The needs of the vulnerable groups in society such as the children, women, persons with disabilities and HIV-AIDS, gays and lesbians, older persons and victims of racism are enlisted among the human rights. They belong to the pastoral care of the Church as well.[72] The services provided by the Catholic charitable institutions are provided to all without distinction as part of the Church's social apostolate.

The number of charitable institutions reflects the vitality of religious institutes of Sisters, Brothers and Priests, who often provide staff or sponsor such institutions as part of their particular mission. Social work seems to have made a significant contribution to the development of the Northeast and the empowerment of the poor. This mission is appreciated for fostering people's participation, networking with NGOs, and enabling the Church to cross boundaries and collaborate with all.

Health and Family Welfare

The Sisters, through their apostolate of the sick make healing present to those who need it the most. Through their dedicated service to the sick, they incarnate the most attractive aspect of the figure of Jesus to the sick and the needy.[73] In the field of health and family welfare, the

Sisters have rendered services in the Civil Hospitals as well as in the dispensaries. The Church run hospitals in the Northeast are administered efficiently and they succeed in delivering quality healthcare at affordable rates. The Mercy Home in Dibrugarh, Nazareth hospital in Shillong and the Borgang hospital by the Sisters are worthy of mention. The Nursing School of Shillong has contributed to the preparation of Nurses in the Northeast India.

Catholic Health Care Institutions in India in 2001

TABLE NO. 2

1.	Hospitals	737
2.	Dispensaries	2429
3.	Leprosaria	248
4.	Homes for the aged and the 'differently endowed'	865
5.	Orphanages	2112
6.	Nursing Homes	2021
7.	Marriage counseling centres	587
8.	Special centres for social education and re-education	4969
9.	Other institutions	694

Source: Leonard Fernando and G. Gispert-Sauch, Christianity in India,
Penguin Viking, 2004, pp.232-236

Through a large network of dispensaries, the Sisters have provided medical services in the rural areas. The mobile clinics are a great help to the poor and the sick in the villages. The marriage preparation courses conducted by the Sisters have produced far reaching effects towards good family life. The medical camps at various centre's proved to be effective towards better health and hygiene. It is asserted that the medical care the Sisters give has brought down the level of child mortality. People assume that much more could be done to awaken them to a better understanding of health and family ministries in the particular context of the Northeast India.[74]

Pastoral Care

The term 'pastoral' comes from the Latin word *pastor* meaning 'shepherd'. The term is applied to that action of the Priests and the Sisters with a view to the 'care of souls' exercised by virtue of the faculty granted by the Church.[75] The Pastoral ministry consists of healing, sustaining, guiding and reconciling the troubled persons whose concerns arise in the context of ultimate meaning in life. Pastoral care is distinct from what is called 'humanitarian care' amidst conflict, violence, disaster, although broadly speaking the pastoral care embraces all these.[76] It may be noted that the six areas of the pastoral programme pertain to the care of the needy affected by hunger, thirst, being strangers, nakedness, sickness and imprisonment. The Pastoral actions thus consist of giving food and drink to the hungry and thirsty persons, welcoming the strangers, clothing the naked, visiting the sick and the imprisoned. These are considered as authentic expressions of concern, generating from the heart and, the depth of the person. The sense of sharing and the courage to do it is an act of the will and of the intellect.

Christians believe that they have the obligation to get involved in the kind of ministry to love, to share and to care.[77] They consider that the well being of the individual person and of the human society is intimately linked with the healthy condition of the community through marriage and family.[78] The Sisters in various Parish centres have marriage preparation courses in order to instruct and prepare couples for married life. In certain places such courses are conducted twice a year and over 1000 couples are prepared for marriage.[79] It is evident that the Sisters render service by organizing youth movements and leadership courses to prepare community leaders.

Considering the growing number of missionaries in the Region, it was felt that the Sisters could develop helpful ways to involve in the Pastoral care and ensure collaboration for the common goal of building up the society. Their charisms and specialized ministries could be of great help for the overall growth of the society and a source of inspiration and insight for others.[80] The changing circumstances and the new challenges call for rethinking in understanding the implications of new trends such as Post-Modernism and New Age. Facing challenges posed by Pentecostal Movements and fundamentalist tendencies and dealing with the dangers of consumerism and materialism appear to demand the need for developing new methods and fresh pastoral strategies.[81]

Today Christianity in the Northeast India is an active force in society as well as in the lives of many people. But missionaries seem to have failed to win a section of the people, isolated societies, marginalized groups or ostracized individuals, who seek to escape the pains of isolation and scorn and to acquire a sense of belonging.[82] The Catholic Church in the Northeast India has witnessed considerable growth during the last century. The Religious Sisters seem to have made a contribution to its growth and the development of the people in this Region.

The Sisters felt that the house visits are becoming a difficult task due to the time factor in modern lifestyle though the tradition of fostering relationships among people is central to the Catholic heritage. The Sisters took it as their special mission to identify and strengthen the relationships that link people with each other, with the rest of the human race and with the whole created universe. It is asserted that if the Sisters could follow the path of inculturation, dialogue, ecumenism and other such wider avenues of involvement, their contribution could be more effective. This calls for further collaboration, participation, and involvement in the life of the people of the Region.

Among the many Congregations of the Sisters working in the Region, the Sisters of the Little Flower of Bethany commonly addressed as Bethany Sisters, were the first Catholic Sisters to venture into missionary activities in Mizoram and in Tripura. They have been involved in humanitarian activities such as Medical Care, Social Work as well as Education. So far no study was undertaken of the activities of these Sisters. No attempt has been made to assess the role of the Bethany Sisters on the socio-economic lives of the people of the Northeast. The need to record the impact of the work and activities of the Sisters was keenly felt. Hence an attempt is made to have an in-depth study on the activities of the Bethany Sisters and to assess their role in the lives of the people of the Northeast.

Endnotes

[1] C.Becker SDS, *History of the Catholic Missions in Northeast India (1890-1915), op cit.,* p.39.

[2] *Ibid.,* p. 170.

[3] Dr Francis Fernandez, S.D.B. & Dr Jose Varickasseril, S.D.B., (eds.) *Mission: A Service of Love, Essays in Honour of George Kottuppallil, S.D.B.,* Vendrame Institute Publications, Shillong, 1998, p.101.

[4] C. Becker, SDS, *Father Otto Hopfenmueller,* Salvatorian Spirituality & Charism Series, No.12, Society of the Divine Saviour, Bangalore, 2008, p.53.

[5] Dr Julian Bednarz SDS, "Salvatorian contribution to the Church in the Northeast India" in *Centenary of the Catholic Church in the North-East India 1890-1990: A Souvenir.*

[6] *Op.cit.*

[7] National Monthly for Christian Leadership, *op.cit.,* p. 6.

[8] Thomas Manjaly, Graviour Augustine, Tomy Palely, (eds.), *Challenges of Faith Formation in the North-East India,* Oriens Publications, Shillong, 2009, p. 183.

[9] C. Becker, SDS, *Father Otto Hopfenmueller, op.cit.,* p. 159.

[10] *Quarterly Magazine,* 'Mission Today', January-March 2005, Vol.VII No.1, p.4.

[11] Jane Mary Thadathil, *A Great Missionary Legacy: A Brief History of the Origin, Growth and Charism of the Missionary Sisters of Mary Help of Christians founded by Archbishop Stephen Ferrando,* Centre for Indigenous Peoples and Missionary Sisters Publications, Shillong and Guwahati, 1997, p.24.

[12] O.L. Snaitang, *op.cit.,* p.127.

[13] S. Ferrando, *Letter to the Rector Major,* dated 18th March 1932, Salesian Central Archives, Rome.

[14] Amrit Kumar Goldsmith, *Article: The Christians in the Northeast India: A Historical Perspective, 1819-2004,* accessed 20 June 2013.

[15] Thomas Manjaly, Peter Haokip, James Thoppil, *op.cit.,* pp.153-154.

[16] Gratian Carlo S.J., Paul Raj S.J. *Formation of Priests and Religious in the North East India: An Exploratory Study,* Jesuit Institute of Religious Formation, Guwahati, 2005, p. Foreword.

[17] C. Becker SDS, *Father Otto Hopfenmueller, op.cit,* p.53.

[18] Sebastian Karotemprel S.D.B., *Albizuri Among the Lyngams: A Brief History of the Catholic Missions among the Lyngams of the Northeast India,* Vendrame Missiological Institute, Shillong, 1985, p.vii.

[19] C. Becker SDS, *History of the Catholic Missions in the Northeast India, op.cit.,* p.x.

[20] *Op.cit.,* p.vii.

[21] T.B.Subba, Joseph Puthenpurakal, Shaji Joseph Puykunnel, (eds.), *Christianity and Change in Northeast India*, Concept Publishing Company, New Delhi, 2009, p.8.

[22] F.S.Downs, *Christianity in Northeast India: Historical Perspectives,* ISPCK, New Delhi, 1983, p.151.

[23] O.M. Rao, *Focus on North East Indian Christianity,* Indian Society for Promoting Christian Knowledge, Delhi, 1994, p.7.

[24] Thomas Menamparampil, *An Introduction to the North-East India: Culture and History,* unpublished, Guwahati, 2006, pp. 40-41.

[25] Sachchidananda, *The Changing Munda*, New Delhi, 1979, p.119.

[26] Thomas Menamparampil, *Church in North East India,* unpublished, Shillong, 1974, p.70.

[27] Francis X. Clark S.J, *op.cit.,* p.8.

[28] *Ibid.*, p. 9.

[29] Yoland Randel F.M.M. (trans) *Size and Structures of the Catholic Church in India*, 1982, p.43.

[30] Gratian Carlo S.J. & Paul Raj S.J., Formation of Priests and Religious in North East India: An Exploratory Study, Jesuit Institute of Religious Formation, Guwahati, 2005, p.3.

[31] S.Karotemprel SDB (ed.), *The Catholic Church in Northeast India 1890-1990,*Vendrame Institute Publications, Shillong, 1993, p.296.

[32] *www.bethanymangalore.org* accessed on 11 June 2013.

[33] Dr George Kottupallil 'A Historical Survey of the Catholic Church in North-East India from 1627 to 1983' *Centenary of the Catholic Church in North-East India 1890-1990, Souvenir.*

[34] John Desrochers CSC, *The Social Teaching of the Church in India,* NBCLC/CSA, Bangalore, India, 2006, p.123.

[35] *Op.cit.,* p.303.

[36] *Ibid.,* pp. 272-273.

[37] Thomas Edamattathu and Ida Rodrigues, " Contribution of the Religious Sisters to the Church in Northeast India", in S.Karotemprel(ed.), *The Catholic Church in Northeast India 1890-1990, A Multi-dimensional Study*, Vendrame Institute Publications, Shillong, 1993, p.296.

[38] Mary George, *The F.M.A. Contribution to the Missions in Northeast India*, A paper presented at All India Symposium on Salesian Missions in India, Shillong, 1983, p.53.

[39] *The Catholic Directory of India 2013:* The Catholic Bishop's Conference of India, Claretian Publications, Bangalore, India, p.2413.

[40] Sabastian Karotemprel, S.D.B., (ed.), *op.cit.,* pp.308-309.

[41] David R. Syiemlieh, (ed.), *Diocese of Agartala: Ten Years and Onward*, Don Bosco Press, Shillong, 2005, p.162.

[42] Thomas Edamattathu and Ida Rodrigues, *op.cit.*, p. 304.

[43] *Op.cit.*, p. 164.

[44] *Ibid.*, p.170.

[45] *Op.cit.*, p.299.

[46] O. Paviotti, *The Work of His Hands: The Story of the Archdiocese of Shillong-Guwahati 1934-1984,* Archbishop's House, Shillong, 1987, p.17.

[47] *Souvenir*, Diamond Jubilee of the Prefecture, *op.cit.*, p. 64.

[48] Thomas Edamattathu and Ida Rodrigues, *op.cit.*, pp.296-305.

[49] *Ibid.*, p. 67.

[50] Pushpa George, *The Missionary Sisters of Mary Help of Christians and their Contribution to the Missions, A paper* presented at All India Symposium on Salesian Missions in India, Shillong, 1983, p.127.

[51] Fr William Grimm in "Change is a must for all", *Smart Companion India:* National Monthly for Christian Leadership, June 2012 / Vol.3 / No.5, p.11.

[52] *Ibid.*, p.12.

[53] Angie O' Gorman columnist, USA, in *National Monthly Magazine for Christian Leadership*, Smart Companion- India, July 2012/ Vol.3 / No.6, p.13.

[54] Dr Dominic Jala & Ms Patricia Mukhim in 'Contribution of the Catholic Church Towards Education in North- East India', in *Centenary of the Catholic Church in North-East India 1890-1990: A Souvenir*

[55] Lazar Jeyaseelan, *History of the Catholic Church in Manipur,* Diocese of Imphal, Manipur, 1994, p.155.

[56] *All India Catholic Education Policy 2007,* Catholic Bishop's Conference of India, New Delhi, p.4.

[57] *Report of the General Meeting of the CBCI,* 2006, pp.49-50.

[58] C. Becker SDS, *History of the Catholic Missions in North East India, op.cit.,* p.259.

[59] *Ibid.*, pp.340-341.

[60] Dr Dominic Jala & Ms Patricia Mukhim, op.cit.,

[61] C.Becker SDS, *Early History of the Catholic Missions in Northeast India:* (trans. & ed.), *op. cit.,* p.175.

[62] *Ibid.*, p.88.

[63] Mother Anne, A Seed is Sown, in *St Mary's College Golden Jubilee Souvenir,* Shillong, 1937- 87, p.3.

[64] R.P. Tewari, *Problems of Education in North East India,* quoting from *Education in India,* 1976-77, Prakash Brothers, Ludhiana, p.71.

[65] Dr Dominic Jala & Ms Patricia Mukhim, *op.cit.*

[66] S. Karotemprel SDB, The Catholic School and A Growing Church, in *Indian Missiological Review*, July 1980, p. 249.

[67] Janusz Symonides (ed.), *New Dimensions and Challenge for Human Rights*, Rawat Publications, UNESCO Publishing, New Delhi, 2003, p. 4.

[68] Thomas Manjaly, Peter Haokip, James Thoppil, *Towards Building up the Local Church: Priestly Ministry for 21ˢᵗ Century, op.cit.*, p.43.

[69] *Ibid.*, p.45.

[70] Dr Dominic Jala & Dr J.S.Shangpliang in 'The Contribution of the Catholic Church towards Socio-Cultural Development in North- East India', in *Centenary of the Catholic Church in North-East India 1890-1990, A Souvenir.*

[71] *Ibid.*, p.42.

[72] *Ibid.*, p.89.

[73] S. Karotemprel SDB, The Nurse Sister and Family Welfare in a Growing Church, in *Indian Missiological Review*, January 1980, p.29.

[74] *Ibid.*, pp.31-32.

[75] Thomas Manjaly, Peter Haokip, James Thoppil, *op.cit.*, pp.74-75.

[76] *Ibid.*, p.73.

[77] *Op.cit.*, pp. 80-81.

[78] *Lumen Gentium*, Encyclical Letter of the Vatican II, para 11.

[79] E. Packumala, The Role of the Religious Sisters and their Contribution to the Adivasi Community in the Assam valley, in *Indian Missiological Review*, April 1985, p.182.

[80] Thomas Manjaly, Peter Haokip, James Thoppil, *op.cit.*, p.49.

[81] *Ibid.*, p.63.

[82] Thomas Menamparampil, *An Introduction to North-East India: Culture and History, op.cit.*, pp. 40-41.

Origin, Growth and Activities of the Bethany Sisters

The Congregation of the Sisters of the Little Flower of Bethany – familiarly known as The Bethany Sisters, is a religious family consisting of 1381 members at present. The entry of the Bethany Sisters in Northeast India seemed to have ushered in significant changes in the lives of many people of the Region. The Bethany Congregation in the Northeast is still in its growing stage, predominantly taking roots among the 'tribal's' of the Region. Here an attempt is made to find out the extent to which the Bethany Sisters operated and liaise with elements of the State as well as Civil Society in providing welfare services and provisions. This Congregation is very much involved in developmental activities through its numerous educational institutions, medical care, together with its many charitable and social institutions.

The Origin

The Congregation of the Sisters of the Little Flower of Bethany was founded on 16th July 1921. Bethany was the name of the first house at Bendur, Mangalore where the four pioneers began their common life under the direction of their Founder. He wanted his followers to emulate the spirit of contemplation and loving service practiced by the famous residents of Bethany of the Gospels, namely, Martha, Mary, and Lazarus. It was started by Fr Raymond Francis Camillus Mascarenhas hereafter referred as RFC Mascarenhas in StSebastian's Parish of Bendur, Mangalore (Karnataka). The institute is a Roman Catholic Religious Order founded with a purpose of uplifting the needy and the downtrodden. It was the work of an Indian visionary Priest with purely Indian material and Indian means.[1]

It is believed that like all Founders of Religious Congregations, who were responsive to the needs of the people among whom they lived, RFC Mascarenhas decided to meet the triple needs of the time by starting a Religious Congregation for women.[2] Firstly, a number of young women who wanted to offer themselves for the works of charity were unable to do so owing to financial constraints. Secondly, education for the poor especially the girls was lacking. Thirdly, there was scarcity of dedicated teachers to take care of children's educational needs in remote villages. RFC Mascarenhas had realized that other Religious Congregations involved in the educational apostolate were mainly catering to the needs of the upper and the middle classes. The medium of instruction in their institutions was English and their activities were confined to the developed towns and major cities. No initiatives were taken to provide education with lesser expenses for the poorer students.[3]

Four teachers at St Sebastian's Parish school, Marceline Menezes, Flora Mathias, Alice Mathias, and Regina Gertrude Gonsalves became the pioneers of the new Congregation he founded. After a period of instruction and preparation for the new way of life they were to adapt, these four young women entered their new way of life on 16th July 1921. To signify their new lifestyle, they were given new names as Sr Martha, Sr Clare, Sr Lourdes and Sr Gertrude. These Sisters shared the vision of RFC Mascarenhas and their way of life attracted many more young girls. It answered the triple needs of that period, i.e., providing Catholic education for the poor especially the girls, presenting an opportunity for the girls who had genuine vocation to consecrate their lives to God as Sisters irrespective of their status in society and to supply good, dedicated and qualified permanent teachers to teach in the schools in the rural areas.[4]

Besides, the pastoral and educational needs were to be met by the members, particularly by being in service of the girl children, women and rural masses of Mangalore and the society at large. Thus, the Sisters were involved in educational, social, pastoral, medical apostolate and ministry of hospitality according to the needs of the place.[5] For the first time, the village schools were run entirely by an Indigenous Order of Sisters without foreign control or guidance. Thus, the Bethany Congregation heralded a self-governing Indian Church. The Institute was canonically erected on 28th July 1932.

Raymond Francis Camillus Mascarenhas-The Founder

Mgr RFC Mascarenhas, the Founder of the Bethany Congregation was an educationist. He was intensely concerned with contemporary problems, particularly those of education. He was obsessed with the idea of bringing education within the reach of the marginalized and the underprivileged in the rural areas and to the girls in particular. Through the Bethany Sisters he was able to realize his dream for the development of women, the poor and the marginalized, down-trodden and needy irrespective of caste and creed.[6]

Mgr RFC Mascarenhas was born on 23rd January 1875 in Shimoga, Karnataka. He was ordained priest on 4th March 1900 and worked as a Parish Priest of Bendur in Mangalore, Karnataka and as an assistant parish priest of three parishes of South Kanara, Karnataka. As a Vicar General of the Diocese of Mangalore from 1931-1941, he aimed at bringing the compassionate love of Jesus to the poor and the neglected. Being a man of vision, he foresaw that education was the best means of empowering the poor. He visualized a society where education would be everyone's privilege. He concretized these ideas in as early as 1930, which were later taken up by the government.

Mgr RFC Mascarenhas opened orphanages so that the poor children could be fed, looked after, educated, and thus empowered. He led the Sisters to go into neglected areas where no one wanted to go. His interest in education of the poor did not stop at Primary level. He established craft schools and non-formal education centres for the empowerment of women who could earn their livelihood through arts and crafts. In 1922 he started St Martha's- the first Industrial school for girls at Bendur in Dakshina Kannada District of Karnataka. The purpose was to train women for self-employment resulting in their consequent empowerment and self-reliance.

The establishment of a handloom weaving industry in Bethany was his idea for imparting training in a trade to youngsters in the art of handloom weaving. In 1930 he composed and got printed a booklet in the local language namely Konkani. When the literacy campaign started in 1980, this booklet was used as the material for teaching children and illiterate adults, to read and write. Pope Pius XII conferred on him the honour of Domestic Prelate in 1955. He died on 23rd December 1960 and was buried at St Sebastian's Church, Bendur, Mangalore. His cause of Canonization was taken up in 2007 and he was declared Servant of God by Vatican on 3rd May 2008.[7]

Contribution of Mgr RFC Mascarenhas

The educational endeavours of Mgr RFC Mascarenhas at the beginning of his Priestly ministry at Udyavar and Agrar in Mangalore (Karnataka) were in terms of helping out numerous poor students in their education. In 1927 when universal and compulsory education was introduced in every Province of India, there was increase in demand for teachers for Primary and Secondary education. He was the first to respond to this need by opening new communities and sending Sisters to the remote Elementary schools.

Boarding houses and free orphanages for girls facilitated education for the poor children of the remote villages. He was the first one to establish girls schools in the villages and advocated lady teachers' training. Mgr RFC Mascarenhas focused not only on the literary side of education but also on the industrial education especially for girls through which they were able to earn their living. He envisioned higher education for women. In 1957 he sought permission from the Bishop of Belgaum,

Karnataka to start Women's college at Dharwad realising that there were no colleges exclusively for women.[8]

Within two decades a large number of girl students had their Primary, Higher Primary and Higher education as well. Following the footsteps of Mgr RFC Mascarenhas, the Bethany Sisters have been taking a stand in empowering women through various means especially through education which is the main apostolate of the Congregation. Bethany institute has been one of the first Congregations to start educational institutions in the vernacular for the poor, the marginalized, Dalits and tribal's of South Kanara and later in other parts of India.

Role of Mgr RFC Mascarenhas in Promoting Education

Mgr RFC Mascarenhas held many important responsibilities in the government machinery and in the Diocese. In 1923, he was elected to the Municipal Council and he continued in that post till 1929. He prepared a memorandum of educational and other grievances of the Catholic community and was sent to Madras as a delegate to appear before the Simon Commission. The result of this representation was the government order of 1929, which may be called the *'Magna Carta'* of the Catholic schools in India, recognizing their rights. He was President of the Catholic Association of South Kanara in 1931 and served in that capacity for 10 years. He also figured prominently in the civic activities of the city and was the only Catholic and influential member of the District Education Council, serving for two terms.

He was appointed to different Boards and Commissions of the Diocese. He was a consulter of St Joseph's Inter Diocesan Seminary, Mangalore; Vice-President of Catholic Board of Education, Diocese of Mangalore from 1932 to 1941. From 1932 to 1936, he was the Diocesan supervisor of Catholic Elementary and Secondary schools. He was sent as a Diocesan representative to amicably solve serious disputes and conflicts in the Parishes and was nominated official of the Diocesan Ecclesiastical Court.[9] He became the President of Konkani Catholic Pioneer Truth Society in 1938 and served as the President of the Mangalore Roman Catholic Pioneer Fund from 1941-1942. Through this fund, he gave leadership to plan and execute several projects, especially for the economic self-reliance of the poor in South Kanara. In all these responsibilities he sought to be compassionate towards the marginalised sections of the society.

The Charism of the Bethany Sisters

The educational, pastoral and missionary dimension of Mgr RFC Mascarenhas' mission was guided by the compassionate love of Jesus which captured him. He had love for the poor, especially women of rural areas. This probably urged him to share with the members of the Institute, the elements of his mission through the first Constitutions that he drafted, the letters that he wrote, the messages that he gave, the General Chapters that he guided and the literary works that he undertook. The life lived by the Sisters directed by him and the mission undertaken under his guidance provides some insights into his charism. One of Mgr RFC Mascarenhas' dreams for the Church in India and for his newly founded Congregation was that they should be rooted and developed in Indian culture.

The first four Sisters of Bethany, Sr Martha, Sr Clare, Sr Lourdes, and Sr Gertrude remained in close association with Mgr RFC Mascarenhas once they came to live together as a formal group. Even before that he instructed them on every Friday and shared with them his vision. So, the communication of his aspirations began much earlier than the foundation of Bethany. They saw him, heard him and communicated with him daily. Though not directly, he shared with them during the weekly conferences the contents of his spiritual experiences and invited them to participate in the same. They tried for their part to capture his vision through the personal sharing done and spiritual direction given.

The Pioneers watched from a close distance his dispositions towards religion, attitude towards life, the priorities that he set, the values that he upheld, the compassionate nature that he exhibited when the poor and the needy approached him. In the meantime, they also realized that their call was to become partners in his vision and mission. The Congregation that came into being primarily to educate the poor girls who had no opportunities as well as to dedicate their lives for the service of humanity helped in inculcating in its members a true missionary spirit, besides helping them to acquire the necessary skills and knowledge.

The Growth of the Bethany Congregation

On 21st July 1927 the strength of the Institution that was founded in 1921 had risen to 26.[10] On 1st June 1928 for the first time the Bethany Sisters took charge of St Joseph's school, Kankanady, Mangalore. On 29th July 1932 Bethany was recognized as a religious family in the Church by the Decree of Canonical Erection received after 11 years of its existence as a pious association. On 26th May 1934, fifty-two Sisters who had lived together from the time of the foundation of the Congregation made their religious commitment.[11]

Heeding the invitations, the pioneers ventured into new mission territories in Kerala and North Karnataka. In 1936 the Congregation crossed the boundaries of Mangalore and launched into Wyanad mission in Calicut, Kerala. Eude's Convent in Kerala was inaugurated in 1938 and Sisters began to teach in the existing St Michael's School. The spirit of expansion had gripped Bethany and in 1939, North Karnataka received 8 Bethany Sisters at Dharwad and Guledgudd primarily to teach in schools.

As the mission expanded, Mgr RFC Mascarenhas gave priority to the education and training of the Sisters for the various works of the Institute. Lack of financial resources, illness and death of many young Sisters and other trials did not prevent the young Institute from growing in number and merit.[12] In the 1940's invitations had been received from as far as Patna in North India to send the Sisters to undertake educational services there. However, the possibility of opening convents in North

India was explored only towards the end of 1960. On 28th July 1971, the occasion of the Golden Jubilee of the Institute, the Congregation was declared of Pontifical Rite by a Decree of Praise from *Propaganda Fide*, Rome by which it was placed directly under the Pope.

The Institute experienced unprecedented growth and success in its undertakings. Bethany Sisters extended their activities all over India and even beyond. Many Priests and lay persons familiar with the Congregation's past struggles called this decade as 'the Golden Age of Bethany.'[13] As the number of Sisters increased year after year, at the invitation of Bishops and Priests working in rural areas, Bethany Sisters penetrated the interior villages. They brought comfort and solace to the poor through formal and non-formal education, developmental works, faith formation and medical care.

The Congregation that was started in1921 with just four members in a humble way has today 1381 professed sisters. Bethany Sisters have Novitiates in Mangalore, Mysore, and West Bengal where 60 Novices receive two years intense training to become Sisters. More than 50 Pre-Novices are preparing themselves in 3 Pre-novitiates to become the future Bethany Sisters. There are 181 Candidates in 8 Provinces who have joined the Bethany Sisters in their mission activities.

Presently Bethany has 187 communities in three continents of Asia, Europe, and Africa with its presence in 61 Dioceses (49 in India, Nepal and 12 in Europe, and Africa). In India their presence is felt in the States of Karnataka, Goa, Kerala, Maharashtra, Tamilnadu, Andhra Pradesh, Punjab, Haryana, Uttar Pradesh, Himachal Pradesh, Delhi, Jharkhand, Uttaranchal, Orissa, Gujarat, West Bengal, Assam, Nagaland, Manipur, Tripura, Mizoram, Meghalaya and Arunachal Pradesh. In Europe and Africa, the Sisters serve in Germany, Italy, Austria, France, Belgium and Mauritania in West Africa, Tanzania and Senegal.[14] The Sisters hail from different States as well as tribes of India. For effective administration, the Congregation has been divided into Provinces.

The Administrative Units of the Congregation

TABLE NO 3

1.	Central administration	3 Convents	6.	Southern Province	22 Convents
2.	Delegation Abroad	13 Convents	7.	Northern Province	18 Convents
3.	Mangalore Province	34 Convents	8.	Eastern Province	16 Convents
4.	Bangalore Province	19 Convents	9.	Northeast Province	32 Convents
5.	Western Province	23 Convents			

Source: The Sisters of the Little Flower of Bethany, Mangalore, *Hand Book*, pp. 45-64.

During the tenure of Mother Macrina as leader of the Institute, many ventures were undertaken. They were extending the branches of the Congregation far and wide to the Northeast and North-West of India, as well as Rome and Germany making the Congregation truly missionary. Hence, under her leadership Bethany became the first Sisters' Congregation to enter Mizoram and Tripura.[15] The Congregation that was started in 1921 has spread through the length and breadth of India as far North as Chandigarh, as far South as Kanyakumari, as far East as Tripura and as far West as Gujarat in India.

Mission Oriented Activities of the Bethany Sisters

Education

Before Bethany was founded, there were other Congregations devoted to the education of girls. But their efforts were confined to the well-to-do class of girls, who had the necessary means to avail of the expensive education which they gave. However, the Bethany Sisters' schools were mainly meant for the poor and the needy. Further, Bethany Sisters probably were the pioneers in starting technical, industrial, and vocational training centre's, especially for dropouts, the unemployed and economically backward girls. Fr RFC Mascarenhas had installed weaving looms for self-employment.[16] The purpose of this was to train girls in tailoring, needle work, lacemaking etc. Another great need of the time was in the field of health care and health education of poor villagers and realizing this, he initiated the Sisters in the elementary medical care.[17]

The opening of Convents in rural areas, with schools attached to them, not only in South Kanara District but also in mission areas of Calicut, Belgaum and Mysore helped to bring education to the poor people. As an ardent promoter of primary education, Fr RFC Mascarenhas' main concern was to provide good and efficient teachers for Primary schools. Therefore, he opened a Teachers' Training Institute at Kinnikambla (Karnataka) in 1945 which helped to provide teachers to the various village schools of the Parishes. To facilitate education for the children of the poorer families and remote villages, orphanages, and hostels i.e., free boarding homes, were opened at Kinnigoli, Kinnikambla, Taccode and Kulshekar in Mangalore, Karnataka. These orphanages became centres of learning and education and the girls from these orphanages spread it to their respective villages. These schools and orphanages have become centres of vocations to Sisterhood as well.

Through the determined efforts of Fr RFC Mascarenhas to organise Bethany's educational efforts in a systematic way, Bethany Educational Society (BES) Mangalore, was founded. It was registered on 4th September 1948 with the title, 'The Bethany Educational Society, Mangalore', under the Societies Registration Act, 1860.[18] His vision of education is borne out by the record of institutions listed for the registration in 1948. They numbered 34, including boarding houses, orphanages, industrial and farm schools.[19] Today the BES manages a total of 272 educational institutions.

Educational Institutions of BES

TABLE NO 4

1.	KG schools	58
2.	Primary and Higher Primary schools	46
3.	High schools	53
4.	Senior Secondary/ Pre-university colleges	18
5.	Degree colleges	2
6.	Teachers' Training Institute	1
7.	Balwadies and non-formal education centre's	23
8.	Hostels and orphanages	36
9.	Vocational training centre's	22
10.	Community Colleges	6
11.	Production centre's	6
12.	Crèche	1

Source: The Sisters of the Little Flower of Bethany, Mangalore, *Hand Book*, pp. 45-64.

Through all these institutions, the BES tries to disseminate its Core Values such as God experience, compassionate love for all especially the poor and the marginalized. Communion, collaboration, team spirit, excellence in terms of developing each one's unique potentials to build a just and humane society, truth, love, justice, peace, simplicity of life-style, dignity of labour, respect for life, nature, cultures, religions and love for the nation are some of the Core Values imparted through the educational institutions of BES.[20] Bethany's educational apostolate continues through the various endeavours of BES in the remotest areas of the vast Indian Sub-Continent.

The first National Convention of BES held in 1988 and the second National Convention in 2001, reformulated the vision, goal, and objectives of BES. Its purpose was clarified as 'fullness of life for all' especially the poor, marginalized and women in particular. Here 'all' would mean those who come into the caring fold of the Bethany Sisters-girls and boys as well, whether in schools, vocational or non formal educational centre's, boarding houses, hostels, or social work centre's. The National Conventions further emphasized on the liberation and empowerment of women.[21] Through a long drawn process these Conventions evolved a vision statement.[22] Sr Rose Therese in her article on 'educating students in the changing scenario opines that 'the constant effort of the BES will be to ensure to all, that good education which is an inalienable right of every individual in virtue of one's dignity as a human person.'

In the words of Cardinal Telesphore P. Toppo 'True and faithful to their charism, Bethany Sisters have been able to achieve success in the field of education. Besides this, they are also involved in the pastoral care, socio-medical, hostel and youth ministry. Through these ministries they strive to uplift the condition of the poor and the needy, particularly of the girl children and the women.'[23] The main concern of BES has been bringing modern education to the marginalized, the rural poor, tribal's and girls. Even today vast majority of our schools are in the remote areas, serving the poor and the underprivileged. Education imparted by the BES has opened doors of knowledge to countless marginalized persons and endowed them with dignity and status, competencies, and upward mobility across the nation.

As per the Congregational statistics of 2008-2009, the total student strength of BES schools was 63,271 out of which 34,163 were girls and 29,108 were boys. The ratio reveals that the girls outnumbered the boys which serves as an indication that the Sisters are conscious and make effort to keep alive the charism of the Founder primarily the education of the girls. There were 1,611 teaching faculties out of which 1,318 were female staff and 293 were males. Out of 307 non-teaching staff of BES schools, 204 were females and only 103 were males. At present Bethany Sisters are involved in the work of education in 21 States of India and their presence is felt in Nepal, Europe, and Africa as well.

The BES adapts child-oriented education as the dynamics of class room pedagogy that is, the contents taught are contextualized and relevant, audio-visuals are used in teaching and each student is given individual attention. The content is simplified, probing questions asked, learning made interesting and experiential. Four ways of interaction such as teacher – class, student – student, student – text and group interactions are introduced. Role plays, field trips, workshops, debates, and games are organized and self–evaluation facilitated.

Learner involvement and motivation, adapting classroom situation, introducing activities in the classroom, and encouraging learning in pairs forms an important part of the BES pedagogy. For the slow learners conducting remedial classes, introducing each one teach one, project work and group study, visiting the houses of students to know the family background and providing extrinsic and intrinsic motivation is stressed. Knowledge about the family background of the students, learning environment, their economic condition, cultural set up is taken into consideration while teaching.

Keeping in focus the above mentioned pedagogy, vision, goal and Core Values, the Bethany Sisters also serve in 131 Institutions managed by the various Dioceses and the other Congregations. A total of 399 Sisters are serving in the Institutions of the Congregation and 151 Sisters serve in the Institutions of the Dioceses as well as other Religious Congregations. In the words of Rt Rev. Raphael Cheenath, Archbishop of Cuttack and Bhubaneshwar 'The Sisters are engaged in pastoral, educational, social and evangelical activities.'

Social Welfare and Health Care

Bethany Social Service Trust (BSST) known as Sahodaya was started in 1995 to focus on developmental activities. Through the social work activities, the Bethany Sisters show compassionate love for the people especially the dehumanized poor. The vision of the BSST is to create a just and humane society and the mission is aimed at restoration of human dignity through a process of empowerment to them.

The Sisters are engaged in multiple social works such as family visits, instruction of children, hygiene and childcare for the womenfolk, health care, village touring, providing care for the aged etc. The Sisters are engaged in youth centres, crèches, dispensaries, knitting and sewing centres rendering service in the surrounding as well as far away villages. They have extended their field of activity to vocational training schools and continue to serve the people through various charitable institutions. In the words of Rt Rev Albert D'Souza, Archbishop of Agra 'The Sisters seem to have contributed towards the upliftment of women as the vocational training given in weaving, sewing, tailoring, typing, knitting etc. enables youngsters to earn their livelihood. The missionary collaboration rendered by the Sisters of the Little Flower of Bethany in different fields of apostolates has added vitality and evangelical fruitfulness to the Church through the years.'

According to Rt Rev Anthony Fernandes, Bishop of Bareilly 'The Congregation founded for the education of girl children and women continues its mission of empowering women in India.' A large number of poor girls, mostly school dropouts, are being trained for the government school certificate in cutting, tailoring and embroidery. Besides, issues such as human trafficking are taken up and women in villages are instructed in hygiene, food habits, childcare, first aid, etc., for better living. The Sisters have played a role to raise the dignity of women in society through various conscientisation programmes. Similarly, at the economic level they have enabled many girls to secure adequate employment and reduce the level of poverty.

The focus of the mission of the Bethany Sisters is mainly promotion of communal harmony and peace, education, development through Self Help Groups and Mahila Mandals (women's groups), training of women, youth and others in job-oriented skills. This is done by setting up vocational training and production centres, integrated child welfare and development through promotional schools at all centres of work, education and rehabilitation of street children and slum dwellers' children. These centres are set up in Karnataka, Kolkata, Ludhiana, Faridabad, Silchar and Guwahati. Tribal development initiatives among the tribal's of Northeastern States, West Bengal, Orissa, Jharkhand, Uttaranchal, Maharashtra, Andhra Pradesh, and Kerala are taken up.

There are some community-based rehabilitation of differently-abled at Doddabelavangala, Santibastwad and Guledgudd in North Karnataka. Integrated development of children and micro-entrepreneurial development initiatives through Jyothi Seva Kendra, Chittapur and Gulbarga in Karnataka are taken into consideration. Youth development and leadership programmes are undertaken at all the centres. Sisters are active in prison ministry at Naini in UP, Ludhiana, Dharwad, Chevayur in Kerala, Mangalore, and Aachen in Germany. Sisters have also taken up different works in the area of housing, sanitation and drinking water for the poor at Waynad in Kerala, Chittapur in Karnataka, and Chintalpudi in Andhra Pradesh. Watershed management and organic farming in Mangalore and Badibahal in Orissa are given importance.

Rt Rev Sarat Chandra Nayak, Bishop of Berhampur opines that 'Right from the time of the pioneers till today, the Sisters' continuous service in various fields has contributed greatly to the nation building. The missionary zeal and the courage of the Sisters have brought comfort to our poor tribal people who are marked by poverty, ignorance and illiteracy.'[24]

Bethany Sisters in the Northeast have made efforts to read the signs of the times by undertaking the work of Promotional Schools in Silchar and Guwahati which is a cohesive strategy to reach out to the city migrants. The intervention consists of education of children towards mainstreaming through promotional schools in the slums. Activities of the year include Daily Literacy/study classes, Co-curricular activities/celebrations, Follow up of past students, Self Help Group action, Rights Education and Advocacy. The results were that about 170 children entered formal schools for class 1-4, 240 poor women and men were aware of their rights, improved cleanliness in the slum environment, 14 SHGs were formed among focus parents.

Rights Based Approach (RBA) in relation to promotional schools at the level of economy as means to support the education of the children was taken up. Self Help Groups were organized among the parents of these children. At the level of social exploitation, the Sisters took to educate the parents on human rights, right to life, right to education and find better prospects for their children. At the level of corrupt governance, it was decided to educate and organize the illiterate people of the slums especially women to approach the local government schools to admit their children without being harassed for bribe. At the level of child rights, the parents and adults were educated on the existing child labor prevention act. In cases where supplementing income by the bigger children was essential, study classes were arranged to such children for imparting education.

The significance of the programme was that the teachers at the promotional schools also acted as social work animators as they facilitated the SHG functioning in addition to the particular social workers. Rights education helped the people to some extent to become aware of the available government benefits. In the year 2013 about 120 families re-applied for ration cards, of which 17 received the cards. A few had applied for pension benefits and scholarships. Follow up of promoted students through a study done in January 2013, the mainstreamed ones between 2008-2012 through 8 centers, shows that, of the total 712 students promoted to formal schools, 669 (i.e., 94%) were found regular to schools.

Glimpses of other significant moves of the Bethany Sisters are care of injecting Drug Users (IDUs) Alcoholics and prevention of HIV/AIDS. Bethany Social Welfare Society, Mamit, Mizoram, serves as a drop-in center for IDUs. Here the combined project of Mizoram State AIDS Control Society (MSACS) and National AIDS Control Organization (NACO) is implemented in the care of IDUs, Alcoholics, and HIV/ AIDS patients. There are a total 30 staff including a part time doctor who cover 34 distant villages of Mamit district in Mizoram. Since 1995 Bethany Health cum Rehabilitation Centre at Sihphir, Mizoram conducts the programme on Care of IDUs and alcoholics, and Awareness building towards prevention of HIV/AIDS in about 30 villages around Sihphir (Aizawl Dt.). Since then hundreds of clients have been helped and rehabilitated, accompanied with planned follow up. Vocational and Skill training programmes for rural youth, Self Help Group Action for Women Empowerment, Livelihood creation and Social Progress are undertaken by the Bethany Sisters.

Bethany Social Service Centre at Barasat in West Bengal is the Social Service wing of Bethany Social Service Society (BSSS) of North East India, having its headquarter in Guwahati, Assam. Bethany Sisters initiated the mission work in the rural communities of Kadambagachi Panchayat, Barasat district of West Bengal. The people here belong to the economically and socially lower strata of society. It was a venture of learning the unknown 10 villages in the beginning. Though initially it was a struggle, but Sisters continued the work with persistent efforts. Here Bethany Sisters aim at health care and women empowerment towards sustainable development. After 16 years of Bethany Sisters' presence there, the Sisters have reached to 6 Gram Panchayats rendering both medical and social service to 13 villages in 41 centres, formed 63 Self Help Groups out of which 45 Self Help Groups are functional.

At Kattalcherra, in Tripura which is a hub of social, medical, and educational activities of the Bethany Sisters, leadership training programs, income generating programs, animal rearing, etc are conducted in almost 30 villages every year. Incense sticks making, agriculture, animal husbandry, weaving, tailoring, poultry rearing are a few of the skills taught by the Sisters. Power tiller is given to two areas of this centre, families have profited from the rubber plantation made available to the villagers. Pineapple plantation is provided, there are 20 Self Help Groups and government resources are tapped by the local people with the encouragement of the Sisters involved in social work. Candle making is taught and is carried on for two groups of 12 members each. 200 women are organized into a wing and Sisters are fully in charge of their activities. Leadership, awareness programmes, charitable works are performed by these groups of women. They also sponsor the poor girl students by paying their school fees.

Para legal programs on Right Based Approach (RBA) are undertaken. Para legal personnel and co-ordinators are trained, and they have fought with the government for their rights through Right To Information. The success stories of these programs are that they have succeeded in getting electricity and water for their villages. Indira Awaz Yojana, old age pension schemes have been availed for the people and retailer shops, non-governmental schools have started to function because of these programs. In all this Sisters have acted as grass root level facilitators. Malaria control programs have been successful and there are 5 Co-ordinators, 30 community health volunteers joining their hands with the Sisters and doctor functions as a district project manager.

Archbishop Salvatore Pennacchio, Apostolic Nuncio in his message on the Golden Jubilee of Northeast Province wrote 'Bethany Sisters had set out as a new venture into the Northeastern part of India. It is a proud moment to have 30 convents and being engaged in educational, pastoral, hostel, medical and social apostolates. They have taken up exceedingly difficult and challenging ministries of rehabilitation of Alcoholics, HIV/AIDS victims, drug addicts, prison ministry and other forms of services which are the need of the 50 years. It is a moment to acknowledge having so many centres, educational, pastoral, medical and social apostolates among the less privileged and deprived.'[25]

Pastoral Care

'Sachetana', the pastoral wing of the Congregation focuses on the goal of bringing good news to the poor, to proclaim liberty to the captives and recovery of sight to the blind as proclaimed by Jesus before starting his mission.[26] Pastoral care runs through all the activities of the Bethany Congregation. Pastoral care of the school community involves annual retreats and recollections for staff and students, counseling, visits to the families and value-based education on the core values of BES. Pastoral care of children in the hostels/boarding houses includes moral instruction, counseling, and visits to their families as well. Pastoral care is given to the sick through their spiritual care in hospitals and homes such as visiting and praying with them, empathetic listening, and counseling etc.

The Bethany Sisters take interest in the prison ministry by visiting the prisons, praying with the inmates, listening to them, and providing them with material help. Pastoral care of the migrants is carried on by offering spiritual and emotional support, accompanying them in their pain, isolation, and rehabilitation. The family ministry is carried on through visits, reaching out to the women in distress, rehabilitation of broken families, sharing in their struggles, joys, and sorrows. The pastoral care of the domestic workers involves faith formation, catechesis, payment of just wages, treating them with kindness, respecting their dignity and assisting them to find a better future. Pastoral care is also given priority by the Sisters in countries like Germany, France, and Italy by accommodating the visitors, looking after the elderly and so on.

Bethany Sisters give importance to the role of lay men and women for the growth of the Church and the society. The Bethany Lay Association (BLA) consists of people who are married but participate in the charism of the Sisters by prayer, humanitarian and welfare activities. The Sisters invite people of good will to join them as lay associates to participate in their charism, spirituality and collaborate in their mission. Therefore, lay associates constitute all those Catholic men and women who respond to this invitation to share in the life and mission of the Bethany Sisters. They participate in community development, charitable services, youth ministry, developmental works and Self-Help Groups, counseling at rehabilitation centres, social work, ministry to the sick and giving pre-marital and post-marital guidance at counseling centres etc.

In the words of Bishop Julius Marandi of Dumka Diocese 'The Children in the schools run by the Sisters are given faith formation, human and intellectual formation to stand on their own feet. Many students in general and especially poor and under privileged benefit from Sisters' services.' 'Prompted and motivated by Mgr RFC Mascarenhas' charism, the Sisters according to the needs of the time and place are engaged in the apostolates of Catholic education of the rural poor specially girls, teaching of Catechism in the Parish communities, care of children, the sick and the elderly and socio- developmental works. The Sisters have made a difference in the lives of thousands of people' writes Bishop Felix Toppo of Ranchi.[27]

Bethany Sisters in Northeast India

The year 1960 marked the death of Mgr RFC Mascarenhas-the Founder and it marked an important transition in the life and development of the Bethany Congregation. Since then the Bethany Sisters extended their activities all over India and even beyond.[28] Specifically, the history of Bethany in the Northeast began in 1962, when Mother Macrina, the then Superior General sent four Sisters to Kolasib to open the first convent in the Mizo district of Assam.

Fr Jean Vezina, the Parish Priest of Kolasib wrote to the Mother General on 8th August 1962: 'May I start with a very sincere thanks for the fine religious you have sent over here. They seem to go along together, and they have been tried through sickness. The Sisters are a part of our mission work. These trials and difficulties will seal the blessings of God for the excellent work performed by your loving daughters. We are still very few missionaries and our means are extremely limited. Let your daughters pray that we may be very faithful servants of the Lord in these difficult places.'[29]

For better administration, the General Chapter in 1969 decided to divide the Congregation into Regions. Accordingly, the Northeast mission was raised to the status of a Region in 1971 with Sr Sylvine as the first Regional Superior. On 8th March 1980 Northeast region was annexed to the Northern region with headquarters at Sacred Heart's Convent, Ludhiana in Punjab and Sr Canice became the Regional Superior. In 1986, the Congregation was re-organized into five administrative units. Mangalore, Bangalore, and Northern Regions became Provinces and Northeast and Kerala unit were raised to the status of vice-provinces.

The Northeast Province of the Congregation was established on 14th July 1986. Holy Family Convent in Silchar was chosen as the official Province headquarters and Sr Lillis was installed as the first Provincial Superior. Her priority was to review the situation of Bethany's mission in the Northeast- the achievements, the failures and look for new ways to make the mission relevant. Perceiving the real need of the people led her along with her team members to realize the importance of social service in the Region.

Although Bethany Sisters had been doing some social and medical work from the beginning, the organized way of carrying out this mission started with the use of Sr Noeline's training which she received at Coady international institute of St Francis Xavier University, Canada. During the next decade there was surge in the social work activities of the Province and this mission gained importance. From 1990s the Sisters were sent for training in social work making them sufficiently equipped for the ministry.

The first training house for the aspiring girls of the Region was established on 3rd January 1969 and Pre-novitiate as well as Novitiate houses at Kolkata in the 1990s. While there were six Sisters from Northeast at the time of Province's Silver Jubilee in 1987, there were over sixty Sisters from this Region in the Golden year of the Province in 2012. Sr Noeline, the former Provincial Superior of the Sisters in the Northeast Province opines that 'Walking in the footsteps of the Pioneers, the Sisters over the five decades have left no stone unturned in contributing their share in the making of what Bethany in Northeast India is today.

Fifty years ago, the Sisters of the Little Flower of Bethany in Northeast made an option to share their lives with the people. At a time when existing Congregations think of inter congregational formation houses due to lack of aspirants, Sisters in Northeast India are blessed with good number of vocations from the Region itself.'[30]

Carrying forward the common mission and building on what had been achieved, the Provincial Superiors and their teams continued to give priority to the training of personnel for the various apostolates. Having entered fields like Media, Homeopathic Medicine and many Sisters having completed their Post-graduate degrees, importance was also given to the training of young Sisters of Bethany in the Northeast. Keeping in mind the future thrust, Sisters are now crossing over to areas like Law, Post Certificate in B. Sc. Nursing and a few Sisters have completed research as well.

Education, socio-medical ministry, pastoral care, rehabilitation of drug addicts, hostel and youth ministry and service of charity as per the needs of the society and signs of the times are the works that the Sisters carry on in the Northeast.[31] This study is limited to the fifty years (1962- 2012) of missionary work of the Bethany Sisters in the Northeastern States and West Bengal where the Sisters worked in various mission stations with a variety of missionary activities, methods and strategies.

The mission which started with just four Sisters at Kolasib, Mizoram in 1962, the cradle of Bethany Sisters in Northeastern India, appears to have taken roots in this soil and grown up in stature spreading it's branches across the seven States in the Northeast and over to West Bengal. At present the Bethany Sisters have their foundations at Aizawl, Kolasib, Sihphir and Mamit in Mizoram; Silchar, Guwahati, Lumding and Nalbari in Assam; Agartala, Kattalcherra, Depacherra, Dharmanagar and Khayerpur in Tripura; Dimapur, Kohima and Viswema in Nagaland; Kolkata, Barasat, Behala, Chittaranjan, Sulantu and Siliguri in West Bengal; Shillong, Umsning and Jongksha in Meghalaya; Canchipur in Manipur and Namsai and Manmow in Arunachal Pradesh.

Centres of the Bethany Sisters in the Northeast

TABLE NO.5

SI No	Community	Year of Establishment	SI No	Community	Year of Establishment
1.	Bethany Provincial House, Guwahati	25.3.2004	17.	St Joseph Convent, Viswema	11.02.1977
2.	Bethany Convent, Garchuk	02.02.2000	18.	Avila Convent, Lumding	10.01.1979
3.	Madonna Convent, Kolasib	28.06.1962	19.	Bethany Convent, Kolkata	18.06.1980
4.	Holy Family Convent, Silchar	11.06.1966	20.	Bethany Convent, Kathalcherra	08.07.1983
5.	Holy Cross Convent, Dimapur	17.01.1969	21.	Bethany Convent, Depacherra	13.07.1988
6.	Christ King Convent, Kohima	21.01.1969	22.	Bethany Convent, Canchipur	23.01.1989
7.	Mary Mount Convent, Aizawl	07.06.1969	23.	St Joseph's Convent, Chittaranjan	30.06.1990
8.	Holy Cross Convent, Agartala	15.06.1974	24.	Sacred Heart Convent, Behala	07.06.1991
9.	Bethany Convent, Sihphir	15.08.1991	25.	Bethany Convent, Samoguri, Namsai	16.07.2011
10.	Bethany Cottage, Barasat	13.06.1997	26.	Bethany Convent, Attavar	02.08.2007
11.	Holy Cross Convent, Dharmanagar	11.02.1999	27.	St Theresa Convent, Ngherpet Veng, Mamit	25.03.2011
12.	Bethany Convent Study Centre, Shillong	08.08.2002	28.	Bethany Convent, Khayerpur	09.01.2011
13.	Bethany Convent, Bazar Veng, Mamit	04.03.2003	29.	Bethany Convent, Manmow, Namsai	29.06.2014
14.	Bethany Convent, Jongksha	06.02.2004	30.	Bethany Convent, Umsning, Meghalaya	04.03.2017
15.	Bethany Convent, Sulantu	31.05.2006	31.	Bethany Convent, Biratnagar, Nepal	13.06.1996
16.	Bethany Convent, Nalbari	16.07.2010	32.	Bethany Convent, Siliguri	23.08.2020

It may be probable that for the growth of the Church in Northeast India, the contribution of the Bethany Sisters cannot be underestimated. Sr Wilberta, the former Superior General of the Bethany Congregation opines that 'It was in 1962, when Bethany was merely 41 years old that the Congregation made a leap into Northeast India. During these fifty years Bethany has percolated into the interiors of the Northeastern States. Rt Rev James Knox, the Apostolic Internuncio, invited Bethany to Northeast India. His letter to Mother Macrina, in response to the request made by Mgr George Breen, Prefect Apostolic of Haflong for a Congregation of Sisters to serve in Mizoram reads, 'I thought of appealing to the Bethany Congregation which would be eminently suited for the pioneering work that needs to be done in this part of my jurisdiction. I feel satisfied that Bethany has striven hard to prove her trustworthiness. All the missionary Priests, Diocesan as well as Religious, the Sisters and lay collaborators have always infused in Bethany Sisters a sense of confidence and enthusiasm by their support and solidarity.'[32]

Little did the superiors as well as the pioneer missionaries realize how their new fertile mission field would contribute to their growth in the whole country. After fifty years of that first arrival in 1962, the Northeast Province of the Bethany Congregation today counts about 198 members. The Northeast has emerged as one of the seven Provinces of the Congregation. The increasing number of young girls coming forward to join the team of Bethany Sisters' missionary work is perhaps a proof that the presence of the Sisters and their work is appreciated by the people of the Region. At present, the Bethany Congregation in the Northeast has 98 local Sisters.

Names of the local Bethany Sisters from Northeast India

TABLE NO: 6

SN	Name	State	SN	Name	State
1	Sr Malati Magdalene	Tripura	10	Sr Agatha Methasunu Vitsu	Nagaland
2	Sr Therese Lagardo	"	11	Sr Sulahele Teresa	"
3	Sr Sumitha	"	12	Sr Roselin Dukru	"
4	Sr Sabina Uchoi	"	13	Sr Gladys Viswentso	"
5	Sr Lucy Uchoi	"	14	Sr Kedukhole Christina Kiso	"
6	Sr Melissa Darlong	"	15	Sr M Jubino Rikha	"
7	Sr Elizabeth Uchoi	"	16	Sr Mhalesienuo Martha Zhale	"
8	Sr Sukhi Therese	"	17	Sr Pusale Louisa Kikhi	"
9	Sr Mitila Sangma	"	18	Sr Viketonu Teresa Rhetso	"
10	Sr Therese Darlong	"			
11	Sr Chandita Sangma	"	1	Sr Mary Naulak	Manipur
12	Sr Sorine Sangma	"	2	Sr Lolia Juliana	"
13	Sr Gitarani Monica Sangma	"	3	Sr Ruth Mao	"
			4	Sr Esther Thiankim	"
1	Sr Margaret Mary	West Bengal	5	Sr Therese Meryline	"
2	Sr Rosalia	"	6	Sr Lucy Gonmei	"
3	Sr Mariam Kujur	"	7	Sr Marina Pao Therou	"
4	Sr Carmela Tudu	"	8	Sr Line Raymond	"
			9	Sr Roselima Taimei	
1	Sr Anna Francisca	Nagaland	10	Sr Silvia Pao Daphrou	"
2	Sr Mary Grace Kujur	"	11	Sr Charou Elizabeth Pao	"
3	Sr Lanjiklu Lucy	"	12	Sr Martha Gonmei	"
4	Sr Mary L Kikon	"	13	Sr Veine Veronica	"
5	Sr Catherine Rongmei	"	14	Sr Angela Gonmei	"
6	Sr Susan Maria	"	15	Sr Judith Pamei	"
7	Sr Adu Celine	"	16	Sr Monica Kamei	"
8	Sr Dominica Assumi	"	17	Sr Angelina Pao	"
9	Sr Rose Dukru	"	18	Sr Catherine Pao	"

19	Sr Wairok Remee Maring	Manipur	18	Sr Helen Liansangpuii	Mizoram
20	Sr Veinai Therese	"	19	Sr Lucy Manuni	" (R I P)
21	Sr Ashiphrou Esther	"			
22	Sr M Hriiziini Florence	"	1	Sr Charilin Ryngkhlem	Meghalaya
23	Sr Josyna Paocine	"	2	Sr Bankyntiew Jyrwa	"
24	Sr Teresa Gonmei	"	3	Sr Jessyna Khonglah	"
			4	Sr Aiphimary Rani	"
1	Sr Mary Laldikzuali	Mizoram	5	Sr Veronica Franceline	"
2	Sr Therese Zothanpari	"	6	Sr Piety War	"
3	Sr Lucy Vanlalnghaki	"	7	Sr Pynhunlang Marbaniang	"
4	Sr Irene Therese	"	8	Sr Wanrimon Kharbuli	"
5	Sr Maria Veronica	"	9	Sr Mary Maryline	"
6	Sr Therese Rothangpuii	"	10	Sr Julian Lamare	"
7	Sr Therese C. Liani	"	11	Sr Emelia Wahlang	"
8	Sr Therese Lallianpuii	"	12	Sr Mestamary Thongni	"
9	Sr Veronica Zohmingliani	"	13	Sr Pdiangarti Pathaw	"
10	Sr Rebecca Lalzamliani	"			
11	Sr Juliet N. Ngaihi	"	1	Sr Cicilia Kujur	Assam
12	Sr Margaret Lalthlamuani	"	2	Sr Jyoti Xalxo	"
13	Sr Judith Rinliani	"	3	Sr Anandi Kerketta	"
14	Sr Veronica Kimtei	"	4	Sr Mary Grace Bhengra	"
15	Sr Mary Guite	"	5	Sr Gloria Kisku	"
16	Sr Dominica Siamliani	"	6	Sr Sunitha Edith	"
17	Sr M Veronica Lalbiakhliri	"	7	Sr Imilia Tirkey	"

Keeping in mind the charism of Mgr RFC Mascaren has and in keeping with the original purpose of the Congregation, the Bethany Sisters have concentrated their efforts in the education of girls and the poor. Bishop Anil Couto, of Jalandhar writes, 'Through their educational institutions and their social interventions they have shaped and molded hundreds of young men and women to be responsible citizens of India. They have formed the personalities and made them men and women in character. Through their institutions they endeavor to uplift the poor and the downtrodden and thus bring about a society based on justice and equality.'[33]

House visiting, care of the sick, teaching of Catechism to the little one's, religious instruction to the adults, teaching of hygiene and child care, the settling of irregular marriages and catering to the needs of the hostel children are the usual activities of the Sisters. Staying in the villages they meet the people and sharing their life and struggles, gladly accepting the meager food the villagers offer.

In Northeast India, where medical facilities were poor and infant mortality rate was high, the Sisters took the lead in establishing better living conditions by undertaking first-aid and hygiene programmes, courses on home nursing, cooking and nutrition, mother and child health programme and non- formal education of women and children. The importance given to health care can be seen from the fact that the fully trained doctors and Sister nurses fulfilling their healing ministry in the villages, in the boarding establishments and in village dispensaries. Health care is one of the most important activities the Bethany Sisters have undertaken in this Region, while education is another important field of their activity. Boarding schools, established for the poor children, who have no means of education due to their poverty, are said to be maintained at the cost of facing many difficulties and deprivations.[34]

The headquarters of the Northeast Province of the Bethany Sisters is situated at Guwahati in Assam. The Provincial Superior of Northeast is the overall in charge for the life and mission of the Sisters in the Northeast and is based at Bethany Provincial House Guwahati, Assam. The Congregation has Sisters and Candidates from all over India including Mizoram, Assam, Nagaland, Manipur, Meghalaya, Tripura, Assam and West Bengal.[35] The different centres continue to carry on the mission of the Church through schools, boarding houses and dispensaries.[36] 'The Congregation getting vocations from tribal communities reveals that it does the work of God, fulfilling the Church's missionary character and the responsibility of the local Church' says Rt Rev Binay Kandulna, Auxiliary Bishop of Ranchi.'[37]

The study of the assessment of the Bethany Sisters in Northeast India would be incomplete without a consideration to trace the situation of this Region in the 1960s, when the Bethany Sisters made their entry. Sr Lillis, the Assistant Superior General of the Congregation opines, 'I nostalgically recall my life spent in Northeast as the most challenging yet enjoyable and enriching years of my religious life. The seven hills with multi tribes, their melodious music, open mindedness, the solidarity I felt with the co-missionaries, the challenges of communication system, the frustrations faced in the administration, the joy I experienced seeing sprouting of Christian faith in the people, climbing the hills in the Khasi villages, the deadening night travels with the convoys of Tripura, being stranded on the way to Thanlon in Manipur, the fear psychosis after Fr Mathew Manianchira was shot dead in Imphal were some of the missionary events wherein I could experience the God of hills and valleys.'

According to Rt Rev Lucas Kerketta, Bishop of Sambalpur 'Bethany Sisters lived in an old building for several years. They have been working selflessly with a deep spirit of commitment facing many hardships while catering to the poor and the backward areas.'[38] This situation was applicable to most of the centres where the Bethany Sisters rendered their services. At that time, the sick were unattended to and there were no hospitals or dispensaries to cater to the needs of the common folk. The Sisters had heard about the traumatic experiences of missionaries in the hills. Though the political instability of the place, the non-availability of food, lack of communication facilities, the constant threat to their lives had always caused great distress and anxiety to the Sisters in the past, the friendliness and loving attitude of people made them feel at home among the people. Here below the missionary activities of the Bethany Sisters in the field of education, health, and pastoral care as well as social work are elaborated State-wise.

Bethany Sisters in Mizoram

Letter written by Mother Macrina to Rt Rev J.R. Knox, Apostolic Internuncio on 1st April 1962 states 'Personally I visited the place. There is good scope for missionary effort. Mgr George Breen would have us select any one of the two places viz, Silchar or Kolasib. I chose the latter as there is greater need of Sisters there than at Silchar although there are several difficulties to overcome there.'[39] The dire need of the Church then at Kolasib was to educate the youth of St John's High school run by the Holy Cross Brothers and to staff the girl's hostel. Four Sisters namely Sr Misericors, Sr Sylvine, Sr Dolora and Sr Inviolata were sent to the Mizo district of Assam in 1962 to take charge of the girl's hostel and teach in St John's High School.[40] On 1st July 1962, Sr Misericors, the first superior of the convent wrote to the Superior General: 'I am happy to inform you that the house consists of just a hall, the kitchen is not yet ready. We enquired about milk, eggs, vegetables etc. as we can't get anything here.'

Mgr George Breen, the Apostolic Prefect seeing the need of a Middle School for the mixed population asked the Sisters to open such a school. In January 1963, an English medium middle school was opened by the Bethany Congregation. In March 1963, the superior wrote: 'We have 56 children in the Nursery and in the Middle School we have 24 children.' On 15th February 1965 again, she wrote to the headquarters, 'Last year there were three classes-Nursery A and B and class IV of Middle School. Superior with two aspirants was managing all these classes. The education minister had come to our Mizo Hills this morning; we met him at the inspection bungalow. He has promised a grant for children's park and school building.'[41] The Nursery and the Primary school were housed in temporary sheds; permanent quarters were completed in January 1966. The Sisters gradually picked up the local language and adapted themselves to the culture. This enabled them to identify themselves with the people as they moved into the villages and meeting the people in their families.

On 9th June 1968 Fr P. J. Joseph of St John's wrote to the Superior General: 'May I tell you right now how much we are delighted to see your Sisters among us and how much we expect from them for the good of our girls. Before many years, you will be able to train some local vocations to enlarge the ranks of your dear Congregation. We are so badly in need of teachers in Mathematics and Science and if they are from your Congregation, they would be immensely helpful to give some sort of Catholic education to the students. It is so hard to get a teacher from outside because in a disturbed area like the Mizo district we cannot assure them of their safety. We can't afford to give them lodging and still worse, they wouldn't get food quite easily.'[42]

Gradually Madonna Convent Kolasib founded in 1962, became the centre of various missionary activities. The welcome address accorded to the Mother General by the Catholics of Kolasib Parish states 'Our priests here have kindly provided us with a boarding house for girls since 1961. Quite a number of girls even from interior villages come here as borders to get education and better discipline. But to our great regret so far it has been rather difficult to have suitable guardians for these borders. We are anxious to have this, the only Catholic hostel for girls in the district. It would be a blessing to all in the district.'[43] The number of children in the hostel increased in leaps and bounds as it was the only hostel for girls in Mizoram. In 1987, the National Open School was started at Kolasib, to serve the vast number of high school drop –outs. More than 700 students all over Mizoram have passed out of this institute. A new hostel building was put up in 1991.

During the insurgency period (1966-1986) which spanned roughly twenty years, the missionary activities of the Bethany Sisters were confronted with many problems. No moral support came for the Sisters from anywhere since mail delivery had been suspended. The Sister's school was the only school functioning in the entire Mizo district during those troubled times. Even during the most turbulent period they continued to provide the homeless with food and clothing as far as they could. Although they and the children under their care remained safe during those frightful days, they suffered from anxious moments and inconveniences. Initially the Sisters faced a lot of uncertainty and fear.

On 18th September 1965 Sr Misericors wrote to Superior General: 'Two MNF men entered the convent asking for money and threatening our lives.' Fr John Martin wrote to the Superior General on 13th March 1966: 'Everything is fine at Kolasib and the Sisters are all safe and sound just in case you have not heard from them since the communications were interrupted.' In a letter to the Sisters on 15th February 1984 the then Superior General Sr Sylvine writes: 'I have noted the difficulties of dealing with students whose parents do not cooperate with the teachers. Please do not give up your efforts to make the students morally good.'

The community report of Madonna convent in Kolasib written in 1983 states 'The community consisted of 10 members who were all engaged in teaching apostolate, while two Sisters taught in St John's High School.' Students were given special attention in their studies. They were given free education including all the accessories during the academic year. In one of the community reports it is mentioned that 'Our main apostolate at present is only teaching in the school. We visit the houses of the locality and the sick people in hospital on holidays. No other village work or social work we can do since we are busy with the school work and in the hostel.' The values of personal cleanliness and cleanliness of surroundings were inculcated. With the purpose of making the students fit to earn their living, practical experience was given in manual labour and thus the dignity of labour was upheld. At the demise of students or their parents, prayer hours were conducted in respective families.

The Sisters visited those who were sick and advised the family members. They attended funerals and consoled the members. During the longer holidays, Sisters took turns to visit the nearby villages and spent some days with the people, catechizing and praying with them as well as teaching them hygiene. Since conveyance was a major problem, the Sisters had to reach to the villages on foot, yet sometimes it was not possible to keep in contact with the people of distant villages. They took initiative to help the village schools by guiding the teachers in teaching and even supplying the learning material.

The Sisters worked whole heartedly to impart value-based education and to maintain good educational standard catering to the needs of the students. To tap and exploit the innate qualities and to promote the all round development of the students, regular co-curricular activities were organized and conducted from time to time. Though the school was situated in the rural area, it was a common saying among the people that the school was equivalent to that of a town, which spoke of the rapid progress of the school. It was proved by the merit scholarships achieved by the students for studies outside Mizoram. Physical education was also given equal importance to promote physical development and discipline of the students. Special interest was taken in the backward students in giving coaching classes and visiting their parents to solve their educational problems. Teaching of Moral science was considered a must by the Sisters to instill moral and spiritual values.

The then superior Sr Misericors wrote to the headquarters on 30th May 1963: 'We have just received today Rs.1200 from the Block Development Officer towards our Nursery School. We will also be receiving some teaching aids for the Nursery by the end of the week. We have a request from the Block Development Officer (B.D.O.) to take up some cooking classes to the young girls of Mizo District. They will provide whatever is necessary. We have only to go to the office and give them instruction and teach them how to cook. B.D.O has already opened the Home Craft wing and she had sent her representative here to request us to take up the classes.'

The life of the Sisters was an inspiration to the young girls who desired to collaborate with the Sisters in their missionary activities by joining their order. Sr Misericors wrote on 30th May 1963 'Two of my teachers want to become Sisters. One has already decided to join our

Congregation and we will have to help for her only brothers' education if we take her away from here.'

Requests also came from the government officials for Sisters but there were not sufficient personnel to attend to this need. In one of the requests it was written, 'There is a government dispensary here at Kolasib, but Kolasib is now a big village with more than 5000 population. Though the government dispensary provides good medicines and staff, yet the supply of medicine is always limited as other grouping centres also need the same. Besides, if the Church could run a dispensary, it would be a great blessing and a service to the poor people of Mizoram especially under our present condition.

Secondly, ever since the disturbance in the district, our condition of living has become poor due to many social and economic problems which lead us to poverty, high rate of death and ill health. As a result, many babies and children are now left motherless, homeless and without food. We therefore request you earnestly to kindly open an orphanage here at Kolasib so that at least the Church with the help of some volunteers may accommodate and feed those poor people.'

On 29th September 1968 a welcome address to Mother General by the members of the Catholic Church read: 'We the Catholic community of Kolasib had an opportunity to see the happy faces of Sisters whom we never saw before in Mizo hills. The Sisters teach our children and help us in many other ways. Allow us to ask from you 3 things: Firstly, we feel that one convent to serve the whole Mizo District is quite insufficient. So, we request you to open another convent either at Aijal or at Chhingchhip. Secondly, as you can notice, our living condition in this district is extremely poor. The trouble in our district has made the situation worse, which has resulted in many boys and girls to be orphans. We, therefore, request you to bless us with an orphanage or dispensary at Kolasib and to provide with trained Sisters in this field. Lastly, we request you to remember us always in your prayers, especially the hardships and difficulties we are facing.'

On 15th March 1970, Fr P. J. Joseph of St John's High School, Kolasib wrote to Mother Macrina 'Thanking you for sending such good Sisters who mean really a lot to the Church in Kolasib and the Mizo District.' In a letter to the Superior General written in 1980 the superior mentions 'We try to help the weaker and poorer students by supplying them with books, stationery, fee concessions and special coaching.' Sisters took keen interest in learning the local language. On 30th June 1984 Sr Neomi wrote to Sr Sylvine, 'Over here in Mizoram I feel quite at home. I am trying to know the people and I think learning their language is not so easy. Anyway, we have begun to learn Lushai everyday seriously.'

Kolasib was fast growing into a town and there were many children seeking admission in the school. As the number of students increased, they were accommodated in the hostel but the rooms in the hostel were dark without proper ventilation and congested too. On 24th April 1982, Sr Sylvine wrote to Sr Claudia the superior: 'Why not utilize the hostel building for classrooms?' Hence four classes were put up in the hostel. Though the people were poor and unable to pay the fees, they desired to improve the standard of the school and thus assisted to build the additional block required. The Sisters were also helping in a school which was 8 kms away from the station. Once in 15 days the Sisters used to take up the classes for the students in that school with the intention of helping the other teachers teaching there.

On 22nd June 1983, Br. Jose the then Headmaster of St John's Kolasib wrote to the Superior General Sr Sylvine on the transfer of two Sisters 'I am very happy and pleased, so are all the Brothers, the pupils and their parents with the work and help the two Sisters are giving to the people through this school and have no complaints whatsoever. On the contrary only appreciation and gratitude. I most sincerely thank you and the Sisters for their dedicated and selfless service rendered to this institution. Words are insufficient to describe our appreciation of their services.'

The origin of Mary Mount School at Aizawl can be traced back to the year 1952 when it was a Mizo medium Elementary and Middle school named St Paul's. It was started by the Canadian Brother, Godfrey. In 1968, since the Canadian Brothers had to leave Mizoram for good, Mgr George Breen invited the Bethany Sisters to administer this school. In February 1969, the Sisters took over the school to serve the educational and pastoral needs of the people and of the neighbouring villages. Sr Gretta, the superior writes to Superior General on 24th February 1971: 'I tried with the district council to get a plot for the convent and school. They gave all the hope and assurance to find a suitable plot for us. To buy the land the question does not arise at all. Here the government is ready to give the land free of cost for the purpose of education.'

Report written by the superior of the community in 1970 reads: 'The Mizos are interested in education. The villages are not connected by roads. The houses are built of wood with aluminum sheet roofs, as it is difficult to transport material. They are constructed on slopes or terrains and Sisters have to climb 181 steps from the road to the convent. The road too is like a ramp. The weather is quite cold. Sisters are really having a hard time on account of weather and scarcity of food stuffs.'

When Mary Mount was started, it was the only English medium school in the whole of Aizawl town. There were 300 students from K.G.I to Class VI. Sisters took turns to go to meet the people despite the non availability of conveyance. At times, the whole day was spent for visiting the people of those areas. People were friendly and wanted the Sisters to visit them often and pray with them. Whenever there was a chance to go to the villages, Sisters volunteered and stayed in the villages. Collection of old clothes was done once a year to instill in the students that they should share their goods with the have not's. As it is the custom of the place, children made a collection of money in case some member of their classmate's family expired, bought something worthwhile for the family in remembrance of the deceased member, conducted prayer in their houses with the help of the teachers and thus consoled the family members. House visiting was done according to the free time of the Sister's.

Mary Mount School has produced several doctors, engineers, nurses, Indian Administrative and Civil Service officers and politicians as well. The school at present has a total of 1675 students hailing from Aizawl town as well as the neighbouring villages. They are trained to be the future leaders of the society and the country. The school lays emphasis on value education. Inter house and Inter school competitions are conducted keeping in mind the core values of the Bethany Educational Society. Attention is paid to the all round development of the students to make them good citizens.

School assemblies are conducted with relevant themes in line with the BES core values. Orientation programmes are conducted for the staff. The school has an infrastructure consisting of 4 buildings built in 1980, 1986, 1995 and 2013 respectively with the financial aid from the Congregation, Province, government and partly from the parents. Sisters engage themselves in pastoral apostolate, family visits, organizing the children into some associations and any services the society calls for.

Due to the family visits and interaction with the parents of the students, the services of Bethany Sisters are appreciated by the people. Sisters also collaborate with the Montfort Brothers of St Gabriel by the services of two sisters in St Paul's Higher Secondary School. Br P. J. Abraham, Principal of St Paul's wrote to the Superior General of the Bethany Sisters on 21st June, 1976 'My superiors were so happy to hear about the coming of Sisters and they told that the school has a good future. Their coming will be of great help to the school in general and to our girls in particular. The Sisters are very cooperative, and they help us very much. They are contributing much for the upkeep of the good spirit among the religious families here. We are really privileged to have such understanding and helpful neighbours.'

Bethany convent, Sihphir started in the year 1991 is the third foundation of the Bethany Sisters in Mizoram. Here the Sisters assist in the administration of Holy Angel's Diocesan school and are engaged in Parish activities as well. On 26th November 1990 at the arrival of the Sisters, there were nearly 100 people gathered to admit their children to K.G.I and around 115 children were registered for the school.

The Sisters began their educational work with 4 classrooms. Financial problems, lack of transport, lack of knowledge of the local language were a few of the constraints experienced by the Sisters here. Later on, through constant family visits and conducting of awareness programmes in the villages, change was noticed in the attitude of the people towards the Sisters. People were happy with the education imparted to their children and they were a source of encouragement to the Sisters. The parents co-operated with the Sisters in the character formation of their children. Later on, a hostel was put up both for boys and girls and medical help was made available through mobile clinic by the Sister Nurse.

Several girls were housed and educated under the guidance of the Sisters. Rehabilitation centre provided good treatment for the drug addicts. A dispensary had been set up to extend healing and wholeness to many. People have been empowered in the villages and they are quite supportive in Sisters' mission. Empowerment through various apostolates like pastoral, social, medical, and educational has been carried on. The main apostolate being teaching in the school, Sisters give extra care to the weaker students by visiting their families. All the Sisters are actively involved in visiting the families and the sick and conducting instruction classes to the children. As a part of social work, the Sisters conduct awareness programmes, form Self-Help Groups and support groups, organize counseling sessions to the drug abusers etc. Medical apostolate seems to be a great help to the villagers as they hardly have any access to hospitals or dispensaries in their village.

Bethany Sisters started a school at Bazaar Veng, Mamit in 2003 and a simple wooden structure had been built for Sisters' residence.

A double-storeyed structure was built on the land at Ngharpet Veng, Mamit in 2006 to house the National Institute of Open Schooling (NIOS). In 2007, the office of the Bethany Social Service Society, drop-in-centre and health centre were shifted to this place. Meanwhile, the school had reached High school level and admissions were increasing. Hence the need was felt to shift the High school section to Ngharpet Veng. Two more floors were added to the existing building. On 25th March 2011, the community was bifurcated, and a second Bethany convent named St Theresa's Convent was inaugurated at this place. This building houses the convent, High school and NIOS.

Bethany Sisters in Assam

Fr John Martin CSC, the Parish Priest of Holy Cross Church, Silchar, wrote on 10th September 1962 to the Mother General: 'Two of your Sisters were sick, so they spent few days here in Silchar. I just want you to know how well they impressed me by their simplicity and prayerful spirit. I'm looking forward to the time when we also in Silchar will be blessed with their presence.' Thus, the second foundation of Bethany in the Northeast was at Silchar town. Though the Holy Cross Parish at Silchar was founded in the year 1957, the Fathers of Holy Cross began to reside at Silchar in 1947 and cater to the educational needs of the villagers around it.

In the late fifties, a residential mission school with Khasi as the medium of instruction was started by Fr John Martin CSC to provide education to the Khasi children. By and by, English was found necessary to help the Khasi village children to continue their studies in the neighbouring States where High school education was imparted in English. Realizing this need, in 1966 the Khasi medium school was switched over to English Medium. In the very same year, Mgr George Breen approached the then Superior General of Bethany, Mother Macrina, to send Sisters to this new mission. In response to his invitation, Bethany had its second foundation in Silchar in 1966.

On 11th June 1966, when Sr Sylvine, Sr Hariette and Sr Audrey were sent to Silchar to start a second house in the North East, they were welcomed by the flood refugees sheltered in the Church complex. The mission was started to impart education at the Holy Cross Diocesan School. The Sisters assisted in the day today administration of the school. Eventually when the Holy Cross foreign missionaries had to leave Silchar for good, they entrusted the school to Rt Rev Denzil D'Souza, Bishop of Silchar. The records of Holy Cross School indicate the school's good result and good discipline.

Sr Sylvine, the Superior General wrote in 1986 to Sr Jyoti, the then Principal of the school: 'Holy Cross School has a special place in my heart. I remember with joy all the happy years I spent with the students there. It is indeed a source of pleasure to see the progress and the accomplishments of this institution year after year. I congratulate the students who have walked out of the portals of this school for bringing much credit and glory to their Alma Mater. I am proud and happy to note that every year the academic results have been excellent. However, the progress of the school is not limited merely to excellence in academics. The school has provided opportunities to draw out the talents and abilities in every child and to bring out the best in them. The school can proudly boast of its democratic service to the pupils hailing from a variety of backgrounds and social strata, by developing in them a sense of brotherhood and personal integration.'

Under the patronage and chairmanship of late Bishop Denzil D'Souza followed by his successor Bishop Stephen Rotluanga as well as the co-operation and tenacity of the staff members and the Bethany Sisters, Holy Cross School, Silchar caters to the education of the less fortunate Khasi children and the children of those who work in the tea gardens. The school with a boarding attached to it, imparts value based and quality education to thousands of students. From teaching and administration of the school, gradually the Sisters moved out to the remote Khasi villages, to meet the needs of the tribals, who had neither education nor medical facilities.

The Girl's hostel at Silchar caters to the needs of Khasi village girls studying in Holy Cross English Medium School. Besides the school work, the Sisters were engaged in the village work too. Sisters are set apart for developmental works in the Khasi villages. Sisters spare no pains to master Bengali and Khasi languages. In 1982, Sisters ventured into Balia mission and their strenuous efforts to build up this mission by teaching and identifying with the people seems to bear fruit.

Sr Sylvine wrote to the superior on 25th February 1983 'Sr Marie Celine and Sr Assumpta Maria can be fully engaged in social work. They should not in any way be called for school work. Sr Marie Celine has great capacity for work as she is a nurse, full of zeal. She has keen interest in the poor. Then to one of the Nurse Sisters she wrote: 'Do not wait for the jeep. You can go on your own to the villages and spend a few days there with the Adivasi's. People will appreciate it and if they have nothing to give you, you may use food from the community.' The beginnings were not without difficulties. To start with, the Sisters often felt the pangs of hunger. Water for drinking was brought by bullock-carts from the Parish pond.

Constant floods have caused havoc at times. Sr Justina wrote to Mother General on 1st August 1985: 'The recent flood in Silchar has caused a disaster which brought a great loss to our school, hostel and convent. Our compound wall has been washed away during the floods.' The Sisters are engaged in various activities directed to the upliftment of the poor in and around Silchar. Weaving and tailoring classes are conducted by the Sisters for the benefit of a good number of girls. Holy Family Convent, Silchar served as the first Regional, Provincial and transit house for about 25 years. At present the Sisters manage a full- fledged Diocesan Higher Secondary school, a dispensary and do house visiting in the areas.

The community report of Silchar on 19th April 1984 states: 'We have about 100 tribal children whom Sisters love and give extra coaching to bring them to the standard of the other children. Due to the continuous efforts of the Sisters, the children can continue their studies with ease.

Sr Maria works among the Rongmei and Chorei tribes. Sr Ottilia works for the Khasi tribals and their work is much appreciated by the people. Other Sisters too accompany them during the holidays. Sr Malati's work in the hospital has been appreciated by the doctors and patients. Her selfless services, prayer for healing in the hospital has witness value too. Children are given free accommodation in our hostel. Besides, from time to time help is given according to the means of the community. Most of the people are very poor and do not attend our school. We need to take steps to include them in our circles.'

The Sisters travelling from Nagaland and Manipur to Silchar or Guwahati and vice versa often spent time at the railway station at Lumding as they waited for their connecting trains. The gap between train timings was long and during one such wait, some Sisters befriended an Assamese Catholic gentleman namely Mr. Baruah, an Anglo-Indian male nurse employed in the railway hospital. He was of the place and was instrumental in getting the Sisters to Lumding in Assam. On 10th January 1979, the first batch of Sisters arrived in Lumding. The opening of this convent served the educational needs of the people of the locality and it served as transit house for the Sisters travelling by train. At first the Sisters immersed themselves in the educational work and in no time, they started visiting the families after the school hours, praying for the sick, consoling the sorrowful and the disheartened.

As the school progressed and the mission got established, the Sisters wanted to do more for the rural women and girls. Hence a Vocational Training Centre named Jeevan Jyoti was opened in 1989 for the less privileged girls of the villages. It offers 18 months course in tailoring, weaving, embroidery, knitting, home-management and literacy to school dropouts. Every year at least 15 girls complete this Certificate Course. A hostel for girls was also opened in 1992. Apart from their engagements at the school, hostel, and the training centre, the Sisters reach out to villages around Lumding town. Whenever possible the surrounding villages inhabited by the Garos, Mizos, Nagas, Dimasas, Karbis etc. are visited.

On 1st August 1997, with the intention of starting the slum apostolate in Guwahati, Sr Edleburgh, the Provincial Superior and the would be pioneers namely Sr Assumpta Maria and Sr Sushmita went there. They were to start their work among the slum dwellers of Guwahati. On 8th August 1997, they began to stay in a house used as a store house. Whenever the Sisters could spare a little time, they visited the neighbouring families. The discovery of the city slums and the venue of their future apostolate brought them much joy. The newly renovated house was blessed on 31st October 1997 by the then Archbishop Thomas Menamparambil of Guwahati. Staying in this house, the pioneers catered to eight slums of Guwahati city which were registered under the Municipality. In December of the same year a third Sister joined the community. Her experience in various new missions as well as interest in gardening, preparing food for the Sisters was a great help.

In January 1998, the slum apostolate, and the literacy programme in Fatasil Harijan Colony in Guwahati were begun. About 50 to 60 students between 4-12 years regularly attended the literacy classes taught by the Sisters. They were provided with books, slates, and other necessary materials. Seeing many young girls with no useful employment, a sewing machine was purchased, and tailoring was taught. On 7th September 1998, Slum Literacy Programme for ten slums of Guwahati city was officially launched. The project was sponsored by 'Andheri Hilfe.' Each year about 700 students were getting the benefits of literacy from this project. Every year the children between the age of 4 to 7 years were admitted to the local formal vernacular medium schools. The children above 7 years were taught to read and write, up to class IV syllabus and regular classes were held in all the subjects. Two supervisors were appointed for this work and the project was carried on for three years.

The year 2000 saw the launching of Health and Hygiene programmes and Self-Help Groups. On the social work front, a new project-tailoring for the women of Self-Help Group was started in 2003. In 2007, four workshops were conducted on Right to Information Act in collaboration with Legal Cell for Human Rights, Guwahati where 150 adults participated. In order to focus on youth, especially girls, the first Community College of the Province was opened in 2008. The classrooms of the existing school were used for the purpose initially. 26 girls were admitted in the first batch, out of which 12 were regular. Their curriculum included Life Skills, Work skills, Dressmaking and Computer education. Prison ministry was introduced from late 2007. Once a fortnight, Sisters especially the social work personnel visit the central jail along with the Prison Ministry of India team. They conduct recreational and educational programmes for the inmates.

On 28th January 2000, Bethany Convent School was opened with 16 students in K.G. and the school has reached up to class X. The new Provincial House at Gorchuk was inaugurated on the 25th March 2004 where the sick, the young and the old Sisters are cared for. Being the Provincial House, Bethany Sisters working in other States of the Region go there for medical treatment. The Sisters visit families and guide the youth and children.

Bethany Convent, Nalbari was inaugurated on 2nd March 2009, which was an extension service of the Gorchuk Bethany Community. Their immediate task was to teach in the newly founded St Mary's School at Panigaon. On 23rd December 2010, the community kept up the 50th Death Anniversary of Mgr RFC Mascarenhas and distributed blankets to ten poor families to mark this auspicious occasion. Rt Rev John Moolachira, Archbishop of Guwahati writes 'The institutions and centres where the Bethany Sisters work seem to have contributed for the educational, pastoral, social growth and development of many people. Sisters have also taken up ministries to reach out to the abandoned and the lonely. They carry on rehabilitation of Alcoholics, care of HIV/AIDS victims, prisoners and drug addicts which has been an expression of the Sisters to make the compassion of Jesus a reality in the world of today. The members of the Congregation have proved their generosity in the mission field and social upliftment programmes in remote areas.'[44]

The Mission of the Bethany Sisters in Nagaland

As a response to the invitation of Bishop Hubert Rosario of Dibrugarh in August 1967, Mother Macrina, the then Superior General of Bethany paid a visit to Kohima in October 1968. The next year saw the opening of two convents at Dimapur and Kohima. Understanding all the implications and commitments of the ministry that the Sisters were to shoulder in a place of various ethnic and cultural groups, the Sisters responded to the call in order to offer their service to the people of this sector. The ardent invitation of Most Rev Hubert D'Rosario, Bishop of Dibrugarh, met with an equally fervent response from the Superior General who sent a batch of four young and energetic Sisters, Sr Doreen - the Superior, Sr Lolitta, Sr Lenice and Sr Gleva. Sr Doreen writes to Superior General on the 24th February 1969: 'We live in one of the rooms of the school without sufficient things. We are so happy here in the missions.'

As the apostolate of education is one of the prime apostolate of the Congregation and in fact a way of sharing in the mission of the Church, the first group of Sisters were to undertake the day-to- day administration of the academic activities of Holy Cross School, Dimapur. This school had about 150 students in 5 classes in 1969 and today this school is catering to about 2000 students of the State. It has grown in strength and merit and is a boon to the Nagas as well as to the migrants of Dimapur. On 8th May 1970 Fr P. C. Mani of Dimapur wrote to Superior General: 'The Vicar General, Administrator of the Diocese as well as the Archbishop Hubert Rosario were very pleased with the progress of the school and the way the Sisters manage the school.' The Sisters have also undertaken the day- to- day administration of Christ school. The crowd of kids who flock to this school are themselves a proof of the people's appreciation of the Sisters who dedicate themselves to the care of the children.

Report of the village work at Holy Cross Convent, Dimapur on 1st November 1984 stated: 'The people are very happy for the time we spend with them. Our visit to 4th mile made us to understand that some of the families are completely abandoned. Mrs. Vincent Lotha comes with us whenever she is free to visit the families and helps us to instruct them. The healing ministry is improving, and they do realize that the human power alone is not enough, but the divine power is necessary in life. Some non - Catholics ask us to pray for them and visit the Church in order to have a happy life.

The Sisters render great service to the poor by medical help, by visiting and listening to their problems. Sisters are engaged in teaching and they take special interest in the weaker students by teaching and helping them in their studies. Sisters spend some time every day helping the boarders in their studies and giving them moral instruction on Sundays. The poor from villages and towns are given medical care and lots of marriage problems are settled. Mother and Child Health programme is undertaken to help 100 poor families of the locality.'

Christ King Convent, Kohima was started on 21st January 1969. Sr Loyola, the Superior wrote to Mother General on 25th September 1969: 'We have Evening school for grownup girls from 4.30 to 6.30 p.m. We had many trials and difficulties during the past few weeks. The need for more Sisters is so great which can be understood only by seeing the situation. It is extremely hard to work in the missions and many of the institutions are facing the trials. This is a fast-developing town and hence we want good teachers who can talk English correctly.'

One Sister, being a Nurse was engaged in medical care of the people, while the other three taught in the newly opened Primary School. A classroom served as a dispensary. The few hours after school and weekends were spent in the villages of Nerema, Merema, Lazami, Tseminyiu and Khonoma giving medical care and instructing the villagers on hygiene. Thus, besides education, a lot of importance was given to pastoral care and the impact the work of the Sisters had on the people can be gathered from the memories people share about them.

Half yearly report of Christ King community at Kohima in December 1983 states: 'Free education is given to poor students. Extra coaching is given to poorer and weaker students after class. The value of personal cleanliness has been stressed much in the school. The Sister's visit the student's houses regularly and the parents are informed about the progress of their wards. The house maids are taught to read and write in English. Our students are from the villages, the average number of students in each class is 65 and it is difficult to give special attention during the class hours. They do not have enough facilities to study in their houses.' Mr. Philip Suosahie, one of the first Angami Catholic and a retired Catechist stated: 'I was associated with the Bethany Sisters from the beginning. In the school they taught Catechism besides other subjects. After school they visited families which made people feel familiar with them.'[45]

The personal touch and care of the Sisters seem to have borne fruit as it is evident in the number of past pupils occupying key positions in administration today. Ms Margaret Pienyu, Deputy Director of State Horticulture Nursery, Dimapur claims that the daily Mass and Catechism classes had a great impact on her life and made her what she is today. She recalls those Marathi and Hindi dances taught by the Sisters for the Parents' Day and the school functions when they would get dressed up in sarees, ankle bells and wear lots of makeup.

Ms Azenuo Concepta, recalls the early morning marches to the Church with folded hands, the trip to the pond for a session on dental care with a piece of charcoal in hand, the devotional singing and the lessons in reading and discipline. Dr Kiyasetuo Stephen appreciates the right mix of kindness and discipline practiced by the pioneering Sisters of Kohima, namely Sr Loyola, Sr Jolinta, Sr Conelly and Sr Delia. Speaking about the medical apostolate of the Sisters, he writes that the Sisters took the help of the students in visiting families to treat patients because the children had learnt to communicate in English and thus could act as interpreters.

In 1971, a hostel for girls was opened and two Sisters started teaching in Don Bosco High School run by the Salesian Fathers. The hostel renders invaluable service by offering a home to children from far flung villages who study in Christ King and Don Bosco Higher Secondary Schools. Half yearly report of Christ King Convent, Kohima reads 'Various competitions are held to help the children to develop their hidden talents. During holidays all the Sisters go to visit the far away villages. They teach health and hygiene through slides and pictures. Once a month they visit the Civil Hospital and pray over the sick. Each child is given special attention in his/her studies.' The mission that started with a handful of students has grown and now the stress is on education along with hostel ministry and pastoral work. A lot of time is spent on training the girls of the hostel in various activities.

The mission centre at Viswema was managed by the Jesuits of Karnataka Province. In 1977 when the Bethany sisters set out to collaborate in this mission, Fr Stanley Coelho S.J. was in charge of this mission. After the survey of the area the Sisters realized that the urgent health problems of the people can be solved by a well planned net work of mobile health care system. The transport facilities were limited, and villagers usually cultivated things for themselves. The letter written by Fr A. D'Silva to the Superior General on 22nd November 1976 states: 'The people are very eager to see the school run by Sisters. We get wonderful co-operation from the villagers of Viswema and they wanted to offer their land free. They have done up the road by themselves to facilitate transport to the school.' The sisters began classes on 12th February 1977.

Rt Rev T. Resto SDB, the Bishop of Kohima Diocese wrote to Mother Macrina on 31st January 1969: 'From what I can see, your good Sisters seem to be quite happy and full of enthusiasm. But they must put up with the cold of Viswema. Right from the start they have endeared themselves to the local people and this is a great thing for them and the local people'. The Sisters' reached out to other villages especially on weekends when they could free themselves from school work. On Sundays, each Sister took up Church service in one village or the other since Mass could not be celebrated in every village due to lack of Priests. Along with Bible and prayer book, they also carried a few medicines and catered to the needs of the sick in the villages.

When the Sisters arrived at Viswema in Nagaland St Joseph's school started in 1974 had reached up to class 2 with 89 students on the roll. By 1986 it had reached up to class 8 with 450 students. In 2009, the school was upgraded to Higher Secondary level in Arts stream with 66 students in the first batch. From 1986, young girls from different States of the Northeast admitted to the Bethany Congregation were accommodated here to continue their High school education. From the beginning education was given great importance in Viswema along with co-curricular activities. As early as in 1978, students were taken on excursions to other towns of the State like Dimapur. In later years, trips were arranged to places outside the State and beyond the boundaries of the Region.

Closely attached to the school is the hostel which was started to accommodate the children of Viswema itself. In 1977, there were 13 girls and as the school grew and infrastructure improved, children from outside Viswema village were also admitted. At present there are girls from K.G.I to class XII and boys are admitted up to class 4. The average strength of the hostel is about a 100. Most of them are from the villages where there is no good English medium school or from the towns where busy parents have neither time nor the skill to care for their children, besides struggling to earn their daily bread.

The first batch of Sisters to Viswema, namely Sr Noeline, Sr Peace, Sr Ivan, and Sr A P Theresa were teachers, nurses, social workers all rolled into one. The Sisters started moving out to the villages with medicine in their little bags. It was with the power of medicine that the Sisters were able to enter the villages. Within a few months of their life at Viswema the Sisters felt the need to have a mobile medical unit. Organised medical work started on 29th October 1978. The Sisters extended the much-needed medical assistance to 8 villages of the Southern Angami area of Kohima district. They visited the villages on a regular basis and ministered to the sick. As time went by and the demands of their mission increased, the activities of the Sisters became more organized.

From early 1980s two Sisters were set aside for the socio-medical and pastoral work.

On 30th September 1980 Fr Stany Coelho SJ wrote to Sr Sylvine: 'I wanted to explain to you what we intend to do at Eden garden, Khuzama. Your Sisters have been helping me there as best as they could. I personally am of the opinion that in the long run this will be our best work as it is exclusively for the poor. It is a very promising experiment in rural education and if continued according to the plan over a period of five years, it is bound to produce good results. Nagaland government's department of education is keenly interested in this work of ours and has already recognized the non formal education centre. More and more people are now convinced that non- formal education is the only solution to the problem of educating the masses and unemployment, especially in Nagaland. What we need is a group of Sisters to work full time at this centre. Young and old can all find ample scope for their talents and zeal provided they come prepared for a novel experiment with its uncertainties, risks and possible failures.'

At the early stages, besides treating patients at the dispensary, the Sisters trained selected groups of villagers in health care and hygiene, animal husbandry, weaving and similar activities turning many of them as effective workers. Every weekend the socio-medical and pastoral work personnel extended similar services to one or two villages. The target group was always women and girls. Mother and Child Health programme was taken up with great momentum and school Health programmes were initiated. In the 1990s, sanitation drive was taken up and 70 toilets were constructed in Viswema and Kezoma villages. Dispensaries and weaving centres were constructed at Kezoma and Kidima villages and equipped with the necessary equipments. On the economic front, animal husbandry project was introduced about the same time.

The community report of Viswema on mission activities for the months of July to December 1984 reads: 'Sisters carry on their apostolic activities such as teaching and village visiting faithfully. A Nurse Sister is completely set apart for the work of healing ministry. People have faith in her medicine and so many are attracted towards our dispensary. She also visits the villages with her companion. School going Sisters regularly visit the villages on Thursdays and Sundays. Recently, five Sisters visited two faraway villages and spent three days in teaching singing, film-show, giving talks on health and hygiene.

There was very good response from the people. There is a lot of love and friendship, concern for each other and family consciousness among the boarders and helpers are taken good care of. Sports and games are given due importance in the school under the direction of a good physical educationist. Two Sisters regularly visit the women in two villages and guide them to follow Natural Family Planning (NFP) through periodical explanations. Mother and Child Health (MCH) is another programme carried on by the Sister Nurse in charge.'

The dispensary of the Sisters has become a boon not only to the people of Viswema but even to people across the State Border. Patients come from villages as far as Kaibi, Tadubi and Tungjoy in Manipur's Senapati District bordering the Southern Angami area where the Sisters work. Self Help Groups started in the year 2000 now function in Viswema, Mima and Mitelephe. They had been initiated into income generating activities like surf and candle making besides their traditional practice of animal rearing, handloom, and agriculture.

From 2001 Development Committee was formed in each village and regular meetings were conducted with them. Ways of networking with Government and local Non Governmental Organizations was tried out. Village health workers and members of the Self Help Groups were trained in reproductive health, HIV/AIDS, communicable diseases and herbal medicine. Women Development Programme supported by Caritas India was held in 5 villages of southern Angami area. There were 20 fully functional Self-Help Groups and members were given refresher courses, leadership training and exposure programmes. Education on National Rural Employment Guarantee Act (NREGA) was given to a few villagers.

Through these 58 years in the Northeast, the Sisters seem to have been able to contribute to the field of education, healthcare and social work. 'The Sisters have been doing pioneer work in the Northeast. The Diocese of Kohima was one of the first beneficiaries of the Congregation's apostolate in Northeast India. Many people have benefitted through the good work of the Bethany sisters. Thanks to the selfless, dedicated service rendered for the mission' writes Rt Rev James Thoppil, the Bishop of Kohima.[46]

Bethany Sisters in Tripura

In 1960s the need for the services of the Sisters was felt. Boarding houses both for boys and girls had to be started in 1961. It was at this time that Fr Roger Marcel requested the services of the Bethany Sisters to meet the needs of the Church in Tripura. The Bethany Sisters came to Tripura in 1968 at the invitation of the then Bishop Denzil D'Souza of Silchar and so they were the first religious women to come to work in this State. Today the Sisters serve in Holy Cross Schools at Agartala, Depacherra, Dharmanagar, Kattalcherra and Bethany Convent School, Khayerpur. In each of these centres they are also involved in multi-dimensional apostolates like health care, formal and non-formal education, and women empowerment.[47] Every community had set apart two Sisters for socio-medical work coupled with pastoral work.

The first women religious to enter Tripura were the Bethany Sisters who came to Mariamnager near Agartala, Tripura on 27th July 1968. Sr Eva, Sr Clementia, Sr Maria, and Sr Claudia were the first group of Sisters to arrive in Mariamnagar. Their home was named as Shantir Rani Convent. Their main task was with the boarders who were children from interior villages of Tripura. They also taught in the Bengali medium school of the Parish and other ministries like medical service, and developmental works. Mother Macrina, the then Superior General, accepted the invitation saying 'My Sisters are used to putting up with inconveniences and it does not matter much if little things are wanting. They are young and will know to improvise things to meet the situation.' The need in those years was education, health care, social empowerment and Bethany Sisters were the first to cater to those needs. There was only one mission centre and Sisters reached out to almost all the villages giving medical facilities and non-formal education from this centre.

It seems to have been a great challenge for the Sisters in the land of varied language, culture and lifestyle. They were able to capture the hearts of the people and students by their efforts to speak and teach in the Bengali language. One of the Sisters moved out to the villages for tailoring, social work and instruction on health and hygiene.

Holidays were opportune time for the Sisters to visit the far away villagers. At the onset of Bangladesh War in 1971, Sisters who were engrossed in educational apostolate were called upon to engage in healing apostolate. Having mastered the elements of Nursing, they rushed to the refugee camps and kindled hope in the hearts of thousands. Fr Roger Marcel CSC wrote to Mother Macrina on 28th July 1968: 'I would feel remiss if I did not convey to you the gratitude of our people as well as my own for having selected for our humble Church so fine a group of religious.'

Prof. Vincent Darlong, Vice Chancellor of Martin Luther University in Shillong writes, 'Personally, I have a very special emotional connection with the Bethany Sisters. The first Sisters I ever met in 1968 at Mariamnagar were the Bethany Sisters. They were 'angels' in physical body as explained to us by Fr Roger Marcel CSC just before their arrival at Mariamnagar. As a young boy in Class VII and VIII in 1969 and 1970, I was taught by these Sisters, particularly by Sr Eva and Sr Clementia. Those memories remain fresh in me. They contributed immensely to the foundations of my education and learning. I cannot thank them enough.'

Sr Claudia wrote to Mother General on 9th October 1971: 'Sisters were very busy visiting the camps giving medicines, distributing clothes etc during their school holidays. Some Sisters went to Kumarghat to help the Nurses there. There is lack of medicine. The Nurses from different places were coming and helping. Now all of them are gone back. No hope of anyone coming back. There is need to open a dispensary and appoint a permanent Sister Nurse.' Under the expertise of a Nurse Sister, medical apostolate was re-organized. The Nurse worked in collaboration with the Missionaries of Charity who were engaged in the same apostolate. People flocked at the Parish dispensary. A mobile unit was set in operation for extending medical facilities to the neighboring villages. But the communal riots of 1980 paralyzed all the works of the Sisters.

One of the Sisters, then stationed at Mariamnagar, who was a victim of the riots says, 'On 6th June 1980, there were communal riots between the people of the plains and the hill tribes. On 11th June at 3 pm a large number of young men came by trucks with loud shouts, sharpened knives, bamboos and surrounded the whole compound. From among them a few went ahead with their planned task and set the Parish house ablaze. Seeing the fire close by, we all escaped to the jungle thinking that our convent would be the next target. The whole night we remained in the jungle, helpless and in fear. The next day the Central Reserve Police Force came to our rescue.

We were taken to Holy Cross Convent at Durjoynagar where we stayed for three months till the situation calmed down.' However the mission came to an abrupt end in 1980 due to the communal riots that erupted in June resulting in the permanent closure of the convent. Though the past tribulation evoked fear and disappointment, but the work of the Sisters at Mariamnagar yielded a rich harvest in the persons of Sr Tresa Lagardo, Sr Malati and Sr Sumita who are the vocations that bloomed from that mission.

Fr Roger Marcel CSC of Holy Cross School Agartala wrote to Mother Macrina on 30th April 1970: 'Our proposition of starting an English medium school has brightened up quite a bit and the whole town is fired up with the idea. The response is good and I'm sure that we can make of this institution a living witness. People are very glad over the prospect of having a private English medium school and they are ready to pay whatever it will cost. The Director of education has been after us for years as he wants us to start an English medium school. As this project may still take a year or two, i.e. after the Silchar English medium school is put up on a better footing, he suggests that we help him with his own Central School in Agartala, until such a time as we wish to start our own school. He would provide for transportation to and from town, would give the standard salaries to the Sisters, etc. Education in Tripura is certainly worthy of our efforts.'

He further states 'The Sisters could do a tremendous amount of good, even among the staff of the school, beyond what they could do to the children in the manner of education. Mr. Chatterjee, the director, spoke of 100 children, from ages 3 to 5, whom he would like to admit to the Kindergarten of the said school. He also said that when you start your own school, I'll be behind your project, giving all my strength. He's extremely keen on getting some Sisters since the administration has been trying for years to put up an English medium school of all India standards without success. The Sisters would have to be all trained for Nursery classes. This question of training is extremely important as the school in question is a Central school, formally approved by New Delhi, where wards of officers will come and therefore standards as regards qualifications have to be met.'

In 1970, at the request of Fr Marcel who started the Holy Cross English Medium School, Sisters from Mariamnagar community started teaching in this school situated in Abhoynagar. The Sisters would stay at Abhoynagar during the week and return to Mariamnagar at the weekend. In June 1974 Holy Cross community was established in Abhoynagar with Sr Audrey, Sr Alice D'Souza, Sr Berlinda, Sr Lucious and Sr Carol as members. In 1976 when the school was shifted from Abhoynagar to Durjoynagar, the residence of the Sisters too was shifted. The Sisters taught Catechism and needle work in the school. Later the Sisters studied language and took up teaching as their skill as the language improved.

Fr Roger Marcel wrote to Mother Macrina on 4th March 1971: 'I have only praise for the work of the Sisters, they have worked to the satisfaction, if not the amazement of everybody. By obtaining good results at teaching, their first task and through their whole style of life, the Sisters have contributed a great deal towards fostering better understanding and good will for the Church in this part of Northeast India.'

Kattalcherra village, in the Dhalai District of Tripura wherein the Bethany Convent is situated, has population belonging to different tribes. Though each village has a Bengali medium Primary school, the tribal's who are pushed to the background in this State, have a longing to send their children to English medium schools. With the united efforts of Rt Rev Denzil D'souza, Bishop of Silchar, Fr Mathew Vadakkedom CSC, the Provincial Superior of Holy Cross, Sr Sylvine, the Superior General of Bethany Congregation, Fr Hormis John CSC, the Parish Priest and Sr Canice, the Regional Superior, the long felt need of the tribals of Kattalcherra and nearby villages was met.

On 3rd July 1983, a community at Kattalcherra was erected. Sr Assumpta Maria, Sr Isabella and Sr Malati were the pioneers to this mission. The very next day of their arrival, Sisters took up a plan of action and conducted a socio-economic survey. Sisters were engaged in teaching and hostel apostolate. The school has progressed in leaps and bounds in these years under the management of the Holy Cross Fathers and the leadership of the Bethany Sisters. Two Sisters were set aside for social, medical, and pastoral work.

The Sisters started visiting the villages, forming the women's groups and Self Help Groups, working with the youth and developmental activities like tailoring, weaving, making of incense sticks etc. The Sisters were also involved in medical apostolate, attending to the sick and visiting the villages. Late Sr Irene Teresa strained herself to uplift the people from hunger and poverty by introducing saving scheme, animal husbandry, non formal education and sewing classes.

The Holy Cross Dispensary at Kattalcherra was established in 1984. The dispensary is managed by the Bethany Sisters and is one of the oldest dispensaries in the Diocese of Agartala. In its early stage, the Sisters had a very vast area to reach out with their medical assistance. The Sister Nurse from Kattalcherra with the help of health workers looked after the health needs of the people of Kumarghat, Ambassa and Kattalcherra. In the initial days of the dispensary, there were no other medical facilities available where people could confidently approach to get help for their ailments.

Hence the Holy Cross Dispensary was the only source of consolation for them. The objectives of the Dispensary were to impart knowledge on the preventive, promotive and curative aspects of health, to promote wholeness of health, to motivate the people to practice home remedies and herbal medicine. The Dispensary provides awareness programmes on health, healthy environment and ecology, training to the health workers to assist the villagers and provide first-aid to the people.

The medical care centre of the Bethany Sisters in Kattalcherra covers the area from Bagbassa to Ambassa for social work. It covers 20-25 villages for community health programs such as Immunization, Mother and Child Health care, health camps. Approximately 30-40 patients in each village are catered to. Community health awareness program in each village is undertaken in which 50 to 80 participants are actively involved. Medical treatment is given to each family of 30 villages without any disparity. Sisters pray over the sick and in the locality, 4 villages are provided with day and night medical service. Nutrition program, environment, hygiene program, ecology awareness, alternative system of medicine is taught, 6 herbal gardens in 6 villages are maintained.

Sisters work among the Reang and Garo tribals who are poor, underprivileged, landless people occupying government land and cultivating. 30 Panchayats consisting of 10-12 villages on an average are established. Every year one village is taken for intensive malaria control program and various activities are conducted. The Nurse Sister along with her health workers caters to almost thousand outpatients per year as well as patients from the village. Nearly 10 health camps with 500 participants are conducted every year. Since those who cannot afford to pay for the medicine come to these dispensaries, the Sisters find it difficult to maintain the same.

As the need was felt, Bethany Sisters started one more community in Depacherra, a very remote area in the South District of Tripura in 1988. Initially the Sisters came from Agartala and stayed every month for about 20 to 25 days at Amarpur and extended their services to the neighboring villages. They were engaged in treating patients, conducting immunization camps regularly and instructing people on health and hygiene. Weaker students who were attending Bengali medium schools were given coaching classes by the Sisters.

Adult education classes, teaching about the saving schemes, knitting, tailoring, and weaving, taking an economic survey of the area etc. were a few of the daily activities of the Sisters. Developmental works such as mass immunization programme, saving scheme were organized by the Sisters in collaboration with the Priests who were stationed there. Now the Sisters render their services, in three schools managed by the Holy Cross Fathers but the Sisters have boarding's and social development projects.

The Bethany Sisters started St Joseph's Health Centre at Depacherra, on 8th February 1988. The objectives were to be compassionate, kind and loving to the helpless and needy people, to conduct health awareness programmes, to train community health workers and to form village community health centres. The Nurse Sister conducted a mobile clinic and incidental health teaching to individuals and groups in the families and in the villages. In the past years many health programmes have been conducted both at the centre and in the villages around.

Bethany's mission at Depacherra had been multi-dimensional. While two or three Sisters teach in the Parish school, a Nurse Sister and a social worker attend to the socio-medical and pastoral aspect of the mission which includes varied activities. The Sisters in this field were always on the move, touring the villages to give medical aid, instructions, and conducting seminars. They had built up credibility with the government officials, security personnel and even doctors. That is why the Chief Medical Officer of the District Hospital would provide free medicine to be distributed by the Sisters. Doctors volunteered to give free service in the dispensary and in the villages. The BDO was ever ready to be of help and went out of his way to assist the good works undertaken by the Sisters in the villages of Depacherra. Such was the concern of the officers and they were willing to support a good work when they saw it being done with a good intention.

The Sisters worked in collaboration with the Government as well as Non-governmental Organizations. Every year they conducted training programmes for the health workers, seminars for youth, women, and leaders of the villages. They also made time to to give coaching to school dropouts to continue their education through National Institute of Open Schooling.

On 28th April 1992, a rehabilitation camp for the handicapped was held as part of a government project called Community Approaches to Handicap Development. Under this project, four persons were trained and appointed mainly to identify different types of handicaps. A survey conducted under this programme identified 120 cases of total disability and they were given treatment and taught to rehabilitate themselves in their own villages. The presence of the Sisters seems to have a positive impact on the life of students, parents, and people in general. The Sisters also look after the girls' hostel. In a span of two and a half decades, Depacherra village has offered three girls to work as Bethany Sisters.

It was in June 1986, in response to the request of the Parish Priest of Mariamnagar, Sr Sylvine sent a Sister for a diploma in Grihini Training and a Nurse to continue the medical and developmental works in the villages of South Tripura. They started Nirmala Vocational Training Centre on 10th February 1991. It provides skill training in weaving, tailoring, embroidery and knitting to dropouts and illiterate girls are taught to read and write. Literacy programme for trainees, preparing herbal medicine and food preservation skills, like pickle and juice making are the other activities done to empower women.

In the year 1999 a fourth community of the Sisters was started in Dharmanagar in North Tripura. Sr Gretta D'souza, Sr Janet Mendonca and Sr Shylaja were the pioneering members of this community who mainly worked in the school. The Sisters continue to work hard to give all round development to the students. People seem to be happy with the services and the value-based education as they co-operate well with the administration and support it. On 21st January 2009, a hostel for girls was opened with 13 girls. At present the number has reached to 46. The material, spiritual and emotional needs of the boarders are well taken care of. Through the government stipend provided to tribal children, the hostellers are able to pursue their education without much financial burden on their parents.

During the subsequent years, the school building at Dharmanagar was put up. The works begun by the pioneering Sisters have been carried on, with a few additions made. Local people participate in the celebrations of the school. Despite the challenges, the Sisters have survived the floods, storms and all the hurdles placed on their way. The mission seems to be moving from strength to strength. The local people, the youth, members of the Lion's Club and parents were instrumental in protecting the Sisters when on the 24th October 1999 the miscreants made an attempt to burn the small thatched building which was the residence of the Sisters.

In 2012 when Bethany Sisters in Northeast India celebrated the Golden Jubilee of their first arrival to the Region, they thought to start an educational institution of their own administration. After a gap of thirty years, a new convent was constructed in Khayerpur. Sr Noeline, the then Provincial superior and her team in 2009 under the direction of Bishop Lumen Monteiro - the Bishop of Agartala, purchased a plot of land at East Champamura, Old Agartala for the purpose of starting an English medium School. The new convent at Khayerpur in Agartala was inaugurated on 9th January 2012. The initial work was done and supervised by the Superior of Holy Cross Convent Agartala and her Community members. Sr Assumpta Maria played a vital role in the construction of the boundary wall and building work in spite of all the hurdles. When the campus was getting ready for starting the mission, Sr Noeline the Provincial Superior sent Srs Eva, Harsha and Jessyna to take admission for the academic session 2012.

A Community of three sisters was canonically erected on 9th January 2012, to cater to the needs of the School and the locality. Sr Eva was the first Superior and Headmistress along with Sr Shalini Mary and Sr Charilin. 25th January 2012, Wednesday was a Red-letter day in the annals of Bethany Sisters as the inauguration of Bethany School, East Champamura, Khayerpur, took place with 47 newly admitted children of Nursery and K.G.I. The parents were supportive to this institution. The School has reached up to class VIII and is making steady progress. The presence of Sisters is well appreciated in this area. In addition to attending the pastoral needs of the parish, they render service in the neighborhood by coaching students who attend Bengali Medium schools, Spoken English classes for the youth and purposeful family visits.

Stephen Rotluanga, the Bishop of Aizawl opines that 'We are privileged and indebted to Sisters for quality education, health, social and pastoral ministries. We are grateful for their exemplary and faithful commitment, dedication, selfless sacrifices and for many local vocations to strengthen the local Church. Just a handful of Sisters set foot in Northeast mission in 1962 and today they are grown into a Province. Their membership too has grown and it is a matter of great pride to note that they have promoted local vocations.'[48]

Mission in Manipur

Rt Rev Abraham Alangimattathil, Bishop of Kohima-Imphal Diocese was on the lookout for a religious Congregation to take care of the Thanlon mission, in Manipur's Churachandpur District. Though the Bishop asked Bethany Sisters to take up, the Congregation was not keen due to its extreme isolation. As Bethany had agreed to open a house in Viswema, the Superior General sent the Sisters to Thanlon in Manipur. The beginning was difficult and it took a considerable time for the Sisters to adjust to the new environment, the people and the culture.[49]

A girls boarding was opened in February 1987. Sisters spent time after the school hours in visiting families. They put their best efforts in teaching which was well appreciated. To help the less privileged children who had no option but to continue their higher studies in the local government school, the school was upgraded to High School in 1989. The ethnic conflict between the Kuki and Paite tribes in July 1997 led to showers of bullets on the convent on 16th July 1997. This tension continued for months together and the school could not be reopened even by the beginning of January 1998. Finally, the Sisters officially left Thanlon on 15th April 1998. In their 20 years of existence in Thanlon, Bethany Sisters were blessed with two vocations from the place.

Bethany Convent, Canchipur in Imphal, Bethany's second house in Manipur was opened on 23rd January 1989 with Sr Justinian, Sr Peter, and Sr Anna as the pioneers. The Sisters lived in the classrooms and continued to do so with some modification and additions till a new convent was constructed in recent years. Their main work is teaching in the school. People of the place opine that if not for the Sisters, the school would not have flourished.

When Fr Mathew Manianchira- the Principal of the school was murdered in 1990 by an underground faction, the Sisters manifested their courage and carried on the administration of the school. Apart from schoolwork the Sisters visited houses and prayed with the families.

Demands for money and threats from the various groups of insurgents continue to disturb the Sisters. The convent also serves as a sort of transit house for Candidates from different districts of the State. A good number of girls from Manipur have joined Bethany to carry on the mission work.

'The Bethany Sisters have seen the growth and development of the people in Northeast India. The Congregation has contributed its share in this growth and development of the Region. The Sisters are approachable, cordial, hospitable, accommodative, missionary minded and people friendly. I am particularly grateful to the Sisters who have supported, encouraged and helped me to grow as a Priest in the first years of my priestly pastoral ministry. I must acknowledge that the Congregation stood by us in the most trying circumstances in the history of the Archdiocese-the assassination of Fr Mathew Manianchira, the then Principal of Catholic school, Canchipur as well as the fatal shooting and wounding of Fr Tomy Manjaly, ethnic conflicts, student unrest in Catholic school, Canchipur etc…' says Rt Rev Dominic Lumon, Archbishop of Imphal.[50]

Bethany Sisters in Meghalaya

Shillong was inaccessible to Bethany Sisters despite persistent efforts to set foot into this city and avail the opportunities to educate the young Sisters especially from the Northeast. On 16th July 2002, forty years after Bethany Sisters had set foot in Northeast India, they were privileged to have a house at Nongrimbah in Shillong. This house serves as study cum transit house for the Sisters of the Province. The Sisters started to involve themselves in the life of the people by meeting them in their families, attending funeral rites and taking initiative in praying at the deathbed of the dying in the locality. Regular family visits on Sundays brought them closer to people.

One of the apostolates after learning the need of the people of the locality was to reach out to the children with single parents. Therefore, a project of helping children from K.G to class X was launched with the generous help of Swedish Organization for Individual Relief (SOIR). The project provided the children with monthly school fees, books and uniforms, gifts on occasions like Christmas, sports items etc. Remedial classes for slow learners helped the children to measure up to their counterparts in different schools.[51] The Sisters built rapport with their neighbors and the people felt at home with the involvement of the Sisters in the pastoral activities. Sisters avail themselves for any service as and when required.[52]

The pioneering group of Sisters, namely Sr Therese Simon, Sr Marina, Sr Tresa Martis, Sr Mable and Sr Charilin entered Jongksha in Meghalaya on 2nd February 2004. The community had a Nurse for the dispensary, two Sisters for pastoral work which included touring the villages and two Sisters to teach in the school that had classes up to Higher Secondary. The patients began to drop in for treatment. The Nurse Sister not only treats the patients but also takes classes for the people of the village on health and hygiene. They have formed Self Help Groups in the village.[53] Quality education is imparted with the cooperation of the Holy Cross Fathers. Academic performance of the students over the years has been progressive with good results. Discipline, character formation, all round development and awareness of social concerns are emphasized with much effort applying many tips and measures by the Sisters.

Assemblies are conducted on value-based themes. Prayer experiences are given for the school children through retreats. In-service training for teachers is provided every year to improve the quality of teaching. The women, men, youth and teenagers' associations are guided and supported by the Sisters through mentoring and spiritual guidance. Thus, the families especially the children and youth are helped to form right values and good character. Irregular marriages are rectified and relationships outside the wedlock are on the decrease. There is decrease in the dropouts among the students. Most of them complete their Higher Secondary education, pursue higher education, find jobs and a decent living.[54] Overall the Sisters have built good rapport with people. People render support, cooperation and encourage the Sisters through their appreciation for the services rendered to them.

When the Bethany Sisters took up the hostel ministry there were 35 girls from classes V to XII. Gradually the number in the hostel increased. In 2010, there were 69 girls, and a warden assisted the Sister in charge of the hostel. Sisters spend 20 days in a month visiting 22 villages and are closely in touch with the people. They attend funerals, visit families, visit the sick in their homes and hospitals and pray with families in their special needs. The Sisters have made efforts to learn the local language, the culture and the customs of the people and adapted themselves to the climatic conditions. Apart from instructing, they are helped by giving time to listen to their woes and worries and given counseling when required. Sisters have motivated the parents of boys and girls of the village who did not attend school and were engaged in grazing the cows - for evening literacy classes supported by 'World Vision.' At present the Sisters help about 60 weaker students who do not have the facility for learning in their homes, by taking classes in the evenings regularly.

Though the Bethany Sisters began their work quite recently in Meghalaya, its quite encouraging to see the number of girls who have joined the Congregation to carry forward the work begun by the pioneers. Bethany Congregation has 13 Sisters from Meghalaya in a period of 18 years of work in that State.

Bethany Sisters in Arunachal Pradesh

By 2008, Bethany had established houses in six of the seven Northeastern States and was waiting for an opportunity to serve the people of Arunachal Pradesh. Rt Rev George Palliparambil, the Bishop of Miao Diocese offered an invitation to the Bethany Sisters to work at Namsai in the Diocesan school and the Parish. A thatched mud house and a hostel for girls was offered by the Parish to the Sisters. The school was not getting sufficient students, but the admissions increased when the news spread that Sisters were going to teach in the School.

On 1st June 2009, the school reopened with 54 students in K.G and class I and Sr Christine and Sr Sunitha Jyoti were the pioneers to this mission. Sisters opened a girls' hostel with 13 girls from the neighbouring villages. Thus the 30th Bethany Community in Northeast Province and the first Bethany Convent in Arunachal Pradesh was officially established on 15th July 2011. The main apostolate the Sisters are engaged in are teaching and hostel management along with the pastoral ministry. Sisters have built up good rapport with the parents and the neighborhood community.

In 2012 Rt Rev George Palliparambil, the Bishop of Miao Diocese requested the then Superior General Sr Wilberta to take up the mission of establishing a Degree College in Manmow, Namsai in Arunachal. This opportunity was willingly consented by the Congregation for establishing a unique mission of catering to the youth of Eastern Arunachal.

The vision was soon made possible as Mr C K Manpoong – the ex MLA of Namsai, brought to the notice of the Bishop about the availability of land at Manmow. Making use of this opportunity Bishop George consented to take up this offer on certain conditions. The Bethany Congregation took up this challenge through the Northeast Province. Sr Noeline, the then Provincial Superior looked into further details of taking up the cause of Higher Education in this place. To verify the viability of the mission, the Provincial Superior along with her Councilors undertook many visits to Namsai which was quite remote at that time.

On 13th August 2012, the initial procedure of obtaining the No Objection Certificate (NOC) from the Government of Arunachal to open Venerable Uktara Bethany College (VUBC) as well as Land Possession Certificate (LPC) for 15 acres of land from Mr C K Manpoong began. NOC was granted on 16th October 2012 and the Land Possession Certificate was obtained on 18th February 2013. On 27th March 2013, the

Foundation Stone was laid for VU Bethany College by Bishop George Palliparambil. On the same day, the Convent building which was still under construction was also blessed. The first community was erected on 29th June 2014 with Sr Noeline the first Superior and Sr Teresa Martis, Sr Janet Sylvia and Sr Sukhi Therese as the members.

The College runs a ladies hostel since the inception of the College to provide higher education for ladies from far flung villages. In 2016 a hostel for the College boys was also opened. On 16th July 2014, the new venture was actualized with the inauguration of the Academic Session by Mr Ravi Jha, ADC Namsai with the First batch of 54 B.A. and B. Com Students. The official inauguration of VU Bethany College was held on 2nd August 2014. Shree Nabam Tuki, Chief Minister, Arunachal Pradesh was the Chief Guest. Thus, the farthest mission in the Northeast stands synonymous to Mgr RFC Mascarenhas's vision and life – He took the road less travelled. Indeed, that has made a great difference!

Mission in West Bengal

As direct trains from South India and the Northeast were not available, Sisters working in North East India had to pass through Calcutta and halt there to get their train reservations. Sisters were often stranded at Howrah railway station for several days. They spent time at the railway station or sought accommodation in some convent far away. So, the convent in Calcutta at the Cathedral campus was opened on 27th May 1980. Over the years the convent has become a home away from home for many Sisters passing through Kolkata city and in need of a place to rest. The Sisters offer the hospitality of the original Bethany home of the Gospel through their services.

In the beginning, the Sisters joined to pray with the people while visiting the houses which helped them to discover the plight of the working girls in Kolkata. To improve their condition, Sisters started adult education and sewing classes, but they were on the lookout for a more lasting form of involvement in other fields as well. At the request of Archbishop Henry D'Souza of Calcutta, since 1987 the Sisters are involved in Diocesan schools' administration, supervision and teaching in Loyola school at Kidderpore. In 1988, evening classes for school going students were started and conducted regularly. In 1989 the educational ministry was extended to St Berchman's School, Moulali as well.

Literacy classes for the street children and slum children were also initiated and later organized in 1992 with the acquisition of two classrooms for about 100 children. Students were prepared to get admission for classes I-IV in formal schools by way of awarding Promotion Certificates. In 1993 Sisters gave up teaching in St Berchman's School, Moulali and extended their services to St Aloysius Orphanage and Day School, Howrah where they oversee Primary and Secondary sections, teach, and help in the administration of the school as well. They take active part in conducting assemblies and looking after the discipline. In the 1990s Sisters took up the work of sponsorship for over 90 poor students which was a great help for the children from the lower economic strata.

Individual Health Care (IHC) for elderly was started in 1989. The Sisters give religious instruction to people of different age groups. Thus the institutions of the Bethany Sisters in the major cities like Silchar, Calcutta, Aizawl, Agartala and Dimapur have always been places of welcome to all missionaries and serve as a base and support in transit, for business and contact with government departments. As the number of institutions grew, this service also demanded greater sacrifices on the part of those inmates stationed in the transit houses.

At the invitation of Rt Rev Henry D' Souza, the then Archbishop of Calcutta Diocese, Sr Edleburgh, Mother Justina, Sr Titus, Sr Sandhya, Sr Shwetha, Sr Claudius the first batch of Bethany Sisters reached Chittaranjan in June 1990. They took over the administration and management of St Joseph's Convent High School as well as St Joseph's Hindi Primary School. The Sisters tried to achieve high standards of moral, spiritual, and academic distinction. Much care was taken to keep up quality in all spheres. All round development, value-based education, development of personality, computer education and leadership training were given prime importance.

The institution kept growing in number and merit. All through the years, Chittaranjan Locomotive Works administration saw that every facility was provided within their limits for the education of their wards. In 1998, they began construction of another building to accommodate the growing number of students. To keep the school abreast and to benefit from the latest technology, Smart Class e-learning was introduced in 2009. Computer literacy was introduced from class I.

St Joseph's Hindi School saw remarkable progress. Education is imparted to all types of children who speak 17 different languages with a mixed group of parents to deal with. They hailed from different parts of India as they are the employees of Central Railway Locomotive Engine Producing Company. A few of the lepers' children were attending the Hindi Primary School.[55] The Sisters visit the families of particularly students' and teachers' houses. They pray for them and with them on various occasions. The school has been extending non-formal education to the school dropouts and to the less privileged of the locality through evening school which is organized systematically. The Congregation is blessed with 4 Sisters from West Bengal. Sr Sashi Rosalia who joined the Bethany institute from this place in 1992 now serves in Africa, thereby partaking in the mission of Bethany across the seas.

On 7th June 1991, another community was formally established to run the Diocesan Meghmala Roy Education Centre at Behala and take it up to High School level. Sisters were free to go beyond the school and take up other activities, like tailoring centre, spoken English classes etc. for the upliftment of the poorer sections of the society. Though teaching remains the chief work of the Sisters in Behala, fee concessions and attention to the economically weaker students featured on a priority list where about 10% of the income is spent on them. The quality of education was applauded by an officer of the State Education Department in these words, 'We are never aware of such a good school in Behala! The Sisters are a real boon to the people of Behala who should be grateful to them and cooperate with them in the education of their children.'[56]

At Barasat, the Sisters intensified their friendly visits to the neighborhood and the villages with the purpose of reaching out through some form of ministry. They initiated the work of women –organization with the support of Panchayat Pradhan and ward members. They ventured in getting to know the unknown villages around their convent. They exercised courage and patience in initiating the socio-medical ministry at Barasat. The Sisters took up mobile health care services to 10 villages of Kadambagachi from 1999. Self Help Groups too were initiated in six villages, women animators were selected and trained. From 2005, skill training of women in tailoring and animal rearing was introduced to the women of the villages through Functional Vocational Training Forum, Bangalore. This helped the villagers whereby women came forward to utilize employment opportunities through six months' courses in tailoring. This training is continued by way of shifting the village-based training centre.

The impact has been in terms of women progressing towards a socially and economically just society. The increasing number of Self-Help Groups became a base for adopting more development initiatives in the form of education on socio-political issues, gender justice and skill training for women. The women empowerment activities were conducted in an all inclusive pattern by way of including the Panchayat personnel, local leaders and the men from the villages in the process of planning the change initiatives for the villagers.

The socio-medical endeavor of the community was given official identity as Bethany Janvikas Samiti in 2005. In 2006, 'Limerick Ireland Calcutta Calling Group' a voluntary group of donors from Limerick-Ireland came forward to support the developmental activities of the Sisters in the villages.[57] A few batches of Novices and Pre-novices too had their village exposure programme in these villages which has enhanced the effect on the mission of the Sisters. Spoken English classes for the youth and tailoring classes for girls of the neighbourhood were conducted. Beside productive gardening and other aspects of housekeeping, preparation and practice of home remedies among the members of some Self-Help Groups were introduced. Two Sisters are set apart for the village ministry. Over the years, the Sisters enjoy a cordial rapport with the neighbourhood and have made their presence felt in the society through their ministry of caring for the poor and the marginalized.[58]

On 31st May 2006, the community at Sulantu was erected although the admissions to Nursery started on 18th April and the classes were formally started on 8th May of the same year. When the school re-opened in June after the summer holidays the number of students in the school had increased so much that it became necessary to divide the students into two sections and so the hall was used as classroom. On 7th May 2007, school re-opened in the new building. The number of students in the school had reached to 183. On 3rd April 2008, the new academic session started with two sections in each class. The number of students in the school had reached up to 295. Besides school work, the Sisters at Sulantu are engaged in pastoral works like visiting families in the neighborhood.

Bethany Sisters in the Northeast work in several institutions owned by the institute but managed by the Northeast Province. There are educational institutions both formal and non formal, health centers as well as other centres where they render their service.

Educational Institutions of the Bethany Sisters in Northeast India

TABLE NO: 7

1.	Higher Secondary schools	1
2.	High Schools	4
3.	Primary and Higher Primary schools	3
4.	Kindergarten or Nursery schools	6
5.	Balwadies	4
6.	Non-Formal education centres	2
7.	National Open school	2
8.	Boardings and Orphanages	9
9.	Vocational Training Centres	2
10.	Community College	1
11.	Health centres	5
12.	De-addiction/rehabilitation Centres	2
13.	House for the aged	1
14.	Bethany Social Service Society of Northeast	1

Thus, there are 43 institutions in total managed by the Bethany Sisters in the Northeast. Beside these there are several Diocesan as well as other religious institutions in the Northeast where the Bethany Sisters collaborate and render their service.

Since 1962, the Bethany Congregation despite the upheavals, regularly supplied the missions in this Region with a considerable number of Sisters to enlarge the area of missionary work. This perhaps is no minor contribution and the wisdom and foresight of the administration and training personnel led them to select and train young girls from various parts of India to share the work and ensure the continuity of the developmental work started by them. Thus, there is not only a smooth transition from Sisters from Mangalore to vocations from the Northeast since 1984 onwards. A rapid expansion of various works because of the large number of girls joining the mission, working with the Sisters, learning their method of mission work and even more importantly their spirit of work, sacrifice and service is quite encouraging. The Bethany

Congregation itself and home communities became the support of the Sisters in many ways.

Endnotes

[1] Sr Jessy Rita B.S. *The Ripples: The Origin and Development of the Mangalore Province, The Congregation of the Sisters of the Little Flower of Bethany, Mangalore,* Bethany Publications, Mangalore, 2006, p. 10.

[2] Sr Mary Naulak B.S., *Leaven in the East, Sisters of the Little Flower of Bethany in Northeast India (1962-2012),* Blossom Books(P) Ltd. Guwahati, 2012, p. iv.

[3] Geo Payapilly and Mary Benedict, *Fullness of Life,* Bethany Publications, Mangalore, 2003, p. 32.

[4] *The Compassionate Pastor,* Vol.01, No.01, December 2008, Congregation of the Sisters of the Little Flower of Bethany, Bethany Generalate Publications, Mangalore, *A Magazine.*

[5] *Op.cit.*

[6] *Ibid.,* pp.33-34.

[7] *The Catholic Directory of India 2013, op cit* p.131.

[8] Lillis and Trecilla, 'A Champion of Education- Mgr. Raymond Mascarenhas' Bethany Educational Society- II Convention, Mangalore, Karnataka, November 2008, *A Paper.*

[9] Geo Payyapilly and Mary Benedict, *op.cit.,* pp. 85-87.

[10] *Letter* of Administrator Apostolic of Mangalore, Bishop of Calicut, dated 21st July 1927.

[11] Sr Jessy Rita, *op.cit.,* p.18.

[12] Sr Mary Naulak, *op.cit.,*p.v.

[13] Sr Violette D'Souza, *The Vine That He Planted,* Bethany Publications, Mangalore, Karnataka, 1989, p.148.

[14] *Handbook,* The Congregation of the Sisters of The Little Flower of Bethany, Mangalore, 1921-2010, Bethany Publications, Mangalore, pp. 7-8.

[15] Sr Jessy Rita, *op.cit.,* p.22.

[16] *Ibid.,* p.13.

[17] Geo Payyapilly and Mary Benedict.,*op.cit.,* pp. 76-78.

[18] Diamond Jubilee of Bethany Educational Society (R) Mangalore, 1948-2008, *A Souvenir, p.4.*

[19] Sr Violette D'Souza, *op.cit,* p.87.

[20] Education for fullness of life, second National convention, *Post convention Document 1,* BES vision and core values.

[21] Lillita, 'The Plight of the Girl Child and the Response of Bethany.' Bethany Educational Society II Convention, Mangalore, November, 2008, p.6, *A Paper.*

[22] Diamond Jubilee of Bethany Educational Society (R) Mangalore, *op.cit.,* p. 5.

[23] Golden Jubilee of the Northern Province of Bethany Sisters, *A Magazine.*

[24] Diamond Jottings published on the occasion of the Diamond Jubilee celebration of Bethany Educational Society, *A Magazine,* p.134

[25] Golden Jubilee *Souvenir, op cit* p.10

[26] New Testament in the Bible, *Luke 4:18.*

[27] *Op.cit.*

[28] Sr Violette D'Souza, *The Vine That He Planted, op.cit.,* p.112.

[29] Letter in the Archives of Bethany Congregation

[30] Golden Jubilee of the Bethany Sisters in the Northeast Province, *A Magazine, op cit.*

[31] *www.bethanymangalore.org*

[32] *Op.cit.*

[33] Golden Jubilee of Northern Province, *Magazine, op.cit.*

[34] The description of the various activities of the Bethany sisters has been taken from official reports by the congregation.

[35] Lazar.Jeyaseelan, *op cit.* p.101.

[36] Sr Violette D'Souza, *The vine that He planted, op.cit.,* p.112.

[37] Golden Jubilee of Northern Province, *Magazine, op.cit.*

[38] Golden Jubilee of North East Province, *Magazine,op.cit.* Ref: Golden Jubilee of the Bethany Sisters in the North east Province, A Magazine.

[39] Letter in the Bethany Archives at Mangalore.

[40] Sr Violette D'Souza, *The Vine that He Planted, op.cit.*

[41] Letter in the Bethany Archives, Mangalore.

[42] *Ibid.*

[43] Reports of Communities in Bethany Archives, Mangalore.

[44] Golden Jubilee of North East Province, A *Magazine, op.cit.*

[45] Sr Mary Naulak B.S., *op.cit.,* p. 43-44.

[46] Golden Jubilee of North East Province, A *Magazine, op.cit.*

[47] David R. Syiemlieh, (ed.) *Diocese of Agartala: op.cit.,* p.15.

[48] Golden Jubilee of Northeast Province, A *Magazine, op.cit.*

[49] Sr Mary Naulak B.S., *op.cit.,* p. 67-68.

[50] Golden Jubilee of the Northeast Province of the Bethany Sisters, *op.cit.*

[51] *Op.cit.,* p.162.

[32] *Ibid.,* p.163.

[53] *Ibid.,* p.183.

[54] *Ibid.,* p.186.

[55] *Op.cit.,* p. 117

[56] *Ibid.,* p. 125.

[57] *Ibid.,* pp.143-144.

[58] *Ibid.,* p. 145.

Chapter 5

Assessment of the Work
of the Bethany Sisters

Mgr RFC Mascarenhas was a dedicated Priest who served the poor and the marginalized selflessly till his death on 23rd December 1960. The members of the Institute founded by him are involved in the mission of formal and non-formal education, health care, social work, managing de-addiction centres and prevention of HIV/ AIDS. Some of the questions that arose during the research were how are the Sisters viewed by the beneficiaries of their service, by those who have not benefitted from them, by other denominations, by other congregational organizations or Sisters/Brothers groups. I have assessed these points through the questionnaires and analysed through pie charts and bar diagrams in this last chapter of the book.

From the study it is felt that as far as the knowledge of the missionary activities of the Bethany Sisters is concerned, their involvement with the people plays a crucial role in determining the impact that the Sisters have made on the people. The staff, parents and the public are a witness to the activities of the Sisters in the social, medical and the educational sector. They are appreciative of the missionary activities of the Catholic Missions and the work accomplished by the Bethany Sisters in the Northeast. An honest introspection of the missionary activities carried out over the years would help to be effective and to make genuine contribution towards the society.

This chapter presents an analysis of the data collected from different categories of respondents to address the different objectives set for this research. A few of the objectives of the study were already achieved through the technique of content analysis, the focus of data collection was to investigate the extent to which the Bethany Sisters operated in the Northeast, to study the challenges faced by them and to bring out the position of their mission enterprise in the postmodern world. With this purpose in mind, the data was collected using quantitative and qualitative techniques of questionnaires and interviews.

Data Analysis of the Questionnaires and Interviews

During the field visit I felt that there is significant knowledge among the people about the activities of the Catholic Missions and the Bethany Sisters. The level of understanding about the Catholic Missions and the Bethany Sisters is quite satisfactory. The public is knowledgeable about the work done by the Catholic Church in the field of education, medical, pastoral, and social sector. People in all the centres wherever I went to collect the data are aware of the presence and activities of the Catholic Missions and that of the Bethany Sisters.

Bethany Sisters' Contribution to Education

TABLE NO: 8

5.1. Responses from Staff, Parents of Students and the Past Pupils of the Schools: No. of Respondents: 105	YES	NO	CAN'T SAY
1. The educational institution of the Bethany Sisters is administered effectively and competently	97.14	0.95	1.90
2. The Sisters are role models for the staff and the students	83.81	13.33	2.86
3. Their mission of education has a vision, goal, common thrust and uniform policies	90.48	4.76	4.76
4. There is cooperation among the different educational institutions in our area	65.71	23.81	10.48

	Yes	No	Can't Say
5. Teachers appointed in the school are professionally qualified and competent	62.86	31.43	5.71
6. The school caters to the poor	76.19	17.14	6.67
7. The education imparted is value oriented	45.71	42.86	11.43
8. The Sisters in the school, work as a team	86.67	6.67	6.67
9. The Sisters manifest social commitment and concern for the poor	42.86	49.52	7.62
10. Education is seen as a service	60.95	32.38	6.67
11. The staff are paid just and fair wages	45.71	38.10	16.19
12. The Sisters maintain good relations with the people of the locality	77.14	15.24	7.62
13. The students who pass out of this school are value oriented	71.43	18.10	10.48
14. Poor and weak students are supported to cope with their studies	81.90	14.29	3.81
15. The Sisters have gained recognition and respect in the wider society through education	94.29	2.86	2.86
Average of 105	**70.29**	**22.67**	**7.05**

Figure 1

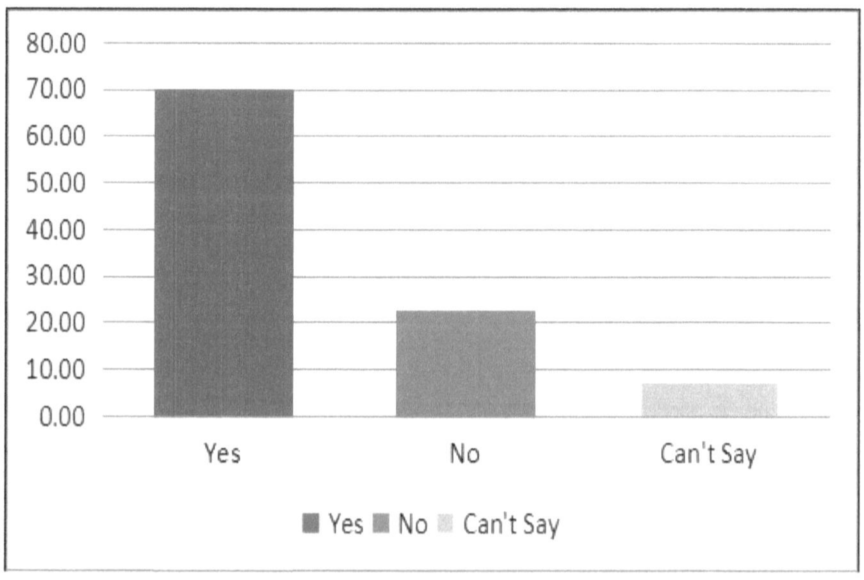

TABLE NO.9

Reponses from Priests and Sisters

No. of Respondents- 28

SI No	Yes %	No %	Can't Say %
1.	92.86	7.14	0.00
2.	70.37	25.93	3.70
3.	92.86	3.57	3.57
4.	64.29	17.86	17.86
5.	64.29	35.71	0.00
6.	46.43	46.43	7.14
7.	42.86	53.57	3.57
8.	71.43	25.00	3.57
9.	35.71	60.71	3.57
10.	17.86	75.00	7.14
11.	64.29	32.14	3.57
12.	88.89	3.70	7.41
13.	64.29	25.00	10.71
15	71.43	25.00	3.57
Average of 28	**65.31**	**29.43**	**5.26**

Figure 2

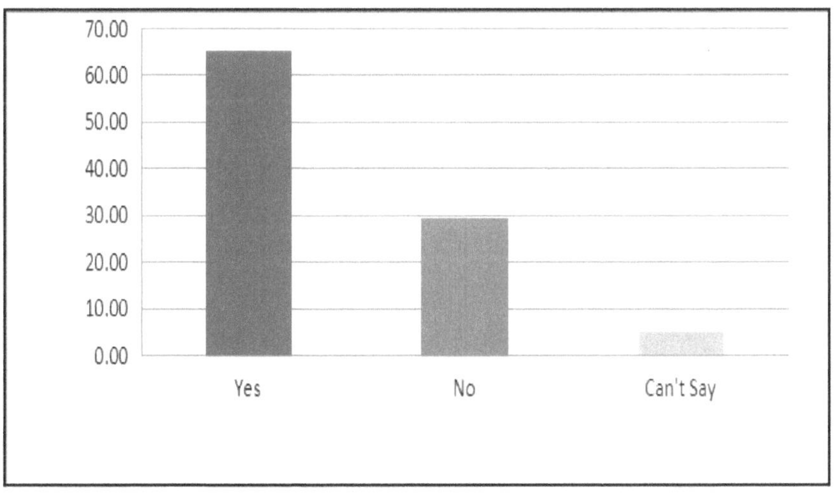

The above figure nos 1 and 2 depict a consensus among the staff, parents, past students, the Sisters as well as Priests regarding the role played by the Bethany Sisters in the educational sector. It is found that 70.29 per cent of the staff, parents, the past pupils and 65.31 per cent of the Priests and the Sisters agree that the educational institutions of the Bethany Sisters are administered effectively and competently. Sisters' mission of education has a vision, goal, common thrust and uniform policies. The Sisters are qualified, and their quality of teaching is appreciated. There is understanding and cooperation among the various educational institutions of the Sisters with the respective State authorities where they render their services.

Sisters in the schools where they serve work as a team and appoint qualified teachers in their educational institutions. Their schools not only cater to the poor, but they are helped and supported to cope with the demands of their studies. Those students who are unable to pay their school fees are either exempted from payment or sometimes are helped out by paying from the salary of the Sisters too. Some less privileged students are also educated without any expenditure from their side.

The Sisters impart value-based education in their institutions and their schools have helped to create a class of citizens with social commitment and concern for the poor. They consider education as service but pay just and fair wages to the staff in their institutions. Good relations are maintained with the people of their locality by admitting all those neighborhood children despite their poor social and economic condition. The students who pass out of Sisters' schools are value based and continue to live those values inculcated in them. Their contribution to the education sector has enabled the Bethany Sisters to be widely recognized and respected in the society and in the Northeast Region as well.

Only 22.67 per cent of the people are not quite satisfied with the quality of education provided by the Sisters. Some of the parents do not seem to be satisfied with the qualification and competence of the teachers appointed by the Sisters in their educational institutions.

The number of respondents who agree that the education imparted by the Sisters is more result oriented also seems to be rather equal with those who agree that the education is value based. But this opinion differs among the Priests and the Religious.

There are an equal number of Priests and Sisters who do not agree that the Bethany Sisters cater to the poor in their educational mission. This would certainly need a serious introspection as Bethany Congregation was founded to cater to the needs of the poor and the marginalized. Overall, 29.43 per cent of Priests and Religious (see Figure no. 2) do not seem to have been satisfied with the education imparted by the Bethany Sisters. It could be that among the respondents 5.26 per cent of the Priests, Sisters and 7.05 per cent of the people are not aware of the education imparted by the Bethany Sisters. This may be as they are not directly associated with the Sisters in their educational work as some of these institutions are managed independently by the Sisters.

The writer also gave out questionnaires to 100 students studying in Bethany Sisters' schools in Assam, Tripura, and Mizoram. The questions generally related to the quality and value-based education imparted to them. The students were from High schools as well as Higher Secondary sections. Out of a hundred, 92 of them responded.

Students' Responses

No. of Respondents: 92

TABLE NO. 10 A

1.	Who is your favorite teacher in the school?	1	2	3
	i. Sister	62		
	ii. Lay teacher		30	
	iii. Don't know			0
2.	What in him/her did you like?			

		1	2	3
	i. Strictness	14		
	ii. Kindness		78	
	iii. Don't know			0
3.	What special quality in a sister did you like?			
	i. Creative teaching	30		
	ii. Compassion		58	
	iii. Can't say			4

From the above Table No. 10 A, it is found that 68 out of 92 students appreciate the Sisters for their kindness and compassion. There are also a significant number of students who are pleased with the creative methods of teaching employed by the Sisters in their teaching ministry.

Students' Responses

No. of Respondents: 92

TABLE NO. 10 B

1.	Are you happy that you are studying in Sisters' school?	1	2	3
	i. Yes	90		
	ii. No		1	
	iii. Can't say			1
2.	What impact has the school had on you?			
	i. Lasting impact	88		
	ii. No impact		2	
	iii. Can't say			2
3	Do you think you would be a better person if studied in another school?			
	i. May be	9		
	ii. No		74	
	iii. Can't say			9

Table No.10 B depicts the difference between educational institutions managed by the Bethany Sisters and others. Out of the 92 students, 90 are happy and satisfied to be a part of the Bethany Sisters' institutions where they study. Again 88 of them feel that these educational institutions have had greater impact on them. A total of 74 of them expressed that they would not have been better if they were studying in some other institution. This is an indication that Bethany Sisters' schools have been making a difference in the lives of those who are part of their institutions perhaps through the values that they inculcate among their students.

Students' Responses

No. of Respondents: 92

TABLE NO. 10 C

		1	2	3
1.	What activities do you have in the school?	1	2	3
	i. Sports and competitions	13		
	ii. Co-curricular activities		75	
	iii. Don't know			4
2.	Do you prefer these activities to teaching?			
	i. Yes	78		
	ii. No		10	
	iii. Can't say			4
3.	Have these activities helped you in your all-round development and character formation			
	i. Yes	86		
	ii. No		5	
	iii. Can't say			1

The above Table No.10 C indicates that the schools of the Bethany Sisters are different as they give importance to lots of co-curricular and extracurricular activities like sports, cultural programmes and competitions. These are preferred by the parents for their wards as it gives them all round development. This is why parents and guardians rush for admissions in Catholic schools. Students on the whole feel happy to participate in these activities and feel that these activities have helped them in their growth and contributed to what they are today. The Catholic schools are well known all over the world for their value based and quality education.

Students' Responses

No. of Respondents: 92

TABLE NO. 10 D

1.	What have you learnt as a student of this school?			
	i. Values	72		
	ii. To compete		20	
	iii. Can't say			0
2.	What values has the school inculcated in you?			
	i. Compassion for the poor and the needy	75		
	ii. Competitiveness		14	
	iii. Can't say			3
3.	How do you live those values in daily situations?			
	i. Awareness	41		
	ii. Desire		48	
	iii. Don't know			3
4.	What values linger in your mind?			
	i. To help others in need	67		
	ii. To adjust with all in the society		25	
	iii. Don't know			0
5.	What gives you purpose in life?			
	i. Values	49		
	ii. Moral Science classes		40	
	iii. Don't know			3

Table No. 10 D indicates that the Bethany Sisters' institutions are known for their value-based education. As mentioned earlier, students are instructed often to help the poor and the needy in whatever way possible. This is a regular feature of the Bethany schools where a week is marked as Social Service Week and whatever the students contribute during that week is distributed to the less fortunate in the villages at least once a year. Most of the students as indicated in the table above feel that they have inculcated values mainly the value of compassion and the desire to help the needy in their own ways. Besides, they feel that the Moral values taught by the Sisters have helped them to imbibe these values and they have not only awareness but also desire to live those values.

Students' Responses

No. of Respondents: 92

TABLE NO. 10 E

1.	In what way are you different from students of other schools?			
	i. Helping those in need	80		
	ii. Same as them		10	
	iii. Don't know			2
2.	Do you like to help the poor and the needy?			
	i. Yes	68		
	ii. Sometimes		20	
	iii. Can't say			4
3.	Do you like to pray?			
	i. Yes	79		
	ii. No		9	
	iii. Can't say			4
4.	Does prayer help you to live better?			
	i. Yes	80		
	ii. No		4	

	iii. Can't say			8
5.	How often do you pray?			
	i. Often	87		
	ii. Never		3	
	iii. Can't say			2

According to Table No.10 E, most of the students feel that they have been different at least in the practice of the value of charity towards those in need. They have also imbibed the value of prayer in their lives and 80 of them expressed that prayer helps them to live better lives.

The Bethany Sisters whom I interviewed expressed that their past is a story of struggle to bring peace and harmony in the society. There were lots of celebrations in the schools. Independence Day which was celebrated with mass drill under the trees was well appreciated by the people who attended it. Generally, the whole village used to be present for any programme in the school without any formal invitation. No tuitions were taken, and no child absented from the school, neither were there any failures in the school. Life was difficult but enjoyable and the moments spent together in the company of each other were happy and joyous.

The above data indicates that the Sisters have maintained good relations with the neighborhood community. The students who pass out from the institutions of the Bethany Sisters are value oriented. The staff in the schools of the Bethany Sisters has high regard for the committed life of the Sisters as a whole and is admirable of the managing capacity of the Sisters. They also find the school as their second home where they are able to forget their worries and concerns. They find that the Sisters are understanding and give due respect to all those who work with them.

The educational institutions of the Bethany Sisters are known for their practical vision and mission statements such as 'Transformative education for fullness of life.' They emphasize on core values like 'Respect for life, nature and culture, excellence in academics, organization as well as co-curricular and extra-curricular activities. Their institutions are well organized and known for discipline, punctuality, cleanliness, strictness, and affection. The Sisters offer a platform for systematic and focused education. They ignite the hearts and minds of the students through whatever they do for the cause of education.

The parents feel that their choice of Bethany Sisters' institutions for the education of their children was due to the discipline they impart and the methods of teaching which seem to be appealing too. The wards are taught the importance of prayer especially during difficult times, to behave well and to be value oriented. The Sisters have inculcated in the students' desire to try their best in whatever they do. They make their classes interesting by the use of stories, posters, and other teaching aids. Students feel free with the Sisters as they mix freely with them.

Some of the parents though they were educated in vernacular government run schools, they had admiration for the students studying in Sisters' institutions. Their disciplined way of life, punctuality in attending to their duties inspired some of those parents to send their children to Sisters' institutions. They feel satisfied with the quality of teaching and the care which the Sisters give to their children. Etiquettes and good manners are given prime importance in Bethany Sisters' Schools. Students who have passed out of such institutions have been successfully coping through life's struggles.

The Sisters give emphasis to spoken English. The general remark of the parents is that 'if someone wants his/her child to be fluent in English and converse, then the option should be a Convent school. Practical knowledge is imparted to the students in the classrooms which helps in better results in the Board Exams. Fee structure is affordable to most of the parents.

Overall, the Catholic Church is forward in the field of education in the Northeastern part of India. Sisters have been able to change the backwardness of the place through their education. Sometimes people of other religions approach the Catholics to get their wards admitted in Sisters' schools as they provide good infrastructure for education of the children. The students belonging to other religions are treated equally and taught to respect all the religions. Most of the students from the villages are accommodated in the hostels managed by the Sisters.

People opine that the Bethany Sisters have been doing commendable job in imparting quality education to the children of the Region and their dedication to the cause of education has been incomparable. They seem to have been impressed by the discipline of the schools as well as the hostels. The Sisters with a vision, goal, common thrust and uniform policies are an example of hard work, commitment, and dedication to the staff. Though the Sisters work under adverse conditions, they bear smiles on their faces. They are trained to work capably in their own field.

Staff is happy to work with the Bethany Sisters and prefer to educate their wards in Sisters' institutions. The love, guidance, and support that the staff receive enables them to give their best in service. The staff give the credit of being what they are today to the Sisters with whom they have worked and who have been a source of strength and encouragement to them. The staff feels that their association with the institutions of the Sisters has been pleasant and fulfilling as well.

Some of the public have known the Sisters' schools through the reading of magazines, books, journals, newspapers, and the Television shows. They are of the opinion that the Convent schools in general are very impressive. The Sisters contribute to the improvement of the society through their social, educational, and medical services. The curriculum provided by the Sisters is advanced, up to date and the way of teaching is student friendly. The rules and regulations of these institutions are appreciable. They have everything in black and white, carefully planned and implemented as well. Their system of education is so close to the hearts of its pupils that there exists a lifelong association between the institution and its students which is so visible even after they leave the institution. The students educated in Catholic schools are found to have achieved success in all walks of life and they even remain indebted to their Alma Mater.

By providing quality education to the children of this Region, the Sisters have helped to improve the standard of living and the condition of the people. Bethany Sisters' schools have helped to develop education in the Region and these schools are preferred by most of the population. They are also dedicated to their responsibilities which make them successful and effective in their mission field. The Sisters have brought about all round development of school children through the education imparted by them. They are committed to the cause of the poor and the marginalized of the society. They always give preference to such class of people in admissions as well as fee concessions.

The missionaries are zealous and enthusiastic for mission, working for the benefit of the State and the Region where they work. They are tolerant towards all religions which they manifest in their love for brotherhood and unity. The education imparted by them is unparallel as they also include in their curriculum humanitarian training like community service. Their education system is effective due to the use of smart technology in the classrooms. Those educated in Convent schools can establish themselves, interact and face the challenges of life.

Sisters' educational institutions differ from other institutions in their way of teaching and in the way the values are inculcated among their students. Studies are given prime importance and taken seriously by those students who study in convent schools. The concept of 'Parents Day' which is meant to honor the parents can be traced back to the Convent schools. In this way the missionaries have been trend setters for Government and schools run by other organizations as they too have started emulating the example of the missionaries.

The Bethany Sisters have taught the value of manual work to their students as well. They make the students to plant trees in the school campus and around their houses to teach the value of caring for mother earth. Time to time, the Sisters take the initiative to motivate the students to contribute generously towards the cause of the poor and the less fortunate of the society by distributing clothes, toilet articles and other stuff. By this action, the students are taught the value of charity and love for the poor. The students are made to realize how fortunate they are and their responsibility to care for their own brothers and sisters.

Working in Sisters' schools has helped the teaching and non-teaching staff to gain knowledge about the Catholic Church and the Catholic Missions. They feel that the school is their second home. School makes them smart and active. They owe their personality development to the missionaries in whose schools they work. They feel fortunate to have associated with the Sisters as they have enabled them to inculcate important values of life. They feel that the Catholic Church is a place to meet people from different parts of the country. Missionary schools provide a serene atmosphere for work.

The members of the staff and the parents were of the opinion that their choice of Catholic schools for themselves as well as their wards was mainly because they themselves received best education from these institutions and were happy and satisfied to have grown up in a Catholic environment. As a result, they also have realized the value of making their children fine human beings through the education they receive in Sisters' schools. They want for their children not just bookish knowledge but more than that to take part in co-curricular activities. In their opinion, this will help their wards to adjust themselves to life and the society in which they live.

Some of the staff members opt to work in Sisters' institutions because of their desire to experience the discipline and the environment of good management along with a desire to develop themselves and their personality. Some of them feel that job satisfaction is what gives them joy, peace and not the amount of salary. They do get opportunities to visit and interact with the staff of other Bethany schools. They also feel that the personnel in Sisters' institutions work more and speak less.

They suggested to increase the level of competition between schools, to employ better qualified teachers and to maintain the experienced teachers without replacing them too often.

Responses from Staff, Parents of Students and the Past Pupils of the Schools

No. of Respondents: 105

TABLE NO.11 A

	School Administration	Yes %	No %	Can't Say %
1.	The Headmistress monitors and coordinates the teaching in the school	94.3	3.81	1.9
2.	Her leadership style inspires trust and confidence	87.6	8.57	3.81
3.	She takes decisions after proper consultation and due deliberation	69.5	19.1	11.4
4.	Is approachable and available to the staff and students	81.9	12.4	5.71
5.	The Headmistress deals with all justly and fairly	74.3	15.2	10.5
6.	She does not hesitate to call to account those who deviate from the norms and policies of the school	78.1	8.57	13.3
7.	Shows special concern for the welfare of the poor and the marginalized	81.9	10.5	7.62
8.	There is openness and transparency in the administration of the school	67.6	17.1	15.2
9.	The management and administration of the school plan and prepare personnel in advance for the needs of the school	80	10.5	9.52
10.	The appointments in the school are made with fairness and impartiality	63.8	18.1	18.1

11.	The teachers are enabled to play their rightful role in the school	69.5	18.1	12.4
	Average of 105	**77.14**	**12.90**	**9.96**

Figure 3

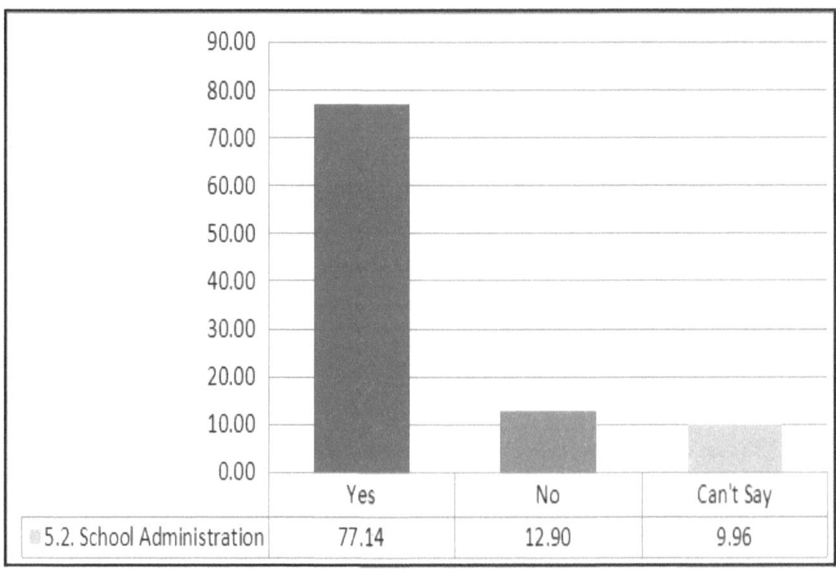

Responses from Priests and Religious

No. of Respondents: 28

TABLE NO. 11 B

SI No	Yes %	No %	Can't Say %
1.	82.1	10.7	7.14
2.	71.4	17.9	10.7
3.	71.4	17.9	10.7
4.	85.7	10.7	3.57
5.	57.1	25	17.9
6.	71.4	7.14	21.4

7.	64.3	25	10.7
8.	67.9	10.7	21.4
9.	60.7	10.7	28.6
10.	71.4	10.7	17.9
Average of 28	**70.5**	**14.6**	**14.9**

Figure 4

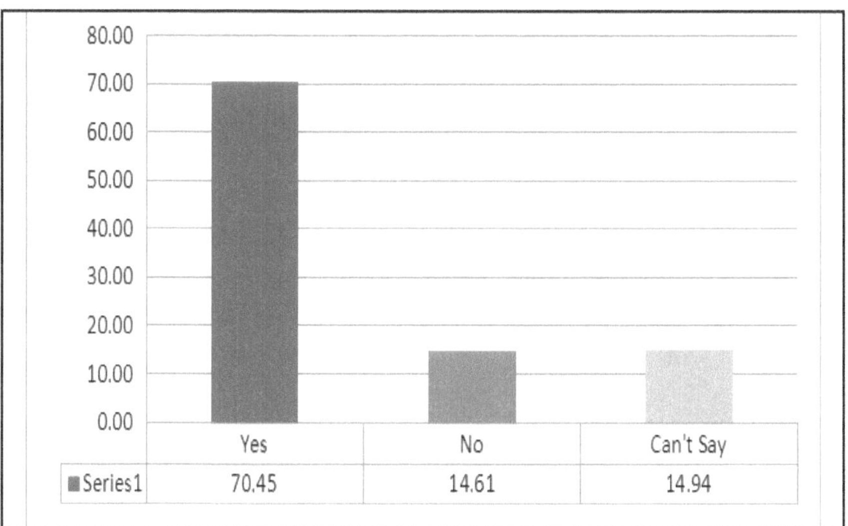

Regarding the administration of the school 77.14 per cent of the people and 70.45 per cent of Priests and the Religious opine that the Bethany Sisters are good administrators and management is quite efficient. The authorities of the school monitor and coordinate the teaching in the schools. Sisters' leadership style inspires trust and confidence. The staff and the students feel that the authorities are approachable and available. There is fairness and justice in the dealings of those who are involved in the administration.

Poor and the marginalized are shown special concern and openness and transparency is found in the administration of the school. The management plans and prepares personnel in advance for the needs of the schools. Teachers are appointed with fairness and impartiality and the teachers are enabled to play their rightful role in the schools.

The administration of the schools is helpful towards the staff and whenever any guidance or advice is sought, the Sisters avail their time for it.

A few of them such as 12.90 per cent of people and 14.94 per cent of Priests and Religious expressed that the school administration is not so efficient. Among all the statements in the table above, some feel that there is no consultation and deliberation while taking decisions especially in matters concerning the schools. The staff is not sufficiently taken into confidence to take disciplinary actions or other decisions to facilitate the teachers to play their rightful role in the school. Some 9.96 percent of the people and 14.61 per cent of the Sisters and Priests also seem to be unaware of the school administration of the Bethany Sisters which could be as mentioned earlier due to non-involvement of these respondents in the educational mission of the Bethany Sisters. Frequent change in the administration of the school due to transfers affects the working of the school as well as the staff.

The strength of the management in Sisters' Schools is found in its infrastructure, manpower, trust, committed staff, sincerity, discipline and proper utilization of time, friendly social environment, loyalty to the mission and service mindedness. The Sisters show their capacity in handling every issue efficiently. There is a homely atmosphere for work in their schools. As a result of the education provided by the Bethany Sisters people have been able to perceive changes in the society. The presence of the Sisters, their visits to the families, listening and talking with the people has helped to improve the condition of the villagers. Sisters seem to have learnt a lot from the people and vice versa.

Though initially there was criticism from the public in some of the places regarding the work of the Sisters, the latter continued with their good work without minding the criticism. This has served as an example for some of the local girls to join the Sisters in their missionary endeavors. Though some of these girls were attracted by the way Sisters taught them, yet they in turn did not get an opportunity to teach after becoming Sisters as they were engaged either in social or medical work.

Hostel Work

Responses from Staff, Parents of Students and the Past Pupils of the Boardings

No. of Respondents: 105

TABLE NO. 12 A

	Views on Hostel Work	Yes %	No %	Can't Say %
1.	The Boarding has played a role in making education accessible to the poor	61.90	9.52	28.57
2.	The Boarding is generally equipped with adequate facilities and infrastructure	58.10	8.57	33.33
3.	The Boarding is administered efficiently	58.10	4.76	37.14
4.	Boarding succeeds in inculcating and maintaining discipline among the students	61.90	8.57	29.52
5.	Today Boarding seems to be more concerned about empowering the poor	25.7	38.1	36.2
	Average of 105	**54.9**	**11.9**	**33.2**

Figure 5

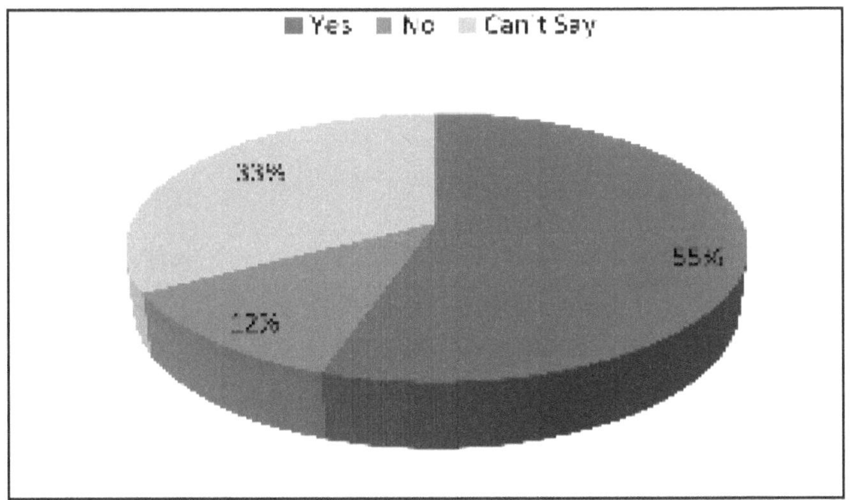

Responses from Priests and Sisters

No. of Respondents: 28

TABLE NO. 12 B

SI No	Yes %	No %	Can't Say %
1	78.6	21.4	0
2	78.6	21.4	0
3	67.9	17.9	14.3
4	75	17.9	7.14
5	37	59.3	3.7
Average of 28	67.7	28.1	4.19

Figure 6

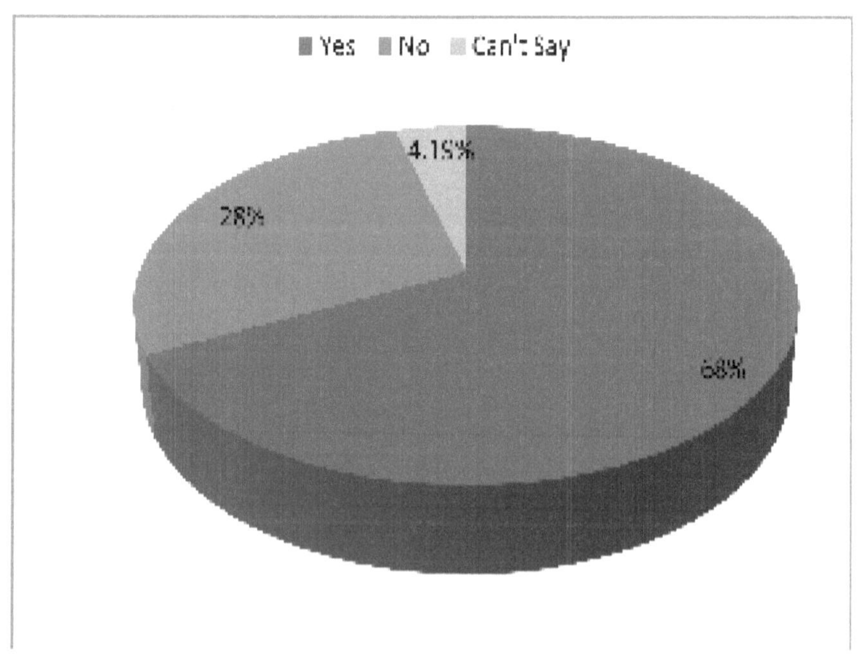

Presently the Congregation is privileged to have 36 hostels in different Provinces of India under the care of the Sisters. These hostels have been a source of religious vocations to Bethany Congregation as well as others. Table No.12 B depicts that 67.7 per cent of the Priests, Sisters and 54.9 per cent of the people agree that the boarding's managed by the Sisters have played a role in making education accessible to the poor. Boarding's are managed efficiently and equipped with adequate facilities and infrastructures.

Discipline has been inculcated and maintained and the poor have been empowered. The hostels of the Bethany Sisters cater to those students who hail from villages and have no facilities for education. Many of the students were and are provided free accommodation and food when they are unable to pay the boarding fees. The boarding's have helped in educating the poor and the slow learners by giving them special attention in their studies.

The Sisters have been a source of inspiration for the young girls of the Region to join the Bethany Congregation in continuing their mission in the Northeast. An insignificant number disagree that the Sisters' boardings are concerned with empowering the rural poor through their hostel ministry. There is need to maintain discipline in the boarding houses. What is more alarming is that 33.2 per cent of people and 4.19 per cent of Priests and Sisters are neither aware nor want to say anything about the hostel ministry of the Sisters. Many of the respondents had left blank the space for statements no. 1-5 regarding the hostel ministry mainly because there were few hostels managed by the Bethany Sisters in those places where the respondents filled up the questionnaire.

Social Work

TABLE 13 A

Responses from Staff, Parents of Students and the Past Pupils of the Schools: No. of Respondents: 105	Yes %	No %	Can't Say %
1. Bethany Sisters give due importance to social ministry; initiatives in social work are encouraged and supported	86.54	6.73	6.73
2. Social Ministry is planned, organized and coordinated well	83.50	5.83	10.68
3. The Sisters involved in social ministry have requisite training and competence	67.62	14.29	18.10
4. Social ministry of the Sisters has contributed to the economic and social development of the people	70.48	13.33	16.19
5. Social ministry has enabled the Bethany Sisters to cross boundaries and collaborate with all	70.48	11.43	18.10
6. The Sisters in the ministry of Social work network and collaborate with other NGOs	57.14	16.19	26.67
7. Social workers are functioning as 'friends of the poor', who identify with them in their struggles	70.48	15.24	14.29
8. Funds are spent for the purpose they are obtained	39.05	10.48	50.48
9. Social ministry is not viewed as a means of income generation	49.52	16.19	34.29
10. Domestic workers are paid just wages	47.62	20.00	32.38
11. There is a system to effectively monitor and coordinate the different social as well as pastoral work	39.42	20.19	40.38
12. Social ministry communicates in action the Sisters'solidarity with the poor and commitment to social justice.	65.71	9.52	24.76
Average of 105	**55.49**	**21.00**	**24.44**

Figure 7

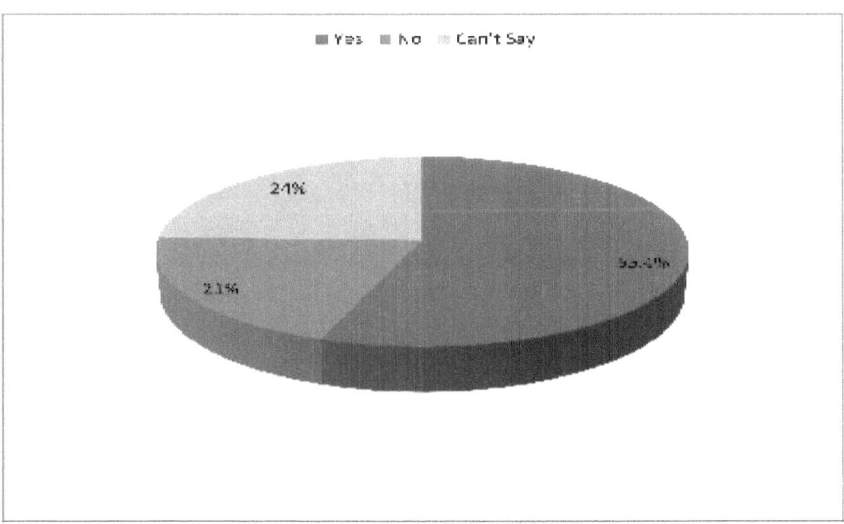

Responses from Priests and Sisters

No. of Respondents- 28

TABLE 13 B

SI No	Yes %	No%	Can't Say%
1	82.14	14.29	3.57
2	75.00	10.71	14.29
3	75.00	17.86	7.14
4	89.29	7.14	3.57
5	89.29	3.57	7.14
6	64.29	25.00	10.71
7	60.71	28.57	10.71
8	21.43	46.43	32.14
9	21.43	57.14	21.43
10	64.29	28.57	7.14
11	35.71	46.43	17.86
12	75.00	10.71	14.29
Average of 28	62.80	24.70	12.50

Figure 8

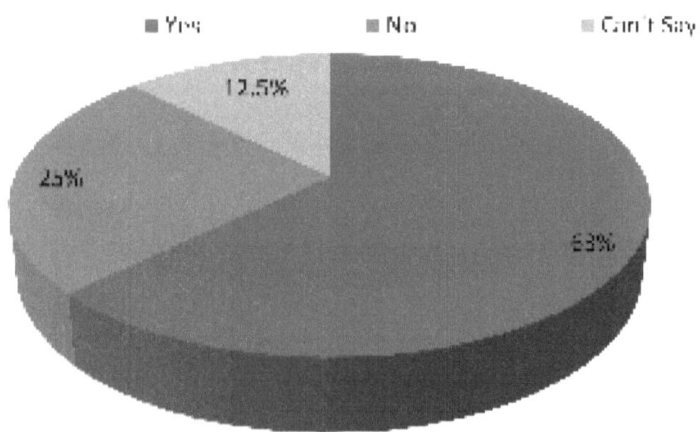

The Bethany Sisters in the social work field at the Congregational level have created visibility for their developmental works. A total of 55.49 per cent of the people and 62.80 per cent of Sisters and Priests agree that the Bethany Congregation and the Northeast Province of the Sisters in particular gives due importance to social work where the Sisters are encouraged and initiatives in social work are supported. This mission of the Sisters is planned and organized well at the Congregational and Province level. The Sisters are given required training and are competent in social work. Social work activities of the Sisters have made a significant contribution to the socio-economic development of the Region. Bethany Sisters seem to have crossed boundaries and collaborated with all in this mission especially by networking with the Non-Governmental Organizations.

The Sisters engaged in social work have become 'friends of the poor', identifying with the people in their struggles. Social work activities are carried on for the welfare of the masses. Domestic workers such as cooks, drivers, watchmen employed by the institutions are paid just wages. The different social and pastoral works are effectively monitored and coordinated at the Generalate and Province level. Above all through this mission Sisters have been communicating in action solidarity with the poor and commitment to social justice.

Yet 21.19 per cent of the people and 24.70 per cent of the Religious personnel do not agree that the Bethany Sisters working in the social field have requisite training and competence. 24.7 per cent of the people and 12.5 per cent of the Priests and Sisters do not seem to be aware of the social work done by the Bethany Sisters. Many of the respondents had marked the column 0- can't say, as they were not sure of the social work done by the Sisters. This is because in some centres where the data was collected, there was no social work centre. Another reason could be that Bethany Sisters are more visible in the educational field rather than social sector. This observation suggests a need for the Sisters of the Northeast Province to get more involved in social welfare activities along with education.

Sisters at the Congregational level are involved in a lot of social work. In places where the Sisters are involved in social and medical activities, there is a lot of appreciation regarding the presence and work of the Sisters. The Bethany Sisters have undertaken various initiatives to help the poor and the needy. They give social awareness to the people. Some of them expressed that they even learnt household works from the Sisters. Some of the Sisters expressed that they were close to people and vice versa. There was a sense of belongingness to each other. People helped the Sisters in many ways especially in the initial stages from carrying water to even preparing the food for them. They would reach out to the Sisters in their difficulties. Children would wait in their houses to see the Sisters visiting their families after school because they felt close to them.

Sisters in the social work field work hard and do a lot of good to the people and society at large through their activities. They are involved in the social life of the people, carry out social obligations and duties satisfactorily. Working with different Non-Governmental Organizations has helped the Sisters working in the social sector to interact with government officials. Sisters feel grateful for the help they received from government officials and sponsorship which they make available to the poor students. A few of the Sisters who work as social workers also provide shelter homes for children with poor and unhealthy home situations. Even the social workers who collaborate with the social work activities of the Sisters have imbibed the spirit of mission work from the Sisters. These volunteers of social work try to maintain good relations with the Church leaders, the leaders of the State and try to do their best as lay leaders.

The Sisters go from door to door in the villages to teach the illiterate by involving themselves in the outreach programme. They work impartially for the welfare of the areas of their concern. The Sisters arrange programmes for the poor and the needy. Collections are done to help the prisoners, for the calamity-stricken masses and to help the poor families. The students are taught the value of not wasting food but rather to share it with the needy. During their family visits, the Sisters do discuss on family issues, give family counseling, and contribute to build up the families. Sisters approach those who are well off to contribute their might to reach out to those in need. Sisters visit the families in the locality and attend the funerals, family functions etc. Thus, good rapport is built with the neighborhood community and the locality.

In earlier days Sisters used to visit the families quite often, every evening they were seen walking from house to house to know the family background of each student, sometimes even to find out why a student absented oneself from the school. While the parents were unable to pay the fees, the Sisters would ask them to pay whatever they could and thus families of students were helped. Knowing the family background of students enabled the Sisters to build rapport with the parents, give fee concessions to the deserving ones and help those who were not financially self sufficient. Students who excelled in studies but were unable to pay the fees were exempted.

Parents at times felt unworthy to accommodate the Sisters in their little huts but on the part of the Sisters, they would accept anything offered by the people, sit with them, and thus identify themselves with the people. The people in the villages expressed that they expect more social services from the Sisters. Sisters are involved in the training of women and youth in job-oriented skills through vocational training thus enabling them to face life meaningfully by standing on their own feet. Cultivation has improved in the villages due to the learning of manual work from the Sisters and people are able to sell their products instead of buying them.

Medical Work

TABLE 14 A

Responses from Staff, Parents of Students and the Past Pupils of the Schools: No. of Respondents: 105	Yes %	No %	Can't Say %
1. The dispensaries run by the sisters are administered effectively	52.38	3.81	43.81
2. These dispensaries deliver quality health care at affordable rates.	68.57	5.71	25.71
3. The personnel in health-care ministry are adequately trained and professionally competent	63.81	6.67	29.52
4. As improved government-sponsored health-care services are now available free of cost, fewer people come to Sisters' health care centre's.	50.48	15.24	34.29
5. Health-care ministry of the Sisters needs to be integrated with social and pastoral ministry.	47.62	10.48	41.90
Average of 105	**56.57**	**8.38**	**35.05**

Figure 9

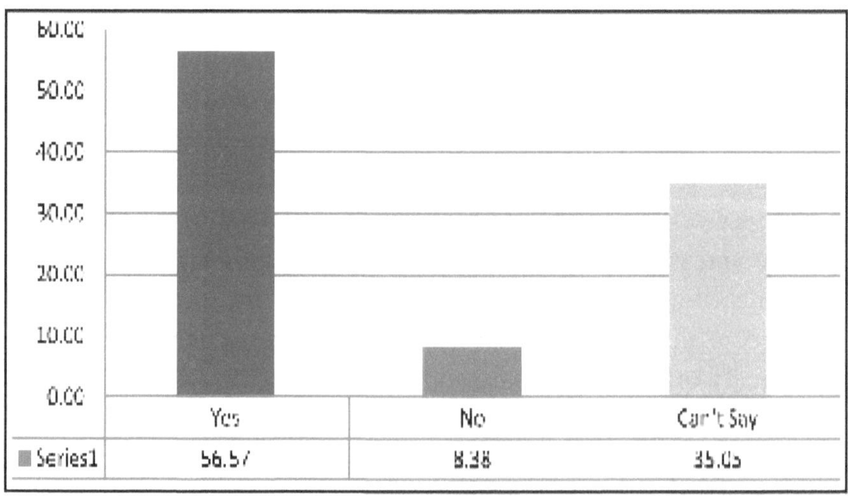

TABLE 12 B

5.5. Medical Work- Responses from Priests and Sisters			
SI No	Yes %	No %	Can't Say %
1.	78.57	14.29	7.14
2.	75.00	17.86	7.14
3.	75.00	17.86	7.14
4.	50.00	39.29	10.71
5.	78.57	14.29	7.14
Average of 28	71.43	20.71	7.86

Figure 10

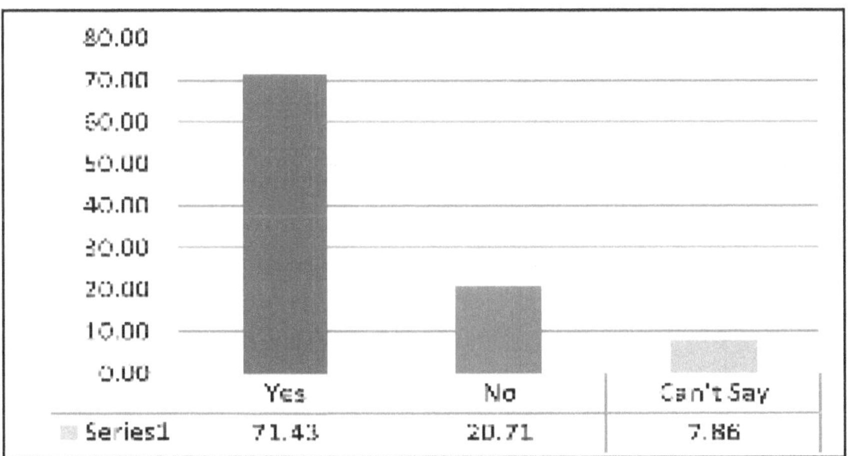

There is a marked difference of opinion among the people and the religious personnel regarding the health care activities of the Bethany Sisters. 71.43 per cent of Priests and Sisters are of the opinion that the dispensaries run by the Bethany Sisters are administered effectively and that they deliver quality health care at affordable rates. Health care seems to be viewed by them as an effective activity and the dispensaries of the Bethany Sisters are managed efficiently. The Nurse Sisters are always available for the patients. What is most alarming is that 35.05 per cent of the people seem to be unaware of the medical services rendered by the Bethany Sisters. This could be due to fewer personnel of Bethany Sisters involved in the medical work and their presence is not felt in health care ministry.

Among the staff and parents, 56.57 per cent feel that the personnel in health care mission are adequately trained and are professionally competent. Though the government-sponsored health care services are made available free of cost in the remote areas, the number of patients coming to the dispensaries of Bethany Sisters has not diminished. The general feeling of the respondents is that there is need to integrate health care activities with the social and pastoral activities which would make the Sisters effective in their mission and make their presence felt among the masses.

The health-related works and especially the services to the addicts by the Sisters are appreciated by the people. Because of the medical care they feel that malaria has been controlled in some areas of the Region. In the opinion of some senior Sisters, medical work was difficult in earlier times due to lack of transportation, personnel and so on but at present the Sisters are making a greater contribution and people are aware of it. People's houses had become their homes as Sisters spent 3-4 days in a village to distribute medicine where medical facilities were totally unavailable.

Health has improved due to the awareness and training on health education provided by the Sisters. The staff employed in the health care centers of the Sisters work hard because Sisters motivate and instruct them periodically. Though they cannot be paid high salary due to lack of funds for medical activities of the Sisters, the medical staff is satisfied. Much of their joy comes from the fact that they are able to work with the missionaries and contribute their services to the society of which they are a part. The Sisters take pains to train them for their work.

The informants at Mamit, Mizoram were happy. Sometimes all the addicts are brought together and programmes are held and medicines, cotton rolls and bandages are distributed. Abscess are cleaned and treated by the Sister Nurses. People opine that all these activities would have been impossible without the presence of the Bethany Sisters and so the activities of the Sisters are well appreciated. Even when the people of the locality hesitate to mingle with the HIV/AIDS patients, addicts and alcoholics, Sisters take a risk for their own lives.

As the de-addiction centre is located in the heart of the village, some locals complain about the presence of the addicts and their treatment as there have been instances of thefts which disturbs the peace and tranquility of that locality. The addicts who are suspected by the local people for stealing their valuables, spreading AIDS and so on are instructed on good values for which they are grateful to the Sisters. Without the presence of the Sisters, the local people feel that more of infectious diseases would continue to exist.

Sisters are doing a good job in social sector especially in the way they care for the addicts is appreciated much by the people who have good rapport with the two Bethany Sisters, namely, Sr Valsal, the pioneer of this de-addiction centre and Sr Premiot- the Headmistress and superior who served at Mamit sacrificed their lives at young age for this mission. Even after their demise they are still missed a lot by the people and are considered as the most dedicated Sisters who gave their all for others despite their illness. They were the benchmark for social work in Mamit district. Sr Premiot had created a history in 2009 and 2010 with 100 per cent result, distinctions and first divisions including letter marks in class X in the district. People feel proud of them for such quality education and medical work.

Drug users feel free to share their problems and difficulties with the Sisters and the health workers who consider themselves as missionaries. The health workers are able to give up alcohol and popping pills. They have developed the ability to empathize with the new clients as they themselves were the victims of drugs and alcohol. The training given to them by the Sisters is a great help in this regard. They feel that the Sisters are pleasant in their dealings.

There is mutual understanding and respect between the health workers and the Sisters. With regard to the changes in the lives of the addicts, they have stopped sharing of needles, save money as needles and vitamins are provided free of cost by the Nurse Sisters and wounds are dressed free of cost. This has inspired the addicts to give up drugs and lead normal lives.

General Impression about the Bethany Sisters

TABLE NO 15 A

Responses from Staff, Parents of Students and the Past Pupils of the Schools: No. of Respondents: 105			
1. Bethany Sisters are just and fair in their dealings	75.24	9.52	15.24
2. Are interested and involved with the people	82.86	10.48	6.67
3. Have special concern for women and girl children	86.67	4.76	8.57
4. They respect and adapt themselves to the culture of the people	87.62	10.48	1.90
5. They play a vital role in the character formation of the students	90.48	7.62	1.90
6. They are simple in their lifestyle	90.48	3.81	5.71
7. They pay special attention to the slow learners and poor	76.19	14.29	9.52
8. The Sisters promote love and respect for all	88.57	5.71	5.71
9. They take interest in the all round development of their students	92.38	5.71	1.90
10. Their presence is a source of comfort and help to the people	84.76	9.52	5.71
11. They are proficient in the local language	53.33	29.52	17.14
12. They cater to the needs of the poor	68.57	13.33	18.10
13. They encourage leadership of people	84.76	6.67	8.57
14. Sisters visit families and help those in need	73.08	12.50	14.42
15. They work to promote harmony and peace	93.33	2.86	3.81
16. Sisters work to empower the weaker sections	78.10	14.29	7.62
17. The Sisters are well informed about the current problems of the society and respond creatively	66.67	14.29	19.05

18. The people appreciate the Sisters for their service	91.43	4.76	3.81
19. Sisters give priority to human empowerment and engage in social work activities	80.95	9.52	9.52
20. Sisters are relevant to the changing times	74.29	10.48	15.24
Average of 105	**77.50**	**11.40**	**11.10**

Figure 11

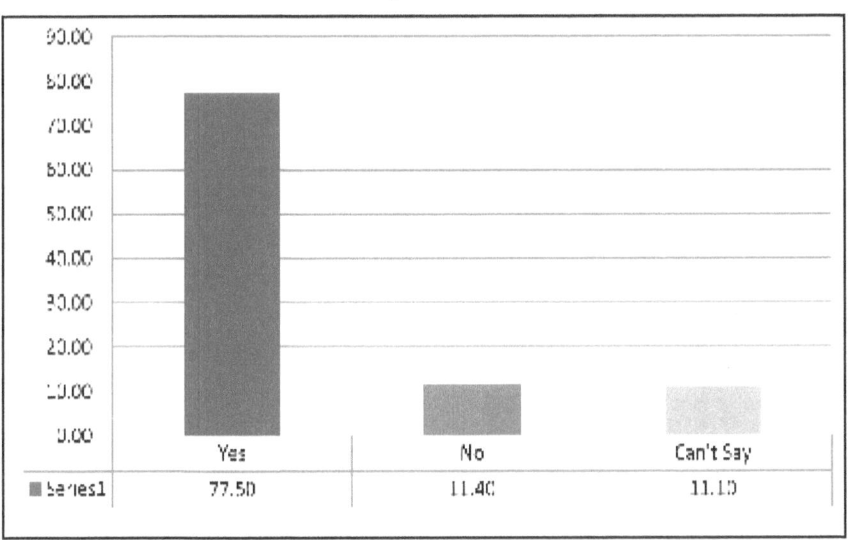

TABLE NO 15 B

Responses from Priests and Sisters: No. of Respondents: 28			
1.	46.43	42.86	10.71
2.	82.14	14.29	3.57
3.	92.86	0.00	7.14
4.	60.71	35.71	3.57
5.	92.86	7.14	0.00
6.	77.78	11.11	11.11
7.	57.14	21.43	21.43
8.	82.14	14.29	3.57
9.	82.14	10.71	7.14

10.	82.14	17.86	0.00
11.	25.00	67.86	7.14
12.	75.00	10.71	14.29
13.	85.71	14.29	0.00
14.	85.71	7.14	7.14
15.	85.71	7.14	7.14
16.	75.00	14.29	10.71
17.	57.14	35.71	7.14
18.	92.86	0.00	7.14
19.	75.00	25.00	0.00
20.	48.15	40.74	11.11
Average of 28	**62.37**	**25.78**	**11.85**

Figure 12

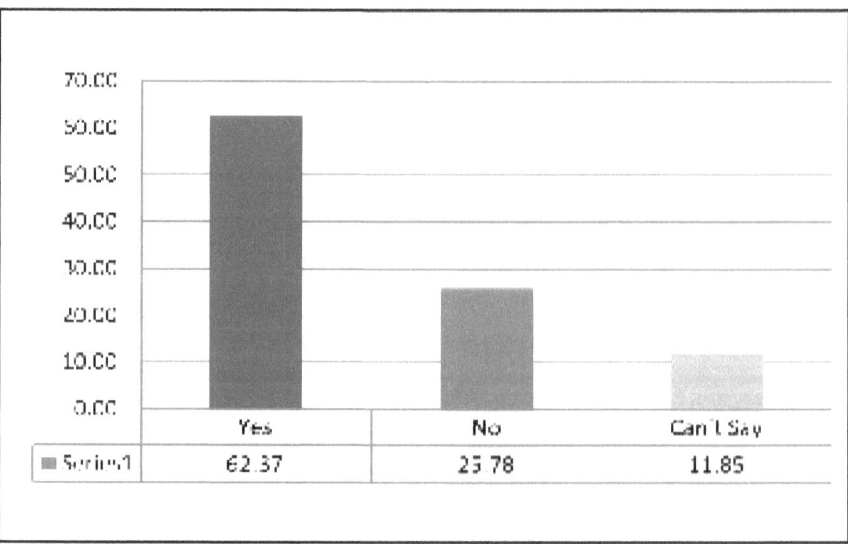

It is satisfying to know that 77.50 per cent of the people are happy to have the presence and services of the Bethany Sisters in their area. They find that the Sisters have genuine religious motivation, are sincere and trustworthy, just, and fair in their dealings. The Sisters are competent in their ministries, rise above differences of language, religion, and culture to reach out and relate to all, take interest and are involved in the welfare of the people. 62.37 per cent of the Sisters and Priests too feel that Bethany Sisters cooperate and relate well with the people, are approachable, available, and helpful. They have special concern for the women and girl children and cope well with the demands of their work. The co-missionaries are happy to work and collaborate with the Bethany Sisters.

The respondents expressed that the Sisters are pleasant and considerate in their dealings with the people. They respect and adapt to the culture of the people. People feel that their acquaintance with the Sisters has made them to be God oriented. Sisters are found to be compassionate, kind, gentle and patient in their dealings. They care for those people who live in their neighborhood, are known for their collaboration and team spirit. Bethany Sisters are simple in their lifestyle, pay special attention to the poor and the slow learners, promote love and respect for all. They also equip themselves and adapt to the new methods of teaching.

The presence of the Sisters is found as a source of comfort and help to the people as they mix well with them. They encourage leadership in people and visiting the families enables them to help those in need. Sisters also work to promote peace and harmony, to empower the weaker sections and to show respect in their dealings. 25.78 per cent of the Sisters and Priests seem to disagree as in their opinion in present days Sisters are less seen going for village visits or even learning the local languages. There is a greater desire on the part of the respondents that the Sisters rise above their individual differences to reach out to all the people. Only 11 per cent of the people as well as the Priests and Sisters feel that they are not quite knowledgeable about the Bethany Sisters and their activities.

People feel that the Sisters are active, friendly, caring, co-operative, impartial, well organized, sincere in their commitment, people oriented, God conscious, efficient in their work and compassionate. Bethany

Sisters make themselves relevant to the times, helpful, down to earth in their approach, loving and ready for any help. They work tirelessly in the mission field. They are innovative in ideas, talented and rich in cultural concepts as well. The Sisters organize good programmes with special ideas. They are an inspiration for the people, staff and they inculcate confidence in them.

People find the Bethany Sisters as disciplined which helps them to inculcate discipline among their students. Bethany Sisters have a human touch in their work, they are amiable, respectful and are good in administration. People feel proud of the work of the Sisters and are inspired by the way Sisters live their lives. Sisters adapt well to the culture and customs of the people of the locality. People appreciate the Sisters for their sacrifice of family and marriage and feel that they are privileged to have the presence and active involvement of the Sisters in their area. They are grateful for the services rendered by the Sisters to their society. Sisters value life in all its forms and work for the upliftment of the girl child.

The teaching and nonteaching faculty members in Sisters' institutions opine that whoever comes in contact with the Bethany Sisters do not remain the same but their life and way of thinking changes due to the encouragement they receive from the Sisters. They do experience care from the Sisters for their well being. The Sisters visit people in the hospitals, pray for them which is a unique feature of the Catholic missionary work. The people desire to have more Sisters in the teaching field as they feel that the Sisters are motherly in their approach and they feel free to approach them. Sisters are seen many times engaged either in cultivating vegetables or looking after flower gardens, thus giving importance to manual labour as well.

Sisters are appreciated for their skills in writing, speaking etc. promoting ambition in life, vision and goal of education and team spirit. Sisters are cooperative, systematic, supportive, teaching the value of the preciousness of life and the public in general are grateful to the

Sisters as they teach them to work for the society. Sisters are active in their mission field, and their policies as well as methods of education encourage students to achieve higher aim in life.

Sisters are known for their quality of education, ability to adapt themselves to any circumstance or situation, capability, and competency in their ministries. Service to the poor in the society and training of women and youth in job-oriented skills through vocational training are their priorities. These are the traits that have adhered the Bethany Sisters to the people of the Northeast. The Sisters respect, cooperate relate well with the people. Through quality education, they strive to bring about national integration.

Social work, health care, de-addiction centres, prevention of HIV/ AIDS, formal and non-formal education are a few of the means used by the Sisters to reach out to people of all strata of the society. The way the Sisters adapt to the alien traditions and cultures is appreciated. Their core values in education and health care ministries are always looked up for emulation by the people of other religions. Their contribution to the economic and social development of the people of Northeast is praiseworthy. Punctuality, planning and organization in work, knowledge about the current issues, taking decisions after proper consultation is appreciated. The staff members too in imitation of the Sisters are service minded, desire to help the poor and build up the character of students.

Quick adaptation to the surroundings is noteworthy of the Bethany Sisters. Dispensaries run by them are effective and help is given to the poor. They are ready for services as and when required of them. Involvement and dedication, interest in the people are the special characteristic features of Bethany Sisters. People find that the core values of their education are practical, their respect for life, nature and culture, love for the poor is worth mentioning. Bethany Sisters are educating the society by imparting all round knowledge and the discipline that is imposed by them in their institutions is practiced by them in their lives. The time spent in Sister's schools as students has huge impact on the personal and professional life of the people and this success is credited to the Bethany Sisters who have taught for many years.

Bethany Sisters played a great role in educating the people of Northeast. When they first came, there were very few English medium schools and they gave moral values to children from rich and poor families alike. They have helped the officers to become what they are today, not only through the schools but also as close acquaintances of the families. Some of the respondents expressed that the Bethany Sister's presence in the Northeast has been God's gift to the area.

The Priests, Brothers and Sisters of other Institutes appreciate the Bethany Sisters for their missionary spirit, witness value, zeal, love for the poor, commitment and dedication to the people and the mission, love, unity, and hard work. They feel that the Sisters are conscious of mission work, take risk and responsiblity, adapt to culture, customs, and the language of the locality. They are hard working, hospitable, self sacrificing and efficient administrators, cordial and welcoming. They possess leadership qualities, love for the mission and are cheerful in service, available, friendly, helpful, daring and put up with inconveniences.

The religious personnel are happy to have known the Bethany Sisters and feel blessed to work with them as they have played a vital role in reforming many lives, concerned about the demands of their work and find ways to uplift the weaker sections of the society. Some of the informants felt that the society acknowledges their sacrifices and cooperates with them and is always obliged and thankful for the innumerable lessons learnt from them. The people seem to have changed their lives after their acquaintance with the Sisters. The pioneer Sisters were courageous and took bold steps to reach to the Northeast and transmit the rich heritage of the Bethany Congregation to the people in their mission.

Bethany Sisters are well trained to teach in the schools and their system of education is inspiring. The poorer sections of the society get an opportunity to receive quality education through the Bethany Sisters and as a consequence many students gain leadership qualities in their institutions. Staff feels that they and their families have always been supported by the presence and loving attitude of the Sisters. The BES has changed the education system by promoting quality and positive, competitive mind among the students. Bethany Sisters have contributed a great deal to the Northeast by reaching out to many remote villages. Sisters share in the struggles of the people. They are rendering yeoman service especially to the villagers. As pioneering women missionaries, Bethany Sisters have played leadership role in the society by taking up the toughest mission in the Northeast which demands many sacrifices on the part of the missionaries.

The informants also suggested certain changes they would like to see in the mission of the Bethany Sisters in the Northeast. Those suggestions were that recruitment of teachers to be done on the basis of quality. The employees need to be given the freedom to put forward their opinions and to treat everyone equally in the mission. They suggested that the Sisters could work to stop child labor and give those children chance for education. The unchanged method of rote learning and homework could be looked into by the Bethany educators. There is need to maintain adequate student - teacher ratio, so that overcrowding of the classrooms could be avoided. Opportunities could be provided for all the teachers to go for in-service training to enhance their knowledge and skills.

Special training is also required for the Sisters involved in the frontier ministries. Greater involvement in the society is needed in order to equip with the modern challenges. Emphasis could be given to learn the local languages so that the Sisters could interact better with the society. Stress on the use of spoken English in the school campuses could help to satisfy the expectations of the parents. More educational institutions need to be established by the Sisters and more of Sisters could involve in classroom teaching. Involve parents and guardians in important decision-making process which concerns the school.

Schools could undertake outreach activities to reach to the poor and help to reduce the poverty of the people. More co-curricular activities, meditation and yoga classes could be introduced. Competitive programs could be arranged to bring out the innate qualities of students and teachers. The Sisters could relate a little more with the students and the common people. Health care ministries could be integrated with NGOs. Syllabus could be reduced to give more opportunities in games and sports, extracurricular activities etc. The Sisters could make their services available in government run institutions as teachers to improve the standard of the government schools run educational institutions as well.

Sisters need to be well trained and there could be more centre's for vocational training. Family apostolate and counseling could be stressed to bind the families together and teach the young ones the meaning of life and importance of living together. The Sisters need to be seen in different social work field and they could have special training for the work they get engaged in. Youth ministry needs more attention and concern for the families could be developed. More young Sisters could work against drug and alcohol addiction and promote harmony and peace in the Northeast. There is also need to give counseling to the adolescents, children and women and be more concerned about the social evils afflicting the society.

Priests and Sisters responded saying that there is need to coordinate education, social and health ministry. Right personnel to right job and collaboration of Sisters as staff members would make them effective in their mission. Sisters could be well equipped, knowledgeable of media and latest electronic gadgets. Sisters could be well trained in one particular field of mission and be equipped in different skills according to their interest so that there is effectiveness in whatever they do. Social work needs to be given importance, train more Sister Doctors in medical field and involve in family counseling. They can equip their schools and keep up the continuity of integrating with the social ministry. Opening more centres in the remote villages, involving more in the pastoral activities is essential as mission field is very vast.

When asked for comments, concerns and suggestions for the Bethany Sisters and their mission in the Northeast, the informants expressed that they were happy to be a part of this research. They hoped that a study of this sort will definitely help to improve the various missionary activities in the Northeast. There is scope for improvement in public relation. Sisters could take up education in rural areas. Sisters' mission has been a success and expected to carry on in the future too.

School administration could take trouble to be aware of the students' problems. Teachers appointed in the schools need to be competent for their profession. Bookish knowledge alone and result oriented education needs to be discouraged. There is need to do away with the method of rote learning and internalization of concepts and application could be introduced. Learning needs to be meaningful, relevant, and useful for students. The missionary spirit of the pioneering Sisters in the field of mission could be emulated by the younger Sisters. Education, pastoral, social and health ministries need to get their due place in order to provide relief to the poor and the needy. Specialized training for youth ministry, counseling etc, need to be given.

There is a sense of satisfaction among the pioneer missionaries that their hard labor has borne fruit and it has resulted in the establishment of standard schools, social service centre's and dispensaries catering to thousands of people in the Northeast. Overall there is satisfaction among the people regarding the activities of the Sisters. According to them the Bethany Sisters manage well the social, medical, or educational sector. Seeing their dedication and commitment quite many young girls from the Northeast have committed their lives as Bethany Sister to collaborate with them in their mission.

Some people have volunteered and joined the Sisters as Bethany Lay Associates to carry on the activities of the Sisters according to their capacity and are satisfied that they can be of some help to the society through their mission. Civil authorities are quite satisfied with the Sisters in the field of education, health, and developmental works. They do not have any expectations from the Sisters instead are grateful for what the Sisters are doing because quite a number of them were trained and educated by the Sisters and they have achieved their aims in life.

Some of the pioneer missionaries of the Bethany Congregation were interviewed by me. A few of them expressed that though providentially they came to Northeast, yet they consider it a blessing in disguise as they had desire and dream to work in the mission stations and to be missionaries. The first challenge they had to face was to teach in mission schools which had vernacular as the medium of instruction. In the beginning the culture, language, people's way of thinking, acting etc. were strange to the Sisters as they came from a South Indian culture. But everything was made possible little by little as long as there was enthusiasm and interest to work.

Some of the Sisters were the witnesses of the Indo- Bangladesh war in 1971-72 and cared for the refugees in the relief camps and were actively involved in the relief work. They are happy that they learnt a lot by being with the medical personnel and serving the people in need. Looking back over those years of mission work they feel fully satisfied and contented for the opportunities provided and for making full use of those chances which have made them strong to face life, challenges, and hardships.

Bethany Sisters were forward in humanitarian works and they set a pattern of going about with the mission work. There were qualified medical personnel, and it was possible to meet the government officials and tap the resources and the assistance through projects. Though it was not so easy to work in the Northeast with the southern background and upbringing but looking back over the challenges faced, it gives the pioneer missionaries a sense of satisfaction of reaching out to those in need. They are quite positive about their mission in this Region and as they have learnt the local language, the Sisters feel quite comfortable with the people and their culture. They feel that of late Bethany Sisters have not been able to venture into new fields in a creative way and have been sticking to the old ways of working.

Young Bethany Sisters feel that the Bethany Congregation has given them platforms to live their vocation to mission. Northeast province has many mission stations to fulfill their aim in life and they share the compassionate love of God to people through their activities. Bethany Sisters are good educators in the Northeast. Witnessing the dedication and hard work of the Sisters many volunteers and well wishers joined them to work hand in hand. They loved to do pastoral work as it involves being with the people in their struggles.

Through the missionary work done by the Sisters in the Northeast, change is noticed in the lifestyle and living standard of the people. There is improvement in all the spheres of the society particularly in health and hygiene. People are educated and given the knowledge to judge and choose between good and evil and in this arena the contribution of the Bethany Sisters cannot be ignored. The people are happy that the Sisters took up the challenge to come to this Region. They adjusted well to new culture, climate, language, inconveniences and have been compassionate, loving and committed to the people. Now that more of facilities are available, the Sisters can do more by reading the signs of the times. There is need for personnel in various fields and more Sisters need to be trained for mission which will help to be more effective in present day society.

Interviews were also conducted with a few of the Bethany Sisters hailing from Nagaland, Manipur, Meghalaya, and Mizoram. They opine that 'from childhood they desired to become Sisters and render service to humanity. They were directed to Bethany through people who had received good education and care from the pioneering Sisters. They do not mind working anywhere as they have one desire to be missionaries in the mission areas like Africa or wherever needed but far away from home town. They expressed that Bethany Sisters have done marvelous work in the society and because of them the society as well as the Region has improved. The State government has recognized the services of the Sisters and helped them. Wherever Bethany Sisters work, people are happy about their mission and Sisters' services are visible as well as appreciated by many.

In order to be relevant to the changing times and the world, Bethany Sisters need to update the knowledge. Socio medical mission seems more in line with Bethany's charism. In some places some parents and people feel that Bethany Sisters are not available to them, perhaps due to workload in a particular field of mission. Hence the Congregation needs to distribute sufficient members in each of the mission field. People expect Sisters to be more connected with them. People look up to the Sisters for advice, guidance and counseling in their struggles and Sisters could be available to listen to their problems.

The local girls have been influenced by the work and mission of the Bethany Sisters which created in them a desire to work in the Northeast, educate their own people in all the spheres of life as done by the missionaries who worked in their own place. They are interested in social work and rehabilitation of addicts. They also expressed dissatisfaction of working as they cannot involve much in the apostolate of their choice, which is to be with the people. They are happy with the activities of the Sisters but feel that Sisters could involve more in the lives of people.

Bethany Sisters' work, mission and their enthusiastic lives motivated some of the girls from the Northeast to choose Bethany for their life career. Being the daughters of the soil it's their joy to be in Northeast and reach out to their own people with the advantage of knowing the cultures, traditions and ways of life as it will make their mission effective. They prefer to be in the villages doing social and pastoral work.

People feel that the Sisters are relevant to the place, time, and culture. The mission that they look ahead is to work for the betterment of the society. Earlier they never thought of life beyond family circles, but they are happy to have become part of Bethany Congregation in serving and loving people. They prefer to work in the Northeast because of the desire to do something for the people associated with them and help them to improve their social life through education. Though interested in teaching but they are not satisfied with the task due to lack of training.

People remember the beginnings, the hard work and the simplicity of the Bethany Sisters but presently as per their observation that enthusiasm and zeal of the earlier missionaries is lacking. Nurse Sisters from the Northeast who render their services to the addicts and the alcoholics in the Region opine that they are in line with their interest to be Nurses and happy to work with drug addicts and HIV/AIDS patients. Their desire is that the Bethany Congregation in the Northeast Province could open more mission centres in remote areas and network with other NGOs. Parents expect more from the Sisters at the pastoral level and in schools and so Sisters could be trained according to their interest of work in specialized fields.

Though they're happy with the work of the Bethany Sisters but feel that it would be better if Sisters could cross the boundaries of classrooms, school campuses so that along with the teaching, children and parents could be helped, educated beyond books and classrooms. Teaching is in line with the charism of the Bethany Sisters as it aims to form human persons with respect to live and responsibility to love, to lift up the poor and the marginalized. People associated with Sisters give lot of encouragement, support and cooperate in the Sister's mission. Sisters could update themselves and be willing to learn in order to adjust and feel comfortable in the mission field.

Catholic Church is much forward in the area of education, health and Catholic institutions reach out to the remotest areas to serve the people selflessly. Earlier or present times do not make work easier or tough but the need to follow the signs of the time and to be present to the era of generation will make a difference. In this modern age, the only way to improve the quality of mission is to make use of all the modern gadgets and reach out to the people. There is satisfaction in working in this Region as people willingly and joyfully accept any service big or small.

Bethany Sisters have carved for many youngsters a path for a better future through education as many are today great leaders and officers. The parents are happy as their children are taken care of. Though most of the informants feel that the Bethany Sisters impart good education, yet value based education that is relevant to the times seems to be the need of the hour. Sisters do teach the students to preserve the forest, treat others as their brothers and sisters and broaden the vision as well as thinking of the people. Sisters are motivated to influence and form the minds of the students with values and convictions by giving them a feeling that the Sisters themselves have lived experience of those values. The students could be given proper motivation and direction for life.

Some of the educational institutions nowadays lack committed individuals. Parents expressed deep concern that the values and care with which they were nurtured as students in these institutions were lacking. As the members of the administration of the school come for a limited period to serve these institutions, there is lack of passion and zeal to bring about a transformation. There is need for coordinated effort on the part of the staff and the administration for respect and appreciation which would help to contribute more to the society than what is being done at present. Frequent family visits of the students and interaction with the parents would enable the Sisters to know their views.

Great desire is expressed by some of the respondents for more Catholic educational institutions to be started in rural areas to cater to the needs of the underprivileged and poorer students of the society. This would serve to give them better education in all respects with a view to help them build stronger societies with their advanced knowledge and also to build stronger families. This is to be done with a view to develop the villages faster and to make the nation stronger in all respects. The need is felt for a close relationship between the management and the staff where the gaps could be built up. The Sisters could be more innovative and reach out to those who do not have an opportunity to come to their schools like the slum and street children through the outreach programmes by involving their own students in programmes like 'Each one teach one.'

Sisters could respond radically to protect and raise their voices for the rights of the people. The need is to work from charity based to rights based approach integrating religious identity and mission by involving in government sectors and government opportunities like Sarva Siksha Abhiyan, Juvenile Justice Board, and Child Welfare Committee etc. could be availed by the Sisters. By becoming network partners, the Sisters may be able to protect and promote the interests of all the Non Governmental Organizations, institutions, schools, hospitals, and social work units irrespective of caste, creed and religious affiliations. Some of the informants observed that the Bethany Sisters have not been forward in social work and that at present Sisters are self sufficient, and do not involve much with the people. The parents desire that their wards be given all the goodness of a human being and make them the most respectful human beings in the society. Sisters could be thinking in line with capitalizing on the social relations as religious and making the people the agents of change through larger networks and regular training programmes.

Catholic institutions are definitely different because of which even pastors and officials having their own schools continue to send their wards to the Catholic schools. Earlier they used to spend the weekends with their families elsewhere, villages were considered unfit to keep their families but at present due to the improvement in the educational facilities, especially because of the existence of Catholic schools, spending the weekends in their own families in villages has become more convenient for them. People cannot separate the Church from the school and the complaint against the school becomes the complaint against the Catholic Church. There needs to be better communication between the Church and the school personnel.

Medical services of the Bethany Sisters is a great help to the society but the society would benefit much more and people would avail such facilities especially in the interior areas if the medical services offered by the Sisters are advertised on social media. Health workers do feel that there should be a bonding and friendliness with the clients in order to make them feel comfortable enough to share their problems. The counseling given to the clients on health and hygiene in the initial stages could be given always. Primary importance could be given on the prevention of HIV/AIDS. The expectations of the people are that the Sisters continue with the Self-Help Groups as it helps poor women folk especially the growing of herbal medicinal plants.

From the responses of the informants, it may be concluded that involvemnt of the Sisters in the families of peoples is impacting their lives more than mere being social workers, educationists, or nurses. People feel free and closer to the Sisters to share their problems when they are one with them in their families. Nowadays there is less contact between the people and the Sisters and a rift is created due to concentration on academic excellence, orientation on results and neglect of interaction with the society which has made the people to point at the Sisters as mere educationists, social workers and health workers.

Bethany Congregation was founded in the cultural context of the people of India. The charism is based on the actual needs of the people of the country. The members who join from other parts of India have been formed in the cultural context of the place and as such they have inculturated themselves to a great extent. The Sisters in the mission stations maintain interaction with the people and with the cultural environment in which they find themselves. In this way they are able to make themselves accepted in the socio-cultural situation of the people.

Besides, the members also exhibit a spirit of cordiality, hard work and dedication. In general, they maintain a non-institutionalized attitude which facilitates their missionary work and allows them greater space and time in their pastoral work. As a specific field of activity, the Congregation chooses the territories, giving preference always to the most difficult and needy mission, so that the missionary aim of the Institute would be faithfully preserved.

Conclusion

Religion is one of the important contributing factor in societal integration as it gives birth to and enriches social values since ancient times. The question under study was whether the presence and works of the Bethany Sisters in the Northeast as a part of the Catholic Missions have contributed to the enrichment of the social values. Hence the focus of the book was the sociological approaches of religion as religion helps to understand social experiences, institutional practices besides serving as a powerful source for explaining a wide range of social attitudes and behaviors. Religions are human and social phenomena regardless of whether the ultimate reality to which they are supposedly oriented has a basis in truth.

What religion has done for the individuals and society was the crux of this research work. Since the topic of investigation was the impact of the work of the Bethany Sisters in Northeast India, it was appropriate to investigate on what the Bethany Sisters with their humanitarian activities were able to do to the society in the Northeast as a whole. How much the Bethany Sisters as part of the Catholic Missions have contributed to the socio-educational and cultural development of the Region in a span of 50 years is recorded in here. It was interesting to note how Catholic Missions and particularly the developmental activities of the Bethany Sisters have helped to fulfill the purposes of religion.

The different aspects and facets of service and the mission of thousands of Catholic organizations across the country manifest that no Religious Congregations neither the diverse ways in which they are trying to meet the challenges of the time are the same. All the Orders show in their missionary work specific peculiarities and characteristic methods which are organically bound up with their very essence and their special aims.

The differences between the Catholic Missions and other Missions are that the Catholic Missions are not confined to any one place and not limited to any one race or social class. Abstaining from marriage and remaining single helps the Catholic Missionaries to give themselves totally for the mission without any reservation. They consider the entire society as their extended family, without any restrictions. They are well known for their commitment, dedication, hard work, service, and sacrifice. They undertake charitable works for the needy and work hard for the poor and the deprived sections of the society. They have better infrastructure, organization, support from Church personnel.

The success rate of the Bethany Congregation in the Northeast India can be assessed from the development of institutions, which indicate the humanitarian work done in the different parts of the Northeast and the extent of mobility achieved. Significant growth is achieved in terms of quality of life for the people because of the education imparted by the Sisters. The Bethany Sisters are in the forefront in the field of quality education, holistic health care and people oriented developmental projects. They have invested in personnel and money. They have proved their dedication and sacrificed their lives for the mission.

Vast human resources have increased along with the number of institutions. Bethany Sisters are managing some of their institutions. The high level of literacy, the low level of infant mortality, improved status of women, the increased desire for ongoing education and health care are signs of integral growth experienced by the people. Better qualified teachers and number of political, educational and governmental leaders of the Region are a few of the products of Sisters' schools. People have offered land for schools and even helped in the building of mission centres.

Some of the similarities and dissimilarities between the Bethany Sisters and other Sisters' Congregations within the Catholic establishment are that the Bethany Sisters focus on the education of the rural poor, especially girls and women empowerment. The Institute is rooted in Indian philosophy and self reliance, dignity of labour, simplicity of life style, education in the vernacular and vocationalisation of education, focus on primary education and adult education, development of villages for the progress of the country and emancipation of women.

These are a few of the noble ideals that were upheld by the Founder and the Founding members.

Today these ideals are manifested in the missionary work of the Bethany Sisters' in the Northeast. Bethany Sisters concentrate on the integral development of students, vocational training to young girls of rural settings, improving the condition and position of women and working for social upliftment. They also work at the empowerment of women through Self Help Groups and try to address the peoples concerns as well as attend to questions of peace and justice.

While technology has taken the world to globalization to make it better, richer, and healthier, it has also created dehumanization and further marginalized the already marginalized people. Today India is afflicted with gender discrimination, female foeticide, infanticide, domestic violence both physical, emotional and harassment, murders for dowry, acid attacks and honour killings. This could be addressed through a mission exercised through compassionate love. The crucial challenge is the growing assertion of ethnic, regional, cultural, and religious identities. As there is more and more intolerance, various forms of communalism, tensions, divisions and even violence, a call to mutual understanding and warm collaboration appears to be timely. There is the urgency to take up the needs of the vulnerable groups in society such as children, women, persons with disabilities and HIV/AIDS, gays and lesbians, older persons and victims of racism as enlisted among the human rights. In this context, this book becomes relevant to the needs of the present Indian society.

The Sisters could consider their overall educational activities which include value formation, non formal education, literacy, skill development, concientization and other forms of peoples empowerment, to make all citizens literate, skilled and competent, socially aware, spiritually motivated and fully involved in the building of a developed and a just society. Some of the needs of the present Indian society are education of the girl children, empowerment of women folk, addressing the issues of human trafficking, poverty, illiteracy, alcoholism, and drugs. Peace and harmony are the core values of our education system. Thousands of students are educated in our educational institutions in order to be leaders of the nation and work towards peace and harmony in our country. Making a major contribution through education towards creating a more just, equitable and harmonious society seems to be the need of the hour.

Bibliography

A.R. Radcliffe-Brown, *Structure and Function in Primitive Society*, Routledge & Kegan Paul, London & Henrey, 1982, Rep.1976.

Alangaram, A. *Religions for Societal Transformation: Interreligious Dialogue from Subaltern Perspectives*, Asian Trading Corporation, Bangalore, 2005.

Aleaz, K.P. *Harmony of Religions: The Relevance of Swami Vivekananda*, Punthi Pustak, Calcutta, 1993.

----------------*Theology of Religions, Bermingham Papers and other Essays*, Moumita Publishers & Distributors, Calcutta, 1998.

Aluckal, Fr Jacob *The Catholic Church in Northeast India*, Archbishop's House, Shillong, July 2006.

Beaver R. Pierce et.al. (eds.), *A Lion Handbook: The World's Religions*, Lion Publishing, England, 1982.

Becker, C. SDS, *History of the Catholic Missions in Northeast India, (1890- 1915)*, (trans. &ed.), G. Stadler SDB & S. Karotemprel SDB, Firma KLM Private Limited, Calcutta, 1980.

---------------- *Father Otto Hopfenmueller*, Salvatorian Spirituality & Charism Series, No.12, Society of the Divine Saviour, Bangalore, 2008.

Beckford, James 'Religion', in Bryan S. Turner (ed.), *The Cambridge Dictionary of Sociology*, Cambridge University Press, UK, 2006.

Berger,Peter L. Luckmann, Thomas 'Sociology of Religion and Sociology of Knowledge', in *Sociology and Social Research*, (Vol.47), 1963. Thomas Luckmann, 'Religion in Modern Society', *Journal for the Scientific Study of Religion*, (Vol. II), April, 1963.

Bokenkotter, Thomas *A Concise History of the Catholic Church*, Image Books, U.S.A, 1977.

Bond, Helen K. et.al., (eds.), *A Companion to Religious Studies and Theology*, Edinburgh University Press, Edinburgh, 2003.

Bottomore, T.B. (ed.) *Karl Marx: Early Writings,* London, 1963.

Carlo, Gratian S.J. & Raj, Paul S.J., *Formation of Priests and Religious in North East India: An Exploratory Study,* Jesuit Institute of Religious Formation, Guwahati, 2005.

Clark, Francis X. S.J, *An Introduction to the Catholic Church of Asia,* Cardinal Bea Publications, Manila, 1987.

Cunningham, Lawrence S. *Introduction to Catholicism,* Cambridge University Press, New York, 2009.

D'Souza, Sr Violette *The Vine That He Planted,* Bethany Publications, Mangalore, Karnataka, 1989.

Davie, Grace "The Evolution of the Sociology of Religion", in Michele Dillon (ed.), *Handbook of the Sociology ofReligion,* Cambridge University Press, United Kingdom, 2003.

Desrochers, John CSC, *The Social Teaching of the Church in India,* NBCLC/CSA, Bangalore, India, 2006.

Dillon, Michele "The Sociology of Religion in Late Modernity" in Michele Dillon (ed.), *Handbook of the Sociology of Religion,* Cambridge University Press, United Kingdom, 2003.

Downs, Frederick S. *Christianity in Northeast India: Historical Perspectives,* ISPCK, New Delhi, 1983.

Downs, Frederick S. *History of Christianity in India,* Vol.V, Part 5, The Church Association of India, Bangalore, 1992.

Durkheim, Emile *The Elementary Forms of Religious Life: A Study in Religious Sociology,* (trans.) Joseph World Swain, George Allen & Unwin, Free Press, New York, 1915.

Edamattathu, Thomas and Rodrigues, Ida " Contribution of the Religious Sisters to the Church in Northeast India", in S. Karotemprel(ed.), *The Catholic Church in Northeast India 1890-1990, A Multi-dimensional Study,* Vendrame Institute Publications, Shillong, 1993.

Everett, John R. 'Religion' in *Encyclopedia Americana,* s.v., Vol.23.

Fernandez, Dr Francis S.D.B. & Varickasseril, Dr Jose S.D.B., (eds.) *Mission: A Service of Love, Essays in Honour of George Kottuppallil, S.D.B.,* Vendrame Institute Publications, Shillong, 1998.

Furseth, Inger & Repstad, Pal *An Introduction to the Sociology of Religion: Classical and Contemporary Perspectives,* Ashgate Publishing Limited, London, 2006.

Galloway, George *Philosophy of Religion,* T &T Clark, Edinburgh, 1956.

Geertz, Clifford *The Interpretation of Cultures,* Basic Books, New York, 1973.

George, Mary *The F.M.A. Contribution to the Missions in Northeast India,* A paper presented at All India Symposium on Salesian Missions in India, Shillong, 1983.

Goldsmith, Amrit Kumar *Article: The Christians in the Northeast India: A Historical Perspective, 1819-2004,* accessed on 20th June 2013.

Gorman, Angie O' columnist, USA, in *National Monthly Magazine for Christian Leadership,* Smart Companion- India, July 2012/ Vol.3 / No.6.

Gregorios, Paulos M. *Religion and Dialogue,* The Rev. Ashish Amos of the Indian Society, ISPCK, 2000.

Grensted, L.W. *The Psychology of Religion,* Oxford University Press, New York, 1952.

Hosten, H. *The Mackensie Manusripts,* Madras, 1926.

Hrangkhuma F. & Joy, Thomas (eds.), *Christ Among the Tribals,* SAIACS Press, Bangalore, 2007.

Isaacson, Walter *Benjamin Franklin: An American Life,* Simon & Schuster, New York, 2003.

J.C.F, W.H. Normaan, *The Philosophy of Religion,* Oklahoma, 1967.

Jeyaseelan, Lazar *History of the Catholic Church in Manipur,* Diocese of Imphal, Manipur, 1994.

Jones, James W., 'Religion, Health, and the Psychology of Religion: How the Research on Religion and Health Helps Us Understand Religion'*Journal of Religion and Health,*(Vol. 3), No.4, 2004.

Jones, Kenneth W. *The New Cambridge History of India: Socio Religious Reform Movements in British India,* Cambridge University Press, Cambridge, 1994.

Karotemprel Sebastian S.D.B., *Albizuri Among the Lyngams: A Brief History of the Catholic Mission among the Lyngams of Northeast India,* Vendrame Missiological Institute, Shillong, 1985.

__________________ "The Impact of Christianity on the Tribes of North East India" in J. Puthenpurakal SDB (ed.), *Impact of Christianity on North East India,* Vendrame Institute Publications, Shillong, 1996.

Karotemprel, S. SDB (ed.), *The Catholic Church in Northeast India 1890-1990,* Vendrame Institute Publications, Shillong, 1993.

Knitter, Paul F. *One Earth, Many Religions: Multi-faith Dialogue and Global Responsibility,* Orbis Books, USA, 1995.

Kunin, Seth O. Watson, Jonathan Miles (eds.), *Theories of Religion: A Reader,* Edinburg University Press, Edinburg, 2006.

Larbeer, P. Mohan *Ambedkar on Religion: A Liberative Perspective,* ISPCK, Delhi, 2003.

Malinowski, Bronislaw D.Sc., *Crime and Customin Savage society,* Littlefield, Adams & Co, Paterson, New Jersey, 1959.

Manimala, Varghese *Toward Mutual Fecundation and Fulfillment of Religions,* Media House & ISPCK, New Delhi, 2009.

Manjaly, Thomas Augustine, Graviour Palely, Tomy (eds.), *Challenges of Faith Formation in North-East India*, Oriens Publications, Shillong, 2009.

McGuire, Meredith B. *Religion, The Social Context*, Fifth Edition, Wadsworth Thomson Learning, USA, 2002

Mckenzie, John L. *The Roman Catholic Church*, Image Books, New York, 1971.

Melton, J. Gordon and Baumann, Martin (ed.), *Religions of the World: A Comprehensive Encyclopedia of Beliefs and Practices,* Oxford, England, 2002.

Menamparampil, Thomas *An Introduction to North-East India: Culture and History,* unpublished, Guwahati, 2006.

_________________________ *Church in North East India,* unpublished, Shillong, 1974.

Miller, Richard W. 'Social and Political Theory: Class, State, Revolution', in Terrell Carver (ed.), *The Cambridge Companion to Marx,* Cambridge University Press, 1991.

Mitchell, Margaret M. & Young, Frances M. (eds.), *The Cambridge History of Christianity, Volume 1, Origins to Constantine,* Cambridge Histories online, Cambridge University Press, 2006.

Mundadhan, A.M. *Sixteenth Century Traditions of St Thomas Christians*, Bangalore, 1970.

Naugle, David K. *Worldview: The History of a Concept,* William B. Eerdmans Publishing Company, Grand Rapids, Michigan /Cambridge, U.K., 2002.

Naulak, Sr Mary B.S., *Leaven in the East, Sisters of the Little Flower of Bethany in Northeast India (1962-2012),* Blossom Books(P) Ltd. Guwahati, 2012.

Neill, Stephen F.B.A., *A History of Christianity in India :The Beginnings to AD 1707,* Press Syndicate of the University of Cambridge, United Kingdom, 1984.

Packumala, E. The Role of the Religious Sisters and their Contribution to the Adivasi Community in the Assam valley, in *Indian Missiological Review*, April 1985.

Pascal, R. (ed.), *Karl Marx and Friedrich Engels, The German Ideology, Parts I and II,* International Publishers, New York 1947.

Patro, Santanu K. (ed.), *A Guide to Religious Thought and Practices,* ISPCK, Delhi, 2011.

Paviotti, O. *The Work of His Hands: The Story of the Archdiocese of Shillong-Guwahati 1934-1984,* Archbishop's House, Shillong, 1987.

Payyapilly, Geo and Benedict, Mary *Fullness of Life,* Bethany Publications, Mangalore, 2003.

Peter, W.L.A. Don *50 Questions about Catholicism,* St Paul Press, Mumbai, 1998.

Pinto, Pius Fidelis *History of Christians in Coastal Karnataka (1500- 1763 a.d.),* Samanvaya, Mangalore, Karnataka, 1999.

Ponraj, S. Devasagayam *Tribal Challenges and Church's Responses,* Mission Educational Books, Madhupur, 1996.

Radhakrishnan, S. *East and West in Religion,* George Allen & Unwin Ltd., London, 1933.

Rahner,Karl Vorgrimler, Herbert (eds.), *Concise Theological Dictionary,* London, 1968.

Raju, T.Swami *The Study of Religion: Methods & Perspectives,* BTESSC / SATHRI, Bangalore, 2004.

Randel, Yoland F.M.M. (trans) *Size and Structures of the Catholic Church in India,* 1982.

Rao, O.M. *Focus on North East Indian Christianity,* Indian Society for Promoting Christian Knowledge, Delhi, 1994.

Rawls, Anne Warfield '*Epistemology and practice: Durkheim's the Elementary Forms of Religious Life.*

Renavikar, Madhavi D. *Women and Religion,* Rawat Publications, Jaipur, 2003.

Rita, Sr Jessy B.S. *The Ripples: The Origin and Development of the Mangalore Province, The Congregation of the Sisters of the Little Flower of Bethany, Mangalore,* Bethany Publications, Mangalore, 2006.

Robertson, Roland '*The Sociological Interpretation of Religion*', Basil Blackwell, Oxford, 1970.

Rosman, Abraham, Rubel, Paula G. and Weisgrau, Maxine *The Tapestry of Culture: An Introduction to Cultural Anthropology,* Ninth Edition,Rowman& Littlefield Publishers, Inc., United Kingdom, 2009.

Sachchidananda, *The Changing Munda,* New Delhi, 1979.

Schmidt, W. *The Origin and Growth of Religion: Facts and Theories,* (trans.) H .J. Rose, Methuen & Co. Ltd., 1931.

Sinha, Raghuvir *Essays in Social Anthropology,* Concept Publishing Company, New Delhi, 1990.

Snaitang, Dr O.L. *Christianity and Social Change in Northeast India,* Vendrame Institute, Shillong, 1993.

Spiro, Melford in M.Benton (ed), *Anthropological Approaches to the Study of Religion,* London, 1966.

Steadman, L.B. and Palmer, C.T. *Beyond Belief, A Review of the Supernatural and Natural Selection: Religion and Evolutionary Success,* Boulder, CO: Paradigm, 2008.

Stuckrad, Kocku Von (ed.), 'Religion' in Introduction: The Academic Study of

Religion- Historical and Contemporary Issues, *The Brill Dictionary of Religion*, (Revised edn.), Metzler Lexikonin (ed.), (trans.) Christoph Auffarth, Jutta Bernard & Hubert Mohr., Vol. III M-R, MartinusNijhoff publishers, Boston, 2006.

Subba, T.B. Puthenpurakal, Joseph Puykunnel, Shaji Joseph (eds.), *Christianity and change in Northeast India*, concept publishing company, New Delhi, 2009.

Syiemlieh, David R. (ed.), *Diocese of Agartala: Ten Years and Onward*, Don Bosco Press, Shillong, 2005.

Symonides, Janusz (ed.), *New Dimensions and Challenge for Human Rights*, Rawat Publications, UNESCO Publishing, New Delhi, 2003.

Tewari, R.P. *Problems of Education in North East India*, quoting from *Education in India*, 1976-77, Prakash Brothers, Ludhiana.

Thadathil, Jane Mary *A Great Missionary Legacy: A Brief History of the Origin, Growth and Charism of the Missionary Sisters of Mary Help of Christians founded by Archbishop Stephen Ferrando*, Centre for Indigenous Peoples and Missionary Sisters Publications, Shillong and Guwahati, 1997.

Thompson, Rev. Newton S.T.D. (ed.) *A Course of Sermons by most Rev. Tihamer Toth B. Herder*, Book Company, 1947.

Tirkey, Christopher Augustus Bixel *Religion / Primal Religions*, ISPCK, Delhi, 2005.

Tiwari, Kedar Nath *Comparative Religion*, Motila lBanarsidass Publishers Pvt. Ltd., Delhi, 1997.

Tylor, Edward Burnett *Primitive Culture*, (Vol. I), New York, 1874.

DOCUMENTS

All India Catholic Education Policy 2007, Catholic Bishops Conference of India, New Delhi.

Education for fullness of life, second National convention, *Post convention Document 1*, BES vision and core values.

Handbook, The Congregation of the Sisters of The Little Flower of Bethany, Mangalore, 1921-2010, Bethany Publications, Mangalore.

The Catholic Directory of India 2013: The Catholic Bishops Conference of India, Claretian Publications, Bangalore, India.

MAGAZINES/SOUVENIRS/JOURNALS

Bednarz, Dr Julian SDS, "Salvatorian contribution to the church in Northeast India" in *Centenary of the Catholic Church in North-East India 1890-1990: A Souvenir.*

Diamond Jottings published on the occasion of the Diamond Jubilee celebration of Bethany Educational Society, *A Magazine.*

Diamond Jubilee of the Prefecture Apostolic of Haflong, 2013, *A Souvenir*

Diamond Jubilee of Bethany Educational Society (R) Mangalore, 1948-2008, *A Souvenir*.

Golden Jubilee of the Bethany Sisters in the North east Province, *A Magazine*.

Golden Jubilee of the Northern Province of Bethany Sisters, *A Magazine*.

Grimm, Fr William in "Change is a must for all", *Smart Companion India:* National Monthly for Christian Leadership, June 2012 / Vol.3 / No.5.

Jala, Dr Dominic & Shangpliang, Dr J.S. in 'The Contribution of the Catholic Church towards Socio-Cultural Development in North- East India', in *Centenary of the Catholic Church in North-East India 1890-1990, A Souvenir.*

Jala, Dr Dominic & Mukhim, Ms Patricia in 'Contribution of the Catholic Church Towards Education in North- East India', in *Centenary of the Catholic Church in North-East India 1890-1990:A Souvenir*

Kottupallil, Dr George 'A Historical Survey of the Catholic Church in North-East India from 1627 to 1983' *Centenary of the Catholic Church in North-East India 1890-1990, Souvenir.*

Mother Anne, A Seed is Sown, in *St Mary's college Golden Jubilee Souvenir*, Shillong, 1937- 87.

National Monthly Magazine for Christian Leadership, *Smart Companion*: India, July 2012/ Vol.3 / No.6.

Quarterly Magazine, 'Mission Today', January-March 2005, Vol.VII No.1.

Strawbridge, W. et.al., *Annals of Behavioral Medicine, Journal of Religion and Health,*(Vol. 3), No.4, 2001.

The Compassionate Pastor, Vol.01, No.01, December 2008, Congregation of the Sisters of the Little Flower of Bethany, Bethany Generalate Publications, Mangalore, *A Magazine*.

REPORTS/REVIEWS

Karotemprel, S. SDB, The Catholic School and A Growing Church, in Indian *Missiological Review*, July 1980.

__________, The Nurse Sister and Family Welfare in a Growing Church, in *Indian Missiological Review,* January 1980.

Report of the Conference of Religious Women India (CRWI) Superiors' General Meet, Bethany Convent Mangalore, 2 January 2008.

Report of the General Meeting of the CBCI, 2006.

Reports of Communities in Bethany Archives, Mangalore

LETTERS

Letters in the Archives of Bethany Congregation

UNPUBLISHED PAPERS

George, Pushpa *The Missionary Sisters of Mary Help of Christians and their Contribution to the Missions*, *A paper* presented at All India Symposium on Salesian Missions in India, Shillong, 1983.

Lillis and Trecilla, 'A Champion of Education- Mgr. Raymond Mascarenhas, Bethany Educational Society- II Convention, Mangalore, Karnataka, November, 2008, *A Paper*.

Lillita, 'The Plight of the Girl Child and the Response of Bethany.' Bethany Educational Society II Convention, Mangalore, November, 2008, A *Paper*.

WEBSITES

http:// en.wikipedia.org /Theories_of_religion#cite_note-Kunin.2C_page_85-61 accessed 20 September 2012.

http://en.wikipedia.org/w/index.php?title=Apostolic_Nuncio_to_ India&action=edit&redlink=1 accessed on 24 September 2011.

http://moses.creighton.edu/JRS/2005/2005-11.html#figures accessed 14 May 2012.

Kevin Schilbrack, "New Directions for Philosophy of Religion: Four Proposals", *Studies in Religion/Sciences Religieuses,* 2012. Accessed on 9 May 2012. Available from http://sir.sagepub.com.

Livesey, Chris "Religion, Functionalist Perspectives."Accessed 14 May 2011.Available from www.sociology.org.uk.

The Oxford Dictionary of the Christian Church, Oxford University Press, 2005. Available from http://en.wikipedia.org/wiki/See_of_Rome.Accessed 19 July 2012

States: Literacy & Population by Religion, 1991 from *indiaonlinepages.com accessed on 3 May 2014.*

www.bethanymangalore.org

*www.bethanymangalore.org*accessed on 11 June 2013.

Other *Lumen Gentium,* Encyclical Letter of the Vatican II.

New Catholic Encyclopedia, Second edn.(Vol.3), The Catholic University of America, 2009.

Oxford English Dictionary

Gregory D. Alles, 'Religion: Further considerations', in Lindsay Jones (ed.), *Encyclopedia of Religion*, Vol.11 (2), 2005.

The Catholic Directory of India 2013: The Catholic Bishops Conference of India, Claretian Publications, Bangalore, India.

Appendix

Major Roman Catholic Countries of the World (% of Population)
Table 2.1

SI No	Country	%	SI No	Country	%
1.	Austria	85	22.	Lesotho	70
2	Belgium	75	23.	Liechtenstein	87.3
3	Belize	65	24.	Lithuania	90
4	Bolivia	84	25.	Luxembourg	97
5	Brazil	74	26.	Malta	95.3
6	Burundi	63.1	27.	Mexico	93
7	Chile	70	28.	Monaco	90.6
8	Colombia	96	29.	Nicaragua	95
9	Costa Rica	90.6	30.	Panama	85
10.	Croatia	85	31.	Paraguay	90
11.	Dominican Republic	95	32.	Peru	81
12.	East Timor	90	33.	Philippines	81
13.	Ecuador	96.5	34.	Poland	96
14.	El Salvador	79.1	35.	Portugal	97
15.	France	90	36.	Puerto Rico	85
16.	Gabon	50.2	37.	San Marino	95
17.	Grenada	65	38.	Seychelles	87
18.	Guatemala	75	39.	Slovakia	68.9
19.	Haiti	80	40.	Slovenia	96
20.	Honduras	97	41.	Spain	99
21.	Hungary	76.6	42.	Uruguay	58

Source: The Catholic Directory of India 2013, The Catholic Bishops Conference of India, Claretian Publications, Bangalore, India, p.96

STATISTICAL DATA (AS PER CONFERENCE OF RELIGIOUS INDIA)					
Name	**Sisters**		**Brothers**	**Priests**	**Total**
	Apostolic	Contemplative			
Number of Congregations	244	9	17	64	334
Number of Major Superiors	569	55	38	160	822

		Candidates 1st year		Novices 2nd year		Professed	Number of Communities
Sisters	Apostolic	9910		2926	2975	93162	12869
	Contemplative	30		17	18	863	63
Brothers	588			128	125	2592	502
Priests	5877			1027	471	18970	2835
Total	**16405**			**4098**	**3589**	**115587**	**16269**

For Priests' Congregations		
Priests	**Brothers**	**Major Seminarians**
13235	1333	5735

The following is a List of the Church's Institutions in India:

1	Mission Stations	17,867
2	Parishes	6,477
3	Religious Congregations	251
4	Major Seminaries	62
5	KG & Nursery schools	3,785
6	Primary Schools	7,319
7	Universities (Colleges)	240
8	Technical Schools	1,514
9	Hostel & Boarding Houses	1,765
10	Hospitals	704
11	Leprosaria	111
12	Rehabilitation Centres	102
13	Homes for the aged & Handicapped	455
14	Creches	228

15	Orphanages	1,085
16	Dispensaries	1,792
17	Weeklies	14
18	Daily Newspapers	3
19	Other Periodicals	272

Source: Mr. Allen Brooks, "Challenges and Opportunities Facing the North East Region", *A Paper Presented in the North East Regional Assembly, 23rd-27th August 2000.*

SI No	Diocese	Total Population	No. of Catholics	% of Catholics	Diocesan Priests	Religious Priests	No. of Priests Congregations	Brothers Congregations	Sisters Congregations	Religious Institutes	Priests	Brothers	Sisters	Secular Educational Insitutions	Social Welfare	Health Services
1.	Agartala	3,200,000	31,848	1	4	53	5	1	12	5	1	12		21	11	14
2.	Aizawl	4,226,960	33,329	0.79	29	20	5	2	12	5	2	12	1	56	37	11
3.	Bongaihgaon	5,500,000	67,077	1.22	28	36	6	2	21	6	2	21	-	47	42	13
4.	Dibrugarh	5,329,982	113,177	2.12	75	52	8	2	13	8	2	13	1	65	14	19
5.	Diphu	1,001,150	57,279	5.72	29	28	6	1	20	6	1	20	-	61	30	22
6.	Guwahati	6,500,000	56,137	0.86	31	105	16	3	37	16	3	37	1	77	30	23
7.	Imphal	2,700,000	90,785	3.36	93	44	6	-	16	6	-	16	-	64	71	30
8.	Itanagar	725,591	82,093	11.31	9	62	9	2	16	9	2	16	-	38	35	13
9.	Jowai	379,294	78,139	20.6	13	16	6	1	10	6	1	10	-	9	2	3
10.	Kohima	198,602	58,090	29.25	32	11	6	1	17	6	1	17	1	137	46	15
11.	Miao	473,120	50,476	10.67	27	57	11	-	16	11	-	16	1	28	24	12
12.	Nongstoin	296,049	123,912	42.86	15	22	6	1	7	6	1	7	-	3	6	13
13.	Shillong	1,082,439	270,353	24.98	31	100	9	4	20	9	4	20	-	91	20	35
14.	Tejpur	822,561	198.972	24.19	59	33	2	-	12	2	-	12	-	44	3	15
15.	Tura	862,473	234,621	27.2	48	41	6	2	17	6	2	17	-	114	85	39

Source: The Catholic Directory of India 2013, The Catholic Bishop's Conference of India, Claretian Publications, Bangalore, India, pp.77-83

	Congregations	Founder	Place of foundation	Year of Foundation	Total Membership	Convents in India	Establishment in the Northeast	Educational centres	Health centres	Social- Welfare centres
1.	Apostolic Carmel (ac)	Mother Mary Veronica of the Passion	Bayonne, France	1868	1605	128	1966	128	4	12
2.	The Daughters of Mary Help of Christians (fma)	Sts John Bosco and Mary Domenica Mazzarello	Mornese, Italy.	1872	1256		1923	107	21	64
3.	Sisters of Franciscan Clarist Congregation (fcc)	Srs Mariam Clara a, Coletha, Agnes, Margareetha, Mariam Thresia, Mariam, Magdelena & Bishop Charles Lavigne, SJ	Changanacherry	1888	6938	689	1966	365	113	132
4.	Missionaries of Charity (mc)	St Mother Teresa	Calcutta	1950	1798		1974			21
5.	Missionary Sisters of Mary Help of Christians (msmhc)	Late Archbishop Stephen Ferrando SDB	Guwahati, Assam.	1942	1044	163	1948	52	30	12
6.	Missionary Sisters, Servants of Holy Spirit (ssps)	St Arnold Janssen, Bl Mother Maria & Josepha	Steyl, Holland.	1889		56	1995			
7.	The Sisters of Charity of Sts Bartholomea Capitanio and Vincenza Gerosa (sccg)	Sts Bartholomea Capitanio & Vincenza Gerosa	Lovere, Italy.	1832		206	1970			
8.	Sisters of our Lady of Fatima (fs)	Msgr Francis Xavier Kroot MHM	Bellary, India	1893	412	77	1988	31	9	23

9.	Srs. of St Joseph of Annecy (sja)	Fr Jeanne Pierre Medaille SJ	Le Puy, France.	1650		16	2007			
10.	Sisters of Adoration of the Blessed Sacrament (sabs)	Servant of God Bishop Thomas Kurialacherry	Champakulam, Kerala	1908	4583	589	1990	308	31	9
11.	Sisters of the Little Flower of Bethany (bs)	Msgr Raymond Francis Camillus Mascarenhas	Mangalore, Karnataka, India	1921	1306	172	1962			
12.	Daughters of Charity of St Vincent de Paul (dc)	Sts Vincent de Paul & Louise de Marillac		1633	20000	62		8	24	52
13.	Missionary Sisters of the Immaculate (Nirmala Sisters) (msi)	Ven Fr Paolo Manna, Mother Giuseppina Dones & Mother Igilda Rodolfi	Milan, Italy	1936		65				
14.	Sisters of Charles Borromeo (scb)	Fr Adrien Bresy	Wez-Velvain, Belgium	1684		60	2005			
15.	Ursuline Franciscan Sisters (ufs)	Fr Urban Stein, SJ	Mangalore, Karnataka, India	1887	800	110	1976	64	14	41
16.	Ursuline Sisters of Tildonk (osu)	St Angela Meric and Fr JMC Lambertz	Tildonk, Belgium	1818		19	1974			
17.	Augustinian Sisters (osa)	Srs Dominika Barth, Kaveria,Luessen Aloysia Tychen & Antonia Sporken	Cologne, Germany	1838	166	26	1997	5	3	2
18.	Clarist Franciscan Missionaries of the Most Blessed Sacrament (cfmss)	Venerable Servant of God Mother Seraphina Farolfi	Bertinoro, Italy	1898	451	69	1974	31	5	11

19.	Congregation of Jesus (cj)	Venerable Mother Mary Ward	Saint Omer, France	1609	232	55	1997	7	5	1
20.	Congregation of Sisters of Nazareth (csn)	Mar Augustine Kandathil, Frs.John Pinakatt & Mathew Mankuzhikkary	Padupuram Kerala	1948	638		1984	9	11	11
21.	Franciscan Servants of Mary (fsm)	Marie Virginie Vaslin	France	1852	237	47	2009	21	13	16
22.	Franciscan Sisters of Our Lady of Graces (fslg)	Archbishop Joseph Bartholomew Evangelisti	Dehradun, India	1965	281	39	2009	9	7	10
23.	Handmaids of Mary (hm)	Fr Edmund Albert Joseph Harrison SJ	Kesaramal, Odisha, India	1944	492	66	1999	9	16	4
24.	Hospitellar Sisters of Mercy (som)	Princess Teresa Orsini Doria	Southern Italy	1821	71	15	1996	4	5	6
25.	Medical Mission Sisters (mms)	Mother Anna Dengel scmm	Washington D.C. USA	1925		35	1972			
26.	Sisters of the Sacred Heart (sh)	Fr.Mathew Kadalikkattil	Pala, Kerala, India	1911	3568	421	1969	57	53	
27.	Sisters of Charity of St Vincent de Paul (scv)	Cardinal Armand Gaston de Rohan	Strasbourg, France	1734	225	20	2011	2	5	1

28.	Sisters of St Ann of Providence (sa)	Marchioness Giulia Faletti Colbert & Marquis Carlo Tancredi of Bardo	Turin, Italy	1834		100	2001			
29.	Sisters of St Joseph of Cluny (sjc)	Blanne Marie Javouhey	Chalon, France	1807			1996			
30.	Sisters of the Cross of Chavanod (scc)	Mother Claudine Echernier	Chavanod, Haute-Savoie, France	1838		145	1979			
31.	Sisters of Mary Immaculate (smi)	Bishop Louis la Ravoire Morrow, SDB	Krishnagar, West Bengal	1948	613	64	1984	28	31	37
32.	Daughters of Presentation of Mary in the Temple (dpm)	Francesca Butti, Maria Rossi	Como, Italy	1833			2010			
33.	Congregation of the Mother of Carmel (cmc)	St Kuriakose Elias Chavara & FrLeopold Boccaro OCD	Koonamavu, Kerala, India	1866	6343	621	1966	682	65	140
34.	Handmaids of Christ (hc)	Msgr Herculano Gonsalves	Calangute, Goa	1935	155	30	2012	12	2	21
35.	Maestre Pie Venerini (Religious Teachers of Bl Rosa Venerini (mpv)	St Rosa Venerin	Viterbo, Italy	1685	260	23	1989	5	1	3
36.	Prabhudasi Sisters of Ajmer (Handmaids of the Lord (psa)	Fr Fortunatus Henry Caumont ofm cap	Ajmer, Rajasthan, India	1906	892	55	2010	10	9	1

37.	The Catechist Missionary Sisters (Salesian Missionaries of Mary Immaculate) (smmi)	Fr.Henri Chaumont & Madame Carre de Malberg	France	1872		120	1987			
38.	Sisters of Notre Dame (snd)	Srs Mary Aloysia & Mary Ignatia	Coesfeld, Germany	1850		32	2005			
39.	The Sisters of Our Lady of the Missions (rndm)	Euphrasie Barbier	Lyons, France	1861		30	1915			
40.	The Sisters of the Destitute (sd)	FrVarghese Payapilly	Chunangamvely, Aluva, Kerala	1927	1396	200	1991	175	72	94
41.	Visitation Sisters of Don Bosco (vsdb)	Archbishop Hubert D'Rosario SDB	Shillong, Meghalaya, India	1983	74	19	1983	1		
42.	Assisi Sisters of Mary Immaculate (asmi)	Very Rev. Msgr Joseph KW Thomas Kandathil	Cherthala, Kerala	1949	765	98	2007	18	70	2
43.	Daughters of Divine Providence (fdp)	Ven Sr Elena Bettini	Rome	1832			2007			
44.	Congregation of the Sisters of the Catholic Apostolate (Pallotines) (csac)	St Vincent Pallotti	Rome	1843	129	12		4	2	
45.	Daughters of St Paul (Dsp)	Bl James Alberione	Alba, North Italy	1915	163	15	1973			

46.	Daughters of the Cross (Liege) (fc)	Bl Mother Marie Therese Haze	Liege, Belgium	1833	489	63		25	15	20
47.	Sister Disciples of the Divine Master (pddm)	Bl James Alberione	Alba, Italy	1924			2005			
48.	Sisters of Charity of Jesus and Mary (scjm)	Fr Peter Joseph Triest	Lovendeghem, Belgium	1803		40	2000			
49.	Sisters of Mercy of the Holy Cross (scsc)	Fr Theodosious Florentini &Bl Maria Theresa Sherer	Bettiah, Bihar	1856		136	1999			
50.	The Congregation of Holy Family (chf)	Bl Mariam Thresia Chiramel Mankidiyan	Thrissur District, Kerala, India	1914	1950	227				
51.	The Fervent Daughters of the Sacred Heart of Jesus (fdshj)	Sr Marykutty of the Sacred Heart	Perunna West, Changanacherry, Kerala, India	1981		22	2009			
52.	Daughters of St Thomas (dst)	Fr Jacob Thazhathel	Aruvithura, Pala, Kerala, India	1969		28	1975			
53.	Ursulines of Mary Immaculate (umi)	Bl Mother Brigida Morello	Piacenza, Northern Italy	1649		84	1996			

54.	Carmelite Sisters of Charity-Vedruna (ccv)	St Joaquina de Vedruna	Barcelona, Spain	1826	194			8	14	18
55.	The Missionary Sisters of the Immaculate Heart of Mary (icm)	Mother Marie Louise de Meester	Mulagumoodu, Tamilnadu	1897		27				
56.	Missionaries of Christ Jesus (mcj)	Mother Pilar Navarro & Fr Angel Ayala SJ	Javier, Spain	1944		15	1948			
57.	Society of the Sisters of St Ann of Luzern, India (sas)	Rector Fr.Wilhelm Meyer		1909	782	108				
58.	The Congregation of the Sisters of St Elizabeth (csse)	Mother Mathilde Otto & Fr Joseph Oechsler	Freiberg, West Germany	1925		14				
59.	Daughters of the Heart of Mary (dhm)	Fr Pierre Joseph de Clonviere & Sr Marie Adlaide de Cice	France	1790	73		2011			
60.	Congregation of the Sisters of St Joseph of Chambery (csj)	Fr John Peter Medaille & Bp Henry de Maupas	Velay, France	1650	482	20		17	15	4
61.	Franciscan Sisters of St Mary of the Angels (fsma)	Sr Marie Chrysostom & Fr John Chrysostom ofm Cap	Angers, France	1892						

No.										
62.	Sisters of Providence (sdp)	St Luigi Scrosoopi	Udine, Italy	1837		16	2009			
63.	Carmelite Missionaries (cm)	Bl Fr Francisco Palau ocd	Spain	1860	131			4	5	1
64.	Congregation of the Sisters of St Martha (csm)	Fr John Kizhakooden	Trichur, Kerala	1948	35	33		3	1	8
65.	Daughters of Our Lady of Marcy (fdm)	St Mary Joseph Rosello	Savona, Italy	1837		28				
66.	Franciscan Missionaries of Service (fmss)	Sr Heide Brauckmann	South Korea	1983		5		1	1	2
67.	Franciscan Missionary Sisters of Sacred Heart (fmsh)	Duchess Laura Leroux de Beufremont & Fr Greigory Floravanti	Gemona, Northern Italy	1861		16				
68.	Sisters of the Holy Spirit (shsp)	Mother Irmina Hoelscher	Germany	1857		28				
69.	Sisters of Holy Cross (menzingem) (hcm)	Fr Theodosious Florentini ofm cap. & Mother Bernarda Heimgartner	Menzingen, Switzerland	1844		80	1959			
70.	Franciscan Sisters of the Sacred Heart (fssh)	Fr Simpliciano ofm	Rome	1886		7	2008			
71.	The Loreto Sisters (ibvm)	Ven Mary Ward	Dublin, Ireland	1821	111	20	1905	14	98	17

72.	Shanti Nilayam Benedictine Abbey, Order of St Benedict (osb)	St Cecilia	Isle of Wight, England	1970		43	1991			
73.	The Salvatorian Sisters (sds)	Fr Francis Mary of the Cross Jordan & Bl Mary of the Apostles	Tivoli, Italy	1888		9	2003			
74.	Augustinian Missionary Sisters (ams)	Srs Clara Canto, Monica Mujal & Querubina Samarra	Madrid, Spain	1890	72	9	2011	1		1
75.	Daughters of St Francis de Sales (dsfs)	Fr Carlo Cavina	Lugo, Italy	1872		25	1994			
76.	The Congregation of the Sisters of the Imitation of Christ (sic)	His Grace the Most Rev. Geevarghese Mar Ivanios	Kerala, India	1925	32	900				
77.	Society of Christ Jesus (scj)	Mother Camino Sanz Orrio		1944			1948			
78.	Sisters of the Holy Cross (ose)						1987			
79.	Sisters of Providence (spg)	Bl Jean Martin Moye	Lorraine, France	1838						
80.	Congregation of the Sisters of the Holy Cross (csc)									

	STATE	BES HSS	DIO/OTH	BES HS	DIO/OTH	BESPRY	DIO/OTH	BESKG	DIO/OTH	BES BALWADI	DIO/OTH	BESVTC	DIO/OTH	BES NIOS	DIO/OTH	BES comty college	DIO/OTH	BES health care	DIO/OTH	BES deadd/reha	DIO/OTH	BES Houses for the needy	DIO/OTH	BES Regd society	DIO/OTH	BES HOSTELS	BES BOARDINGS
1.	Mizoram	-	-	1	2	2	2	2	1	-	-	-	-	1	-	-	-	2	-	2	-	-	-	-	-	2	-
2.	Meghalaya	-	1	-	1	-	-	-	1	1	-	-	-	-	-	-	-	1	-	-	-	-	-	1	-	1	-
3.	Manipur	-	-	-	1	-	-	-	1	-	-	-	-	-	-	-	-	-	-	-	-	-	-	-	-	-	-
4.	Nagaland	1	2	1	2	-	3	1	2	-	-	-	-	-	-	-	-	1	-	-	-	-	-	-	-	3	-
5.	Tripura	-	2	1	2	-	-	1	3	-	-	1	-	-	-	-	-	1	1	-	-	-	-	-	-	-	3
6.	Arunachal Pradesh	-	-	-	-	-	-	-	-	-	-	-	-	-	-	-	-	-	-	-	-	-	-	-	-	-	-
7.	Assam	-	1	1	3	-	-	1	3	2	-	1	-	-	-	1	-	-	-	-	-	-	-	-	-	3	-
8.	West Bengal	-	1	-	4	1	1	1	3	1	-	-	-	-	-	-	-	-	-	-	-	1	-	-	-	-	-
9.	Karnataka	-	-	-	-	-	-	-	-	-	-	-	-	-	-	-	-	-	-	-	-	1	-	-	-	-	-
	Total	1	7	4	15	3	6	6	14	4	-	2	-	1	1	-	-	5	1	2	-	1	-	1	-	9	3

EDUCATIONAL WORK OF THE BETHANY SISTERS

SOCIAL WORK OF THE BETHANY SISTERS

HEALTH CARE AND FAMILY WELFARE OF THE BETHANY SISTERS

PASTORAL WORK OF THE BETHANY SISTERS